WOMEN'S WISDOM:
The New Thought Movement

The Game of Life And How To Play It
How To Live Life And Love It
Life Power and How to Use It

Women's Wisdom:
The New Thought Movement

The Game of Life And How To Play It

By Florence Scovel Shinn

Table of Contents

The Game

Most people consider life a battle, but it is not a battle, it is a game.

It is a game, however, which cannot be played successfully without the knowledge of spiritual law, and the Old and the New Testaments give the rules of the game with wonderful clearness. Jesus Christ taught that it was a great game of Giving and Receiving.

"Whatsoever a man soweth that shall he also reap." This means that whatever man sends out in word or deed, will return to him; what he gives, he will receive.

If he gives hate, he will receive hate; if he gives love, he will receive love; if he gives criticism, he will receive criticism; if he lies he will be lied to; if he cheats he will be cheated. We are taught also, that the imaging faculty plays a leading part in the game of life.

"Keep thy heart (or imagination) with all diligence, for out of it are the issues of life." (Prov. 4:23.)

This means that what man images, sooner or later externalizes in his affairs. I know of a man who feared a certain disease. It was a very rare disease and difficult to get, but he pictured it continually and read about it until it manifested in his body, and he died, the victim of distorted imagination.

So we see, to play successfully the game of life, we must train the imaging faculty. A person with an imaging faculty trained to image only good, brings into his life "every righteous desire of his heart"—health, wealth, love, friends, perfect self-expression, his highest ideals.

The imagination has been called, "The Scissors of The Mind, "and it is ever cutting, cutting, day by day, the pictures man sees there, and sooner or later he meets his own creations in his outer world. To train the imagination successfully, man must understand the workings of his mind. The Greeks said: "Know Thyself."

There are three departments of the mind, the subconscious, conscious and superconscious. The subconscious, is simply power, without direction. It is like steam or electricity, and it does what it is directed to do; it has no power of induction.

Whatever man feels deeply or images clearly, is impressed upon the subconscious mind, and carried out in minutest detail.

For example: a woman I know, when a child, always "made believe" she was a widow. She "dressed up" in black clothes and wore a long black veil, and people thought she was very clever and amusing. She grew up and married a man with whom she was deeply in love. In a short time he died and she wore black and a sweeping veil for many years. The picture of herself as a widow was impressed upon the subconscious mind, and in due time worked itself out, regardless of the havoc created.

The conscious mind has been called mortal or carnal mind.

It is the human mind and sees life as it appears to be. It sees death, disaster, sickness, poverty and limitation of every kind, and it impresses the subconscious.

The superconscious mind is the God Mind within each man, and is the realm of perfect ideas.

In it, is the "perfect pattern" spoken of by Plato, The Divine Design; for there is a Divine Design for each person.

"There is a place that you are to fill and no one else can fill, something you are to do, which no one else can do."

There is a perfect picture of this in the super-conscious mind. It usually flashes across the conscious as an unattainable ideal—"something too good to be true."

In reality it is man's true destiny (or destination) flashed to him from the Infinite Intelligence which is within himself.

Many people, however, are in ignorance of their true destinies and are striving for things and situations which do not belong to them, and would only bring failure and dissatisfaction if attained.

For example: A woman came to me and asked me to "speak the word" that she would marry a certain man with whom she was very much in love. (She called him A. B.)

I replied that this would be a violation of spiritual law, but that I would speak the word for the right man, the "divine selection," the man who belonged to her by divine right.

I added, "If A. B. is the right man you can't lose him, and if he isn't, you will receive his equivalent." She saw A. B. frequently but no headway was made in their friendship. One evening she called, and said, "Do you know, for the last week, A. B. hasn't seemed so wonderful to me." I replied, "Maybe he is not the divine selection—another man may be the right one." Soon after that, she met another man who fell in love with her at once, and who said she was his ideal. In fact, he said all the things that she had always wished A. B. would say to her.

She remarked, "It was quite uncanny."

She soon returned his love, and lost all interest in A. B.

This shows the law of substitution. A right idea was substituted for a wrong one, therefore there was no loss or sacrifice involved.

Jesus Christ said, "Seek ye first the Kingdom of God and his righteousness; and all these things shall be added unto you," and he said the Kingdom was within man.

The Kingdom is the realm of right ideas, or the divine pattern.

Jesus Christ taught that man's words played a leading part in the game of life. "By your words ye are justified and by your words ye are condemned."

Many people have brought disaster into their lives through idle words.

For example: A woman once asked me why her life was now one of poverty of limitation. Formerly she had a home, was surrounded by beautiful things and had plenty of money. We found she had often tired of the management of her home, and had said repeatedly, "I'm sick and tired of things—I wish I lived in a trunk," and she added: "Today I am living in that trunk." She had spoken herself into a trunk. The subconscious mind has no sense of humor and people often joke themselves into unhappy experiences.

For example: A woman who had a great deal of money, joked continually about "getting ready for the poorhouse."

In a few years she was almost destitute, having impressed the subconscious mind with a picture of lack and limitation.

Fortunately the law works both ways, and a situation of lack may be changed to one of plenty.

For example: A woman came to me one hot summer's day for a "treatment" for prosperity. She was worn out, dejected and discouraged. She said she possessed just eight dollars in the world. I said, "Good, we'll bless the eight dollars and multiply them as Jesus Christ multiplied the loaves and the fishes," for He taught that every man had the power to bless and to multiply, to heal and to prosper.

She said, "What shall I do next?"

I replied, "Follow intuition. Have you a 'hunch' to do anything, or to go anywhere?" Intuition means, intuition, or to be taught from within. It is man's unerring guide, and I will deal more fully with its laws in a following chapter.

The woman replied: "I don't know—I seem to have a 'hunch' to go home; I've just enough money for carfare." Her home was in a distant city and was one of lack and limitation, and the reasoning mind (or intellect) would have said: "Stay in New York and get work and make some money." I replied, "Then go home—never violate a hunch." I spoke the following words for her: "Infinite Spirit open the way for great abundance for —— ——. She is an irresistible magnet for all that belongs to her by divine right." I told her to repeat it continually also. She left for home immediately. In calling on a woman one day, she linked up with an old friend of her family.

Through this friend, she received thousands of dollars in a most miraculous way. She has said to me often, "Tell people about the woman who came to you with eight dollars and a hunch."

There is always plenty on man's pathway; but it can only be brought into manifestation through desire, faith or the spoken word. Jesus Christ brought out clearly that man must make the first move.

"Ask, and it shall be given you, seek, and ye shall find, knock, and it shall be opened unto you. (Mat. 7:7.)

In the Scriptures we read:

"Concerning the works of my hands, command ye me.

Infinite Intelligence, God, is ever ready to carry out man's smallest or greatest demands.

Every desire, uttered or unexpressed, is a demand. We are often startled by having a wish suddenly fulfilled.

For example: One Easter, having seen many beautiful rose-trees in the florists' windows, I wished I would receive one, and for an instant saw it mentally being carried in the door.

Easter came, and with it a beautiful rose-tree. I thanked my friend the following day, and told her it was just what I had wanted.

She replied, "I didn't send you a rose-tree, I sent you lilies!"

The man had mixed the order, and sent me a rose-tree simply because I had started the law in action, and I had to have a rose-tree.

Nothing stands between man and his highest ideals and every desire of his heart, but doubt and fear. When man can "wish without worrying," every desire will be instantly fulfilled.

I will explain more fully in a following chapter the scientific reason for this and how fear must be erased from the consciousness. It is man's only enemy—fear of lack, fear of failure, fear of sickness, fear of loss and a feeling of insecurity on some plane. Jesus Christ said: "Why are ye fearful, oh ye of little faith?" (Mat. 8:26.) So we can see we must substitute faith for fear, for fear is only inverted faith; it is faith in evil instead of good.

The object of the game of life is to see clearly one's good and to obliterate all mental pictures of evil. This must be done by impressing the subconscious mind with a realization of good. A very brilliant man, who has attained great success, told me he had suddenly erased all fear from his consciousness by reading a sign which hung in a room. He saw printed, in large letters this statement—"Why worry, it will probably never happen." These words were stamped indelibly upon his subconscious mind, and he has now a firm conviction that only good can come into his life, therefore only good can manifest.

In the following chapter I will deal with the different methods of impressing the subconscious mind. It is man's faithful servant but one must be careful to give it the right orders. Man has ever a silent listener at his side—his subconscious mind.

Every thought, every word is impressed upon it and carried out in amazing detail. It is like a singer making a record on the sensitive disc of the phonographic plate. Every note and tone of the singer's voice is registered. If he coughs or hesitates, it is registered also. So let us break all the old bad records in the subconscious mind, the records of our lives which we do not wish to keep, and make new and beautiful ones.

Speak these words aloud, with power and conviction: "I now smash and demolish (by my spoken word) every untrue record in my subconscious mind. They shall return to the dust-heap of their native nothingness, for they came from my own vain imaginings. I now make my perfect records through the Christ within—The records of Health, Wealth, Love and perfect self-Expression." This is the square of life, The Game completed.

In the following chapters, I will show how man can change his conditions by changing his words. Any man who does not know the power of the word, is behind the times.

"Death and Life are in the power of the tongue." (Prov. 18:21.)

The Law of Prosperity

"Yea, the Almighty shall be thy defense and thou shalt have plenty of silver."

One of the greatest messages given to the race through the scriptures is that God is man's supply and that man can release, through his spoken word, all that belongs to him by divine right. He must, however, have perfect faith in his spoken word.

Isaiah said, "My word shall not return unto me void, but shall accomplish that where unto it is sent." We know now, that words and thoughts are a tremendous vibratory force, ever moulding man's body and affairs.

A woman came to me in great distress and said she was to be sued on the fifteenth of the month for three thousand dollars. She knew no way of getting the money and was in despair.

I told her God was her supply, and that there is a supply for every demand.

So I spoke the word! I gave thanks that the woman would receive three thousand dollars at the right time in the right way. I told her she must have perfect faith, and act her perfect faith. The fifteenth came but no money had materialized.

She called me on the 'phone and asked what she was to do.

I replied, "It is Saturday, so they won't sue you today. Your part is to act rich, thereby showing perfect faith that you will receive it by Monday." She asked me to lunch with her to keep up her courage. When I joined her at a restaurant, I said, "This is no time to economize. Order an expensive luncheon, act as if you have already received the three thousand dollars."

"All things whatsoever ye ask in prayer, believing, ye shall receive." "You must act as if you had already received. "The next morning she called me on the 'phone and asked me to stay with her during the day. I said "No, you are divinely protected and God is never too late."

In the evening she 'phoned again, greatly excited and said, "My dear, a miracle has happened! I was sitting in my room this morning, when the doorbell rang. I said to the maid: 'Don't let anyone in.' The maid however, looked out the window and said, 'It's your cousin with the long white beard.'

So I said, 'Call him back. I would like to see him.' He was just turning the corner, when he heard the maid's voice, and he came back.

He talked for about an hour, and just as he was leaving he said, 'Oh, by the way, how are finances?'

I told him I needed the money, and he said, 'Why, my dear, I will give you three thousand dollars the first of the month.'

I didn't like to tell him I was going to be sued. What shall I do? I won't receive it till the first of the month, and I must have it tomorrow." I said, "I'll keep on 'treating.'"

I said, "Spirit is never too late. I give thanks she has received the money on the invisible plane and that it manifests on time." The next morning her cousin called her up and said, "Come to my office this morning and I will give you the money." That afternoon, she had three thousand dollars to her credit in the bank, and wrote checks as rapidly as her excitement would permit.

If one asks for success and prepares for failure, he will get the situation he has prepared for. For example: A man came to me asking me to speak the word that a certain debt would be wiped out.

I found he spent his time planning what he would say to the man when he did not pay his bill, thereby neutralizing my words. He should have seen himself paying the debt.

We have a wonderful illustration of this in the bible, relating to the three kings who were in the desert, without water for their men and horses. They consulted the prophet Elisha, who gave them this astonishing message:

"Thus saith the Lord—Ye shall not see wind, neither shall ye see rain, yet make this valley full of ditches."

Man must prepare for the thing he has asked for, when there isn't the slightest sign of it in sight.

For example: A woman found it necessary to look for an apartment during the year when there was a great shortage of apartments in New York. It was considered almost an impossibility, and her friends were sorry for her and said, "Isn't it too bad, you'll have to store your furniture and live in a hotel." She replied, "You needn't feel sorry for me, I'm a superman, and I'll get an apartment."

She spoke the words: "Infinite Spirit, open the way for the right apartment." She knew there was a supply for every demand, and that she was "unconditioned," working on the spiritual plane, and that "one with God is a majority."

She had contemplated buying new blankets, when "the tempter," the adverse thought or reasoning mind, suggested, "Don't buy the blankets, perhaps, after all, you won't get an apartment and you will have no use for them." She promptly replied (to herself): "I'll dig my ditches by buying the blankets!" So she prepared for the apartment—acted as though she already had it.

She found one in a miraculous way, and it was given to her although there were over two hundred other applicants.

The blankets showed active faith.

It is needless to say that the ditches dug by the three kings in the desert were filled to over-flowing. (Read, II Kings.)

Getting into the spiritual swing of things is no easy matter for the average person. The adverse thoughts of doubt and fear surge from the subconscious. They are the "army of the aliens" which must be put to flight. This explains why it is so often, "darkest before the dawn."

A big demonstration is usually preceded by tormenting thoughts.

Having made a statement of high spiritual truth one challenges the old beliefs in the subconscious, and "error is exposed" to be put out.

This is the time when one must make his affirmations of truth repeatedly, and rejoice and give thanks that he has already received. "Before ye call I shall answer." This means that "every good and perfect gift" is already man's awaiting his recognition.

Man can only receive what he sees himself receiving.

The children of Israel were told that they could have all the land they could see. This is true of every man. He has only the land within his own mental vision. Every great work, every big accomplishment, has been brought into manifestation through holding to the vision, and often just before the big achievement, comes apparent failure and discouragement.

The children of Israel when they reached the "Promised Land," were afraid to go in, for they said it was filled with giants who made them feel like grasshoppers. "And there we saw the giants and we were in our own sight as grass-hoppers." This is almost every man's experience.

However, the one who knows spiritual law, is undisturbed by appearance, and rejoices while he is "yet in captivity." That is, he holds to his vision and gives thanks that the end is accomplished, he has received.

Jesus Christ gave a wonderful example of this. He said to his disciples: "Say not ye, there are yet four months and then cometh the harvest? Behold, I say unto you, lift up your eyes and look on the fields; for they are ripe already to harvest." His clear vision pierced the "world of matter" and he saw clearly the fourth dimensional world, things as they really are, perfect and complete in Divine Mind. So

man must ever hold the vision of his journey's end and demand the manifestation of that which he has already received. It maybe his perfect health, love, supply, self-expression, home or friends.

They are all finished and perfect ideas registered in Divine Mind (man's own superconscious mind) and must come through him, not to him. For example: A man came to me asking for treatments for success. It was imperative that he raise, within a certain time, fifty-thousand dollars for his business. The time limit was almost up, when he came to me in despair. No one wanted to invest in his enterprise, and the bank had flatly refused a loan. I replied: "I suppose you lost your temper while at the bank, therefore your power. You can control any situation if you first control yourself." "Go back to the bank," I added, "and I will treat." My treatment was: "You are identified in love with the spirit of everyone connected with the bank. Let the divine idea come out of this situation." He replied, "Woman, you are talking about an impossibility. Tomorrow is Saturday; the bank closes at twelve, and my train won't get me there until ten, and the time limit is up tomorrow, and anyway they won't do it. It's too late." I replied, "God doesn't need any time and is never too late. With Him all things are possible." I added, "I don't know anything about business, but I know all about God." He replied: "It all sounds fine when I sit here listening to you, but when I go out it's terrible." He lived in a distant city, and I did not hear from him for a week, then came a letter. It read: "You were right. I raised the money, and will never again doubt the truth of all that you told me."

I saw him a few weeks later, and I said, "What happened? You evidently had plenty of time, after all." He replied "My train was late, and I got there just fifteen minutes to twelve. I walked into the bank quietly and said, 'I have come for the loan,' and they gave it to me without a question."

It was the last fifteen minutes of the time allotted to him, and Infinite Spirit was not too late. In this instance the man could never have demonstrated alone. He needed someone to help him hold to the vision. This is what one man can do for another.

Jesus Christ knew the truth of this when he said: "If two of you shall agree on earth as touching anything that they shall ask, it shall be done for them of my Father which is in heaven." One gets too close to his own affairs and becomes doubtful and fearful.

The friend or "healer" sees clearly the success, health, or prosperity, and never wavers, because he is not close to the situation.

It is much easier to "demonstrate" for someone else than for one's self, so a person should not hesitate to ask for help, if he feels himself wavering.

A keen observer of life once said, "no man can fail, if some one person sees him successful." Such is the power of the vision, and many a great man has owed his success to a wife, or sister, or a friend who "believed in him" and held without wavering to the perfect pattern!

The Power of the Word

"By thy words thou shalt be justified, and by thy words thou shalt be condemned."

A person knowing the power of the word, becomes very careful of his conversation. He has only to watch the reaction of his words to know that they do "not return void." Through his spoken word, man is continually making laws for himself.

I knew a man who said, "I always miss a car. It invariably pulls out just as I arrive."

His daughter said: "I always catch a car. It's sure to come just as I get there." This occurred for years. Each had made a separate law for himself, one of failure, one of success. This is the psychology of superstitions.

The horse-shoe or rabbit's foot contains no power, but man's spoken word and belief that it will bring him good luck creates expectancy in the subconscious mind, and attracts a "lucky situation." I find however, this will not "work" when man has advanced spiritually and knows a higher law. One cannot turn back, and must put away "graven images." For example: Two men in my class had had great success in business for several months, when suddenly everything "went to smash." We tried to analyze the situation, and I found, instead of making their affirmations and looking to God for success and prosperity, they had each bought a "lucky monkey." I said: "Oh I see, you have been trusting in the lucky monkeys instead of God." "Put away the lucky monkeys and call on the law of forgiveness," for man has power to forgive or neutralize his mistakes.

They decided to throw the lucky monkeys down a coalhole, and all went well again. This does not mean, however, that one should throw away every "lucky" ornament or horse-shoe about the house, but he must recognize that the power back of it is the one and only power, God, and that the object simply gives him a feeling of expectancy.

I was with a friend, one day, who was in deep despair. In crossing the street, she picked up a horseshoe. Immediately, she was filled with joy and hope. She said God had sent her the horseshoe in order to keep up her courage.

It was indeed, at that moment, about the only thing that could have registered in her consciousness. Her hope became faith, and she ultimately made a wonderful demonstration. I wish to make the point clear that the men previously mentioned were depending on the monkeys, alone, while this woman recognized the power back of the horseshoe.

I know, in my own case, it took a long while to get out of a belief that a certain thing brought disappointment. If the thing happened, disappointment invariably followed. I found the only way I could make a change in the subconscious, was by asserting, "There are not two powers, there is only one power, God, therefore, there are no disappointments, and this thing means a happy surprise." I noticed a change at once, and happy surprises commenced coming my way.

I have a friend who said nothing could induce her to walk under a ladder. I said, "If you are afraid, you are giving in to a belief in two powers, Good and Evil, instead of one. As God is absolute, there can be no opposing power, unless man makes the false of evil for himself. To show you believe in only One Power, God, and that there is no power or reality in evil, walk under the next ladder you see." Soon after, she went to her bank. She wished to open her box in the safety-deposit vault, and there stood a ladder on her pathway. It was impossible to reach the box without passing under the ladder. She quailed with fear and turned back. She could not face the lion on her pathway. However, when she reached the street, my words rang in her ears and she decided to return and walk under it. It was a big moment in her life, for ladders had held her in bondage for years. She retraced her steps to the vault, and the ladder was no longer there! This so often happens! If one is willing to do a thing he is afraid to do, he does not have to.

It is the law of nonresistance, which is so little understood.

Someone has said that courage contains genius and magic. Face a situation fearlessly, and there is no situation to face; it falls away of its own weight.

The explanation is, that fear attracted the ladder on the woman's pathway, and fearlessness removed it.

Thus the invisible forces are ever working for man who is always 'pulling the strings" himself, though he does not know it. Owing to the vibratory power of words, whatever man voices, he begins to attract. People who continually speak of disease, invariably attract it.

After man knows the truth, he cannot be too careful of his words. For example: I have a friend who often says on the 'phone, "Do come to see me and have a fine old-fashioned chat." This "old-fashioned chat" means an hour of about five hundred to a thousand destructive words, the principal topics being loss, lack, failure and sickness.

I reply: "No, I thank you, I've had enough old-fashioned chats in my life, they are too expensive, but I will be glad to have a new-fashioned chat, and talk about what we want, not what we don't want." There is an old saying that man only dares use his words for three purposes, to "heal, bless or prosper." What man says of others will be said of him, and what he wishes for another, he is wishing for himself.

"Curses, like chickens, come home to roost."

If a man wishes someone "bad luck," he is sure to attract bad luck himself. If he wishes to aid someone to success, he is wishing and aiding himself to success.

The body may be renewed and transformed through the spoken word and clear vision, and disease be completely wiped out of the consciousness. The metaphysician knows that all disease has a mental correspondence, and in order to heal the body one must first "heal the soul."

The soul is the subconscious mind, and it must be "saved" from wrong thinking.

In the twenty-third psalm, we read: "He restoreth my soul." This means that the subconscious mind or soul, must be restored with the right ideas, and the "mystical marriage" is the marriage of the soul and the spirit, or the subconscious and super-conscious mind. They must be one. When the subconscious is flooded with the perfect ideas of the superconscious, God and man are one. "I and the Father are one." That is, he is one with the realm of perfect ideas; he is the man made in God's likeness and image (imagination) and is given power and dominion over all created things, his mind, body and affairs.

It is safe to say that all sickness and unhappiness come from the violation of the law of love. A new commandment I give unto you, "Love one another," and in the Game of Life, love or good-will takes every trick.

For example: A woman I know, had, for years an appearance of a terrible skin disease. The doctors told her it was incurable, and she was in despair. She was on the stage, and she feared she would soon have to give up her profession, and she had no other means of support. She, however, procured a good engagement, and on the opening night, made a great "hit." She received flattering notices from the critics, and was joyful and elated. The next day she received a notice of dismissal. A man in the cast had been jealous of her success and had caused her to be sent away. She felt hatred and resentment taking complete possession of her, and she cried out, "Oh God don't let me hate that man." That night she worked for hours "in the silence."

She said, "I soon came into a very deep silence. I seemed to be at peace with myself, with the man, and with the whole world. I continued this for two following nights, and on the third day I found I was healed completely of the skin disease!" In asking for love, or good will, she had fulfilled the law, ("for love is the fulfilling of the law") and the disease (which came from subconscious resentment) was wiped out.

Continual criticism produces rheumatism, as critical, inharmonious thoughts cause unnatural deposits in the blood, which settle in the joints.

False growths are caused by jealousy, hatred, unforgiveness, fear, etc. Every disease is caused by a mind not at ease. I said once, in my class, "There is no use asking anyone 'What's the matter with you?' we might just as well say, 'Who's the matter with you?'" Unforgiveness is the most prolific cause of disease. It will harden arteries or liver, and affect the eye-sight. In its train are endless ills.

I called on a woman, one day, who said she was ill from having eaten a poisoned oyster. I replied, "Oh, no, the oyster was harmless, you poisoned the oyster. What's the matter with you?" She answered, "Oh about nineteen people."

She had quarrelled with nineteen people and had become so inharmonious that she attracted the wrong oyster.

Any inharmony on the external, indicates there is mental inharmony. "As the within, so the without."

Man's only enemies are within himself. "And a man's foes shall be they of his own household." Personality is one of the last enemies to be overcome, as this planet is taking its initiation in love. It was Christ's message—"Peace on Earth, good will towards man." The enlightened man, therefore, endeavors to perfect himself upon his neighbor. His work is with himself, to send out goodwill and blessings to every man, and the marvelous thing is, that if one blesses a man he has no power to harm him.

For example: A man came to me asking to "treat" for success in business. He was selling machinery, and a rival appeared on the scene with what he proclaimed, was a better machine, and my friend feared defeat. I said, "First of all, we must wipe out all fear, and know that God protects your interests, and that the divine idea must come out of the situation. That is, the right machine will be sold, by the right man, to the right man." And I added, "Don't hold one critical thought towards that man. Bless him all day, and be willing not to sell your machine, if it isn't the divine idea." So he went to the meeting, fearless and nonresistant, and blessing the other man. He said the outcome was very remarkable. The other man's machine refused to work, and he sold his without the slightest difficulty. "But I say unto you, love your enemies, bless them that curse you, do good to them that hate you, and pray for them which spitefully use you and persecute you."

Good-will produces a great aura of protection about the one who sends it, and "No weapon that is formed against him shall prosper. "In other words, love and good-will destroy the enemies within one's self, therefore, one has no enemies on the external!

"There is peace on earth for him who sends goodwill to man!"

The Law of Nonresistance

"Resist not evil. Be not overcome of evil, but overcome evil with good."

Nothing on earth can resist an absolutely nonresistant person.

The Chinese say that water is the most powerful element, because it is perfectly nonresistant. It can wear away a rock, and sweep all before it.

Jesus Christ said, "Resist not evil," for He knew in reality, there is no evil, therefore nothing to resist. Evil has come of man's "vain imagination," or a belief in two powers, good and evil.

There is an old legend, that Adam and Eve ate of "Maya the Tree of Illusion," and saw two powers instead of one power, God.

Therefore, evil is a false law man has made for himself, through psychoma or soul sleep. Soul sleep means, that man's soul has been hypnotized by the race belief (of sin, sickness and death, etc.) which is carnal or mortal thought, and his affairs have out-pictured his illusions.

We have read in a preceding chapter, that man's soul is his subconscious mind, and whatever he feels deeply, good or bad, is outpictured by that faithful servant. His body and affairs show forth what he has been picturing. The sick man has pictured sickness, the poor man, poverty, the rich man, wealth.

People often say, "why does a little child attract illness, when it is too young even to know what it means?"

I answer that children are sensitive and receptive to the thoughts of others about them, and often outpicture the fears of their parents.

I heard a metaphysician once say, "If you do not run your subconscious mind yourself, someone else will run it for you."

Mothers often, unconsciously, attract illness and disaster to their children, by continually holding them in thoughts of fear, and watching for symptoms.

For example: A friend asked a woman if her little girl had had the measles. She replied promptly, "not yet!" This implied that she was expecting the illness, and, therefore, preparing the way for what she did not want for herself and child.

However, the man who is centered and established in right thinking, the man who sends out only good-will to his fellow-man, and who is without fear, cannot be touched or influenced by the negative thoughts of others. In fact, he could then receive only good thoughts, as he himself, sends forth only good thoughts.

Resistance is Hell, for it places man in a "state of torment."

A metaphysician once gave me a wonderful recipe for taking every trick in the game of life, it is the acme of nonresistance. He gave it in this way; "At one time in my life, I baptized children, and of course, they had many names. Now I no longer baptize children, but I baptize events, but I give every event the same name. If I have a failure I baptize it success, in the name of the Father, and of the Son, and of the Holy Ghost!"

In this, we see the great law of transmutation, founded on nonresistance. Through his spoken word, every failure was transmuted into success.

For example: A woman who required money, and who knew the spiritual law of opulence, was thrown continually in a business-way, with a man who made her feel very poor. He talked lack and limitation and she commenced to catch his poverty thoughts, so she disliked him, and blamed him for her failure. She knew in order to demonstrate her supply, she must first feel that she had received—a feeling of opulence must precede its manifestation.

It dawned upon her, one day, that she was resisting the situation, and seeing two powers instead of one. So she blessed the man and baptized the situation "Success"! She affirmed, "As there is only one power, God, this man is here for my good and my prosperity" (just what he did not seem to be there for). Soon after that she met, through this man, a woman who gave her for a service rendered, several thousand dollars, and the man moved to a distant city, and faded harmoniously from her life. Make the statement, "Every man is a golden link in the chain of my good," for all men are God in manifestation, awaiting the opportunity given by man, himself, to serve the divine plan of his life.

"Bless your enemy, and you rob him of his ammunition." His arrows will be transmuted into blessings.

This law is true of nations as well as individuals. Bless a nation, send love and good-will to every inhabitant, and it is robbed of its power to harm.

Man can only get the right idea of nonresistance, through spiritual understanding. My students have often said: "I don't want to be a door-mat." I reply "when you use nonresistance with wisdom, no one will ever be able to walk over you."

Another example: One day I was impatiently awaiting an important telephone call. I resisted every call that came in and made no out-going calls myself, reasoning that it might interfere with the one I was awaiting.

Instead of saying, "Divine ideas never conflict, the call will come at the right time," leaving it to Infinite Intelligence to arrange, I commenced to manage things myself—I made the battle mine, not God's and remained tense and anxious. The bell did not ring for about an hour, and I glanced at the 'phone and found the receiver had been off that length of time, and the 'phone was disconnected. My anxiety, fear and belief in interference, had brought on a total eclipse of the telephone. Realizing what I had done, I commenced blessing the situation at once; I baptized it "success," and affirmed, "I cannot lose any call that belongs to me by divine right; I am under grace, and not under law."

A friend rushed out to the nearest telephone, to notify the Company to reconnect.

She entered a crowded grocery, but the proprietor left his customers and attended to the call himself. My 'phone was connected at once, and two minutes later, I received a very important call, and about an hour afterward, the one I had been awaiting.

One's ships come in over a calm sea.

So long as man resists a situation, he will have it with him. If he runs away from it, it will run after him.

For example: I repeated this to a woman one day, and she replied, "How true that is! I was unhappy at home, I disliked my mother, who was critical and domineering; so I ran away and was married—but I married my mother, for my husband was exactly like my mother, and I had the same situation to face again."

"Agree with thine adversary quickly."

That means, agree that the adverse situation is good, be undisturbed by it, and it falls away of its own weight. "None of these things move me," is a wonderful affirmation.

The inharmonious situation comes from some inharmony within man himself.

When there is, in him, no emotional response to an inharmonious situation, it fades away forever, from his pathway.

So we see man's work is ever with himself.

People have said to me, "Give treatments to change my husband, or my brother." I reply, "No, I will give treatments to change you; when you change, your husband and your brother will change."

One of my students was in the habit of lying. I told her it was a failure method and if she lied, she would be lied to. She replied, "I don't care, I can't possibly get along without lying."

One day she was speaking on the 'phone to a man with whom she was very much in love. She turned to me and said, "I don't trust him, I know he's lying to me." I replied, "Well, you lie yourself, so someone has to lie to you, and you will be sure it will be just the person you want the truth from." Some time after that, I saw her, and she said, "I'm cured of lying."

I questioned: "What cured you?"

She replied: "I have been living with a woman who lied worse than I did!"

One is often cured of his faults by seeing them in others.

Life is a mirror, and we find only ourselves reflected in our associates.

Living in the past is a failure method and a violation of spiritual law.

Jesus Christ said, "Behold, now is the accepted time." "Now is the day of Salvation."

Lot's wife looked back and was turned into a pillar of salt.

The robbers of time are the past and the future. Man should bless the past, and forget it, if it keeps him in bondage, and bless the future, knowing it has in store for him endless joys, but live fully in the now.

For example: A woman came to me, complaining that she had no money with which to buy Christmas gifts. She said, "Last year was so different; I had plenty of money and gave lovely presents, and this year I have scarcely a cent."

I replied, "You will never demonstrate money while you are pathetic and live in the past. Live fully in the now, and get ready to give Christmas presents. Dig your ditches, and the money will come." She exclaimed, "I know what to do! I will buy some tinsel twine, Christmas seals and wrapping paper." I replied, "Do that, and the presents will come and stick themselves to the Christmas seals."

This too, was showing financial fearlessness and faith in God, as the reasoning mind said, "Keep every cent you have, as you are not sure you will get any more."

She bought the seals, paper and twine, and a few days before Christmas, received a gift of several hundred dollars. Buying the seals and twine had impressed the subconscious with expectancy, and opened the way for the manifestation of the money. She purchased all the presents in plenty of time.

Man must live suspended in the moment.

"Look well, therefore, to this Day! Such is the salutation of the Dawn."

He must be spiritually alert, ever awaiting his leads, taking advantage of every opportunity.

One day, I said continually (silently), "Infinite Spirit, don't let me miss a trick," and something very important was told to me that evening. It is most necessary to begin the day with right words.

Make an affirmation immediately upon waking.

For example:

"Thy will be done this day! Today is a day of completion; I give thanks for this perfect day, miracle shall follow miracle and wonders shall never cease."

Make this a habit, and one will see wonders and miracles come into his life.

One morning I picked up a book and read, "Look with wonder at that which is before you!" It seemed to be my message for the day, so I repeated again and again, "Look with wonder at that which is before you."

At about noon, a large sum of money, was given me, which I had been desiring for a certain purpose.

In a following chapter, I will give affirmations that I have found most effective. However, one should never use an affirmation unless it is absolutely satisfying and convincing to his own consciousness, and often an affirmative is changed to suit different people.

For example: The following has brought success to many:

"I have a wonderful work, in a wonderful way, I give wonderful service, for wonderful pay!"

I gave the first two lines to one of my students, and she added the last two.

It made a most powerful statement, as there should always be perfect payment for perfect service, and a rhyme sinks easily into the subconscious. She went about singing it aloud and soon did receive wonderful work in a wonderful way, and gave wonderful service for wonderful pay.

Another student, a business man, took it, and changed the word work to business.

He repeated, "I have a wonderful business, in a wonderful way, and I give wonderful service for wonderful pay." That afternoon he made a forty-one-thousand dollar deal, though there had been no activity in his affairs for months.

Every affirmation must be carefully worded and completely "cover the ground."

For example: I knew a woman, who was in great need, and made a demand for work. She received a great deal of work, but was never paid anything. She now knows to add, "wonderful service for wonderful pay."

It is man's divine right to have plenty! More than enough!

"His barns should be full, and his cup should flow over!" This is God's idea for man, and when man breaks down the barriers of lack in his own consciousness, the Golden Age will be his, and every righteous desire of his heart fulfilled!

The Law of Karma
And
The Law of Forgiveness

Man receives only that which he gives. The Game of Life is a game of boomerangs. Man's thoughts, deeds and words, return to him sooner or later, with astounding accuracy.

This is the law of Karma, which is Sanskrit for "Comeback." "Whatsoever a man soweth, that shall he also reap."

For example: A friend told me this story of herself, illustrating the law. She said, "I make all my Karma on my aunt, whatever I say to her, some one says to me. I am often irritable at home, and one day, said to my aunt, who was talking to me during dinner. 'No more talk, I wish to eat in peace.'"

"The following day, I was lunching with a woman with whom I wished to make a great impression. I was talking animatedly, when she said: 'No more talk, I wish to eat in peace!'"

My friend is high in consciousness, so her Karma returns much more quickly than to one on the mental plane.

The more man knows, the more he is responsible for, and a person with a knowledge of Spiritual Law, which he does not practice, suffers greatly, in consequence. "The fear of the Lord (law) is the beginning of wisdom." If we read the word Lord, law, it will make many passages in the Bible much clearer.

"Vengeance is mine, I will repay, saith the Lord" (law). It is the law which takes vengeance, not God. God sees man perfect, "created in his own image," (imagination) and given "power and dominion."

This is the perfect idea of man, registered in Divine Mind, awaiting man's recognition; for man can only be what he sees himself to be, and only attain what he sees himself attaining.

"Nothing ever happens without an on-looker" is an ancient saying.

Man sees first his failure or success, his joy or sorrow, before it swings into visibility from the scenes set in his own imagination. We have observed this in the mother picturing disease for her child, or a woman seeing success for her husband.

Jesus Christ said, "And ye shall know the truth and the truth shall make you free."

So, we see freedom (from all unhappy conditions) comes through knowledge—a knowledge of Spiritual Law.

Obedience precedes authority, and the law obeys man when he obeys the law. The law of electricity must be obeyed before it becomes man's servant. When handled ignorantly, it becomes man's deadly foe. So with the laws of Mind!

For example: A woman with a strong personal will, wished she owned a house which belonged to an acquaintance, and she often made mental pictures of herself living in the house. In the course of time, the man died and she moved into the house. Several years afterwards, coming into the knowledge of Spiritual Law, she said to me: "Do you think I had anything to do with that man's death?" I replied: "Yes, your desire was so strong, everything made way for it, but you paid your Karmic debt. Your husband, whom you loved devotedly, died soon after, and the house was a white elephant on your hands for years."

The original owner, however, could not have been affected by her thoughts had he been positive in the truth, nor her husband, but they were both under Karmic law. The woman should have said (feeling the great desire for the house), "Infinite Intelligence, give me the right house, equally as charming as this, the house which is mine by divine right."

The divine selection would have given perfect satisfaction and brought good to all. The divine pattern is the only safe pattern to work by.

Desire is a tremendous force, and must be directed in the right channels, or chaos ensues.

In demonstrating, the most important step is the first step, to "ask aright."

Man should always demand only that which is his by divine right.

To go back to the illustration: Had the woman taken this attitude: "If this house, I desire, is mine, I cannot lose it, if it is not, give me its equivalent," the man might have decided to move out, harmoniously (had it been the divine selection for her) or another house would have been substituted. Anything forced into manifestation through personal will, is always "ill-got," and has "ever bad success."

Man is admonished, "My will be done not thine," and the curious thing is, man always gets just what he desires when he does relinquish personal will, thereby enabling Infinite Intelligence to work through him.

"Stand ye still and see the salvation of the Lord" (law).

For example: A woman came to me in great distress. Her daughter had determined to take a very hazardous trip, and the mother was filled with fear.

She said she had used every argument, had pointed out the dangers to be encountered, and forbidden her to go, but the daughter became more and more rebellious and determined. I said to the mother, "You are forcing your personal will upon your daughter, which you have no right to do, and your fear of the trip is only attracting it, for man attracts what he fears." I added, "Let go, and take your mental hands off; put it in God's Hands, and use this statement:" "I put this situation in the hands of Infinite Love and Wisdom; if this trip is the Divine plan,

I bless it and no longer resist, but if it is not divinely planned, I give thanks that it is now dissolved and dissipated." A day or two after that, her daughter said to her, "Mother, I have given up the trip," and the situation returned to its "native nothingness."

It is learning to "stand still," which seems so difficult for man. I will deal more fully with this law in the chapter on nonresistance.

I will give another example of sowing and reaping, which came in the most curious way.

A woman came to me saying, she had received a counterfeit twenty-dollar bill, given to her at the bank. She was much disturbed, for, she said, "The people at the bank will never acknowledge their mistake."

I replied, "Let us analyze the situation and find out why you attracted it." She thought a few moments and exclaimed: "I know it, I sent a friend a lot of stagemoney, just for a joke." So the law had sent her some stagemoney, for it doesn't know anything about jokes.

I said, "Now we will call on the law of forgiveness, and neutralize the situation."

Christianity is founded upon the law of forgiveness—Christ has redeemed us from the curse of the Karmic law, and the Christ within each man is his Redeemer and Salvation from all inharmonious conditions.

So I said: "Infinite Spirit, we call on the law of forgiveness and give thanks that she is under grace and not under law, and cannot lose this twenty dollars which is hers by divine right."

"Now," I said, "Go back to the bank and tell them, fearlessly, that it was given you, there by mistake."

She obeyed, and to her surprise, they apologized and gave her another bill, treating her most courteously.

So knowledge of the Law gives man power to "rub out his mistakes." Man cannot force the external to be what he is not.

If he desires riches, he must be rich first in consciousness.

For example: A woman came to me asking treatment for prosperity. She did not take much interest in her household affairs, and her home was in great disorder.

I said to her, "If you wish to be rich, you must be orderly. All men with great wealth are orderly—and order is heaven's first law." I added, "You will never become rich with a burnt match in the pincushion."

She had a good sense of humor and commenced immediately, putting her house in order. She rearranged furniture, straightened out bureau drawers, cleaned rugs, and soon made a big financial demonstration—a gift from a relative. The woman, herself, became made over, and keeps herself keyed-up financially, by being ever watchful of the external and expecting prosperity, knowing God is her supply.

Many people are in ignorance of the fact that gifts and things are investments, and that hoarding and saving invariably lead to loss.

"There is that scattereth and yet increaseth; and there is that withholdeth more than is meet, but it tendeth to poverty."

For example: I knew a man who wanted to buy a fur-lined overcoat. He and his wife went to various shops, but there was none he wanted. He said they were all too cheap-looking. At last, he was shown one, the salesman said was valued at a thousand dollars, but which the manager would sell him for five-hundred dollars, as it was late in the season.

His financial possessions amounted to about seven hundred dollars. The reasoning mind would have said, "You can't afford to spend nearly all you have on a coat," but he was very intuitive and never reasoned.

He turned to his wife and said, "If I get this coat, I'll make a ton of money!" So his wife consented, weakly.

About a month later, he received a ten-thousand-dollar commission. The coat made him feel so rich, it linked him with success and prosperity; without the coat, he would not have received the commission. It was an investment paying large dividends!

If man ignores these leadings to spend or to give, the same amount of money will go in an uninteresting or unhappy way.

For example: A woman told me, on Thanksgiving Day, she informed her family that they could not afford a Thanksgiving dinner. She had the money, but decided to save it.

A few days later, someone entered her room and took from the bureau drawer the exact amount the dinner would have cost.

The law always stands back of the man who spends fearlessly, with wisdom.

For example: One of my students was shopping with her little nephew. The child clamored for a toy, which she told him she could not afford to buy.

She realized suddenly that she was seeking lack, and not recognizing God as her supply!

So she bought the toy, and on her way home, picked up, in the street, the exact amount of money she had paid for it.

Man's supply is inexhaustible and unfailing when fully trusted, but faith or trust must precede the demonstration. "According to your faith be it unto you." "Faith is the substance of things hoped for, the evidence of things not see—"for faith holds the vision steady, and the adverse pictures are dissolved and dissipated, and "in due season we shall reap, if we faint not."

Jesus Christ brought the good news (the gospel) that there was a higher law than the law of Karma—and that that law transcends the law of Karma. It is the law of grace, or forgiveness. It is the law which frees man from the law of cause and effect—the law of consequence. "Under grace, and not under law."

We are told that on this plane, man reaps where he has not sown; the gifts of God are simply poured out upon him. "All that the Kingdom affords is his." This continued state of bliss awaits the man who has overcome the race (or world) thought.

In the world thought there is tribulation, but Jesus Christ said: "Be of good cheer; I have overcome the world."

The world thought is that of sin, sickness and death. He saw their absolute unreality and said sickness and sorrow shall pass away and death itself, the last enemy, be overcome.

We know now, from a scientific standpoint, that death could be overcome by stamping the subconscious mind with the conviction of eternal youth and eternal life.

The subconscious, being simply power without direction, carries out orders without questioning.

Working under the direction of the superconscious (the Christ or God within man) the "resurrection of the body" would be accomplished.

Man would no longer throw off his body in death, it would be transformed into the "body electric," sung by Walt Whitman, for Christianity is founded upon the forgiveness of sins and "an empty tomb."

Casting the Burden

Impressing the Subconscious

When man knows his own powers and the workings of his mind, his great desire is to find an easy and quick way to impress the subconscious with good, for simply an intellectual knowledge of the Truth will not bring results.

In my own case, I found the easiest way is in "casting the burden."

A metaphysician once explained it in this manner. He said, "The only thing which gives anything weight in nature, is the law of gravitation, and if a boulder could be taken high above the planet, there would be no weight in that boulder; and that is what Jesus Christ meant when he said: "My yoke is easy and my burden is light."

He had overcome the world vibration, and functioned in the fourth dimensional realm, where there is only perfection, completion, life and joy.

He said: "Come to me all ye that labor and are heavy laden, and I will give you rest." "Take my yoke upon you, for my yoke is easy and my burden is light."

We are also told in the fifty-fifth Psalm, to "cast thy burden upon the Lord." Many passages in the Bible state that the battle is God's not man's and that man is always to "stand still" and see the Salvation of the Lord.

This indicates that the superconscious mind (or Christ within) is the department which fights man's battle and relieves him of burdens.

We see, therefore, that man violates law if he carries a burden, and a burden is an adverse thought or condition, and this thought or condition has its root in the subconscious.

It seems almost impossible to make any headway directing the subconscious from the conscious, or reasoning mind, as the reasoning mind (the intellect) is limited in its conceptions, and filled with doubts and fears.

How scientific it then is, to cast the burden upon the superconscious mind (or Christ within) where it is "made light," or dissolved into its "native nothingness."

For example: A woman in urgent need of money, "made light" upon the Christ within, the superconscious, with the statement, "I cast this burden of lack on the Christ (within) and I go free to have plenty!"

The belief in lack was her burden, and as she cast it upon the Superconscious with its belief of plenty, an avalanche of supply was the result.

We read, "The Christ in you the hope of glory."

Another example: One of my students had been given a new piano, and there was no room in her studio for it until she had moved out the old one. She was in a state of perplexity. She wanted to keep the old piano, but knew of no place to send it. She became desperate, as the new piano was to be sent immediately; in fact, was on its way, with no place to put it. She said it came to her to repeat, "I cast this burden on the Christ within, and I go free."

A few moments later, her 'phone rang, and a woman friend asked if she might rent her old piano, and it was moved out, a few minutes before the new one arrived.

I knew a woman, whose burden was resentment. She said, "I cast this burden of resentment on the Christ within, and I go free, to be loving, harmonious and happy." The Almighty superconscious, flooded the subconscious with love, and her whole life was changed. For years, resentment had held her in a state of torment and imprisoned her soul (the subconscious mind).

The statement should be made over and over and over, sometimes for hours at a time, silently or audibly, with quietness but determination.

I have often compared it to winding-up a victrola. We must wind ourselves up with spoken words.

I have noticed, in "casting the burden," after a little while, one seems to see clearly. It is impossible to have clear vision, while in the throes of carnal mind. Doubts and fear poison the mind and body and imagination runs riot, attracting disaster and disease.

In steadily repeating the affirmation, "I cast this burden on the Christ within, and go free," the vision clears, and with it a feeling of relief, and sooner or later comes the manifestation of good, be it health, happiness or supply.

One of my students once asked me to explain the "darkness before the dawn." I referred in a preceding chapter to the fact that often, before the big demonstration "everything seems to go wrong," and deep depression clouds the consciousness. It means that out of the subconscious are rising the doubts and fears of the ages. These old derelicts of the subconscious rise to the surface, to be put out.

It is then, that man should clap his cymbals, like Jehoshaphat, and give thanks that he is saved, even though he seems surrounded by the enemy (the situation of lack or disease). The student continued, "How long must one remain in the dark" and I replied, "until one can see in the dark," and "casting the burden enables one to see in the dark."

In order to impress the subconscious, active faith is always essential.

"Faith without works is dead." In these chapters I have endeavored to bring out this point.

Jesus Christ showed active faith when "He commanded the multitude to sit down on the ground," before he gave thanks for the loaves and the fishes.

I will give another example showing how necessary this step is. In fact, active faith is the bridge, over which man passes to his Promised Land.

Through misunderstanding, a woman had been separated from her husband, whom she loved deeply. He refused all offers of reconciliation and would not communicate with her in any way.

Coming into the knowledge of Spiritual law, she denied the appearance of separation. She made this statement: "There is no separation in Divine Mind, therefore, I cannot be separated from the love and companionship which are mine by divine right."

She showed active faith by arranging a place for him at the table every day; thereby impressing the subconscious with a picture of his return. Over a year passed, but she never wavered, and one day he walked in.

The subconscious is often impressed through music. Music has a fourth dimensional quality and releases the soul from imprisonment. It makes wonderful things seem possible, and easy of accomplishment!

I have a friend who uses her victrola, daily, for this purpose. It puts her in perfect harmony and releases the imagination.

Another woman often dances while making her affirmations. The rhythm and harmony of music and motion carry her words forth with tremendous power.

The student must remember also, not to despise the "day of small things."

Invariably, before a demonstration, come "signs of land."

Before Columbus reached America, he saw birds and twigs which showed him land was near. So it is with a demonstration; but often the student mistakes it for the demonstration itself, and is disappointed.

For example: A woman had "spoken the word" for a set of dishes. Not long afterwards a friend gave her a dish which was old and cracked.

She came to me and said, "Well, I asked for a set of dishes, and all I got was a cracked plate."

I replied, "The plate was only signs of land. It shows your dishes are coming—look upon it as birds and seaweed," and not long afterwards the dishes came.

Continually "making-believe," impresses the subconscious. If one makes believe he is rich, and makes believe he is successful, in "due time he will reap."

Children are always "making believe," and "except ye be converted, and become as little children, ye shall not enter the Kingdom of Heaven."

For example: I know of a woman who was very poor, but no one could make her feel poor. She earned a small amount of money from rich friends, who constantly reminded her of her poverty, and to be careful and saving. Regardless of their admonitions, she would spend all her earnings on a hat, or make someone a gift, and be in a rapturous state of mind. Her thoughts were always centered on beautiful clothes and "rings and things," but without envying others.

She lived in the world of the wondrous, and only riches seemed real to her. Before long she married a rich man, and the rings and things became visible. I do not know whether the man was the "Divine Selection," but opulence had to manifest in her life, as she had imaged only opulence.

There is no peace or happiness for man, until he has erased all fear from the subconscious.

Fear is misdirected energy and must be redirected, or transmuted into Faith.

Jesus Christ said, "Why are ye fearful, O ye of little faith?" "All things are possible to him that believeth."

I am asked, so often by my students, "How can I get rid of fear?"

I reply, "By walking up to the thing you are afraid of."

"The lion takes its fierceness from your fear."

Walk up to the lion, and he will disappear; run away and he runs after you.

I have shown in previous chapters, how the lion of lack disappeared when the individual spent money fearlessly, showing faith that God was his supply and therefore, unfailing.

Many of my students have come out of the bondage of poverty, and are now bountifully supplied, through losing all fear of letting money go out. The subconscious is impressed with the truth that God is the Giver and the Gift; therefore as one is one with the Giver, he is one with the Gift. A splendid statement is, "I now thank God the Giver for God the Gift."

Man has so long separated himself from his good and his supply, through thoughts of separation and lack, that sometimes, it takes dynamite to dislodge these false ideas from the subconscious, and the dynamite is a big situation.

We see in the foregoing illustration, how the individual was freed from his bondage by showing fearlessness.

Man should watch himself hourly to detect if his motive for action is fear or faith.

"Choose ye this day whom we shall serve," fear or faith.

Perhaps one's fear is of personality. Then do not avoid the people feared; be willing to meet them cheerfully, and they will either prove "golden links in the chain of one's good," or disappear harmoniously from one's pathway.

Perhaps one's fear is of disease or germs. Then one should be fearless and undisturbed in a germ-laden situation, and he would be immune.

One can only contract germs while vibrating at the same rate as the germ, and fear drags men down to the level of the germ. Of course, the disease laden germ is the product of carnal mind, as all thought must objectify. Germs do not exist in the superconscious or Divine Mind, therefore are the product of man's "vain imagination."

"In the twinkling of an eye," man's release will come when he realizes there is no power in evil.

The material world will fade away, and the fourth dimensional world, the "World of the Wondrous," will swing into manifestation.

"And I saw a new heaven, and a new earth—and there shall be no more death, neither sorrow nor crying, neither shall there be any more pain; for the former things are passed away."

Love

Every man on this planet is taking his initiation in love. "A new commandment I give unto you, that ye love one another." Ouspensky states, in "Tertium Organum," that "love is a cosmic phenomenon," and opens to man the fourth dimensional world, "The World of the Wondrous."

Real love is selfless and free from fear. It pours itself out upon the object of its affection, without demanding any return. Its joy is in the joy of giving. Love is God in manifestation, and the strongest magnetic force in the universe. Pure, unselfish love draws to itself its own; it does not need to seek or demand. Scarcely anyone has the faintest conception of real love. Man is selfish, tyrannical or fearful in his affections, thereby losing the thing he loves. Jealousy is the worst enemy of love, for the imagination runs riot, seeing the loved one attracted to another, and invariably these fears objectify if they are not neutralized.

For example: A woman came to me in deep distress. The man she loved had left her for other women, and said he never intended to marry her. She was torn with jealousy and resentment and said she hoped he would suffer as he had made her suffer; and added, "How could he leave me when I loved him so much?"

I replied, "You are not loving that man, you are hating him," and added, "You can never receive what you have never given. Give a perfect love and you will receive a perfect love. Perfect yourself on this man. Give him a perfect, unselfish love, demanding nothing in return, do not criticise or condemn, and bless him wherever he is."

She replied, "No, I won't bless him unless I know where he is!"

"Well," I said, "that is not real love."

"When you send out real love, real love will return to you, either from this man or his equivalent, for if this man is not the divine selection, you will not want him. As you are one with God, you are one with the love which belongs to you by divine right."

Several months passed, and matters remained about the same, but she was working conscientiously with herself. I said, "When you are no longer disturbed by his cruelty, he will cease to be cruel, as you are attracting it through your own emotions."

Then I told her of a brotherhood in India, who never said, "Good morning" to each other. They used these words: "I salute the Divinity in you." They saluted the divinity in every man, and in the wild animals in the jungle, and they were never harmed, for they saw only God in every living thing. I said, "Salute the divinity in this man, and say, 'I see your divine self only. I see you as God sees you, perfect, made in His image and likeness.'"

She found she was becoming more poised, and gradually losing her resentment. He was a Captain, and she always called him "The Cap."

One day, she said, suddenly, "God bless the Cap wherever he is."

I replied: "Now, that is real love, and when you have become a 'complete circle,' and are no longer disturbed by the situation, you will have his love, or attract its equivalent."

I was moving at this time, and did not have a telephone, so was out of touch with her for a few weeks, when one morning I received a letter saying, "We are married."

At the earliest opportunity, I paid her a call. My first words were, "What happened?"

"Oh," she exclaimed, "a miracle! One day I woke up and all suffering had ceased. I saw him that evening and he asked me to marry him. We were married in about a week, and I have never seen a more devoted man."

There is an old saying: "No man is your enemy, no man is your friend, every man is your teacher."

So one should become impersonal and learn what each man has to teach him, and soon he would learn his lessons and be free.

The woman's lover was teaching her selfless love, which every man, sooner or later, must learn.

Suffering is not necessary for man's development; it is the result of violation of spiritual law, but few people seem able to rouse themselves from their "soul sleep" without it. When people are happy, they usually become selfish, and automatically the law of Karma is set in action. Man often suffers loss through lack of appreciation.

I knew a woman who had a very nice husband, but she said often, "I don't care anything about being married, but that is nothing against my husband. I'm simply not interested in married life."

She had other interests, and scarcely remembered she had a husband. She only thought of him when she saw him. One day her husband told her he was in love with another woman, and left. She came to me in distress and resentment.

I replied, "It is exactly what you spoke the word for. You said you didn't care anything about being married, so the subconscious worked to get you unmarried."

She said, "Oh yes, I see. People get what they want, and then feel very much hurt."

She soon became in perfect harmony with the situation, and knew they were both much happier apart.

When a woman becomes indifferent or critical, and ceases to be an inspiration to her husband, he misses the stimulus of their early relationship and is restless and unhappy.

A man came to me dejected, miserable and poor. His wife was interested in the "Science of Numbers," and had had him read. It seems the report was not very favorable, for he said, "My wife says I'll never amount to anything because I am a two."

I replied, "I don't care what your number is, you are a perfect idea in divine mind, and we will demand the success and prosperity which are already planned for you by that Infinite Intelligence."

Within a few weeks, he had a very fine position, and a year or two later, he achieved a brilliant success as a writer. No man is a success in business unless he loves his work. The picture the artist paints for love (of his art) is his greatest work. The pot-boiler is always something to live down.

No man can attract money if he despises it. Many people are kept in poverty by saying: "Money means nothing to me, and I have a contempt for people who have it."

This is the reason so many artists are poor. Their contempt for money separates them from it.

I remember hearing one artist say of another, "He's no good as an artist, he has money in the bank."

This attitude of mind, of course, separates man from his supply; he must be in harmony with a thing in order to attract it.

Money is God in manifestation, as freedom from want and limitation, but it must be always kept in circulation and put to right uses. Hoarding and saving react with grim vengeance.

This does not mean that man should not have houses and lots, stocks and bonds, for "the barns of the righteous man shall be full." It means man should not hoard even the principal, if an occasion arises, when money is necessary. In letting it go out fearlessly and cheerfully he opens the way for more to come in, for God is man's unfailing and inexhaustible supply.

This is the spiritual attitude towards money and the great Bank of the Universal never fails!

We see an example of hoarding in the film production of "Greed." The woman won five thousand dollars in a lottery, but would not spend it. She hoarded and saved, let her husband suffer and starve, and eventually she scrubbed floors for a living.

She loved the money itself and put it above everything, and one night she was murdered and the money taken from her.

This is an example of where "love of money is the root of all evil." Money in itself, is good and beneficial, but used for destructive purposes, hoarded and saved, or considered more important than love, brings disease and disaster, and the loss of the money itself.

Follow the path of love, and all things are added, for God is love, and God is supply; follow the path of selfishness and greed, and the supply vanishes, or man is separated from it.

For example; I knew the case of a very rich woman, who hoarded her income. She rarely gave anything away, but bought and bought and bought things for herself.

She was very fond of necklaces, and a friend once asked her how many she possessed. She replied, "Sixty-seven." She bought them and put them away, carefully wrapped in tissue paper. Had she used the necklaces it would have been quite legitimate, but she was violating "the law of use." Her closets were filled with clothes she never wore, and jewels which never saw the light.

The woman's arms were gradually becoming paralyzed from holding on to things, and eventually she was considered incapable of looking after her affairs and her wealth was handed over to others to manage.

So man, in ignorance of the law, brings about his own destruction.

All disease, all unhappiness, come from the violation of the law of love. Man's boomerangs of hate, resentment and criticism, come back laden with sickness and sorrow. Love seems almost a lost art, but the man with the knowledge of spiritual law knows it must be regained, for without it, he has "become as sounding brass and tinkling cymbals."

For example: I had a student who came to me, month after month, to clean her consciousness of resentment. After a while, she arrived at the point where she resented only one woman, but that one woman kept her busy. Little by little she became poised and harmonious, and one day, all resentment was wiped out.

She came in radiant, and exclaimed "You can't understand how I feel! The woman said something to me and instead of being furious I was loving and kind, and she apologized and was perfectly lovely to me.

No one can understand the marvelous lightness I feel within!"

Love and good-will are invaluable in business. For example: A woman came to me, complaining of her employer. She said she was cold and critical and knew she did not want her in the position.

"Well," I replied, "Salute the Divinity in the woman and send her love."

She said "I can't; she's a marble woman."

I answered, "You remember the story of the sculptor who asked for a certain piece of marble. He was asked why he wanted it, and he replied, 'because there is an angel in the marble,' and out of it he produced a wonderful work of art."

She said, "Very well, I'll try it." A week later she came back and said, "I did what you told me to, and now the woman is very kind, and took me out in her car."

People are sometimes filled with remorse for having done someone an unkindness, perhaps years ago.

If the wrong cannot be righted, its effect can be neutralized by doing some one a kindness in the present.

"This one thing I do, forgetting those things which are behind and reaching forth unto those things which are before."

Sorrow, regret and remorse tear down the cells of the body, and poison the atmosphere of the individual.

A woman said to me in deep sorrow, "Treat me to be happy and joyous, for my sorrow makes me so irritable with the members of my family that I keep making more Karma."

I was asked to treat a woman who was mourning for her daughter. I denied all belief in loss and separation, and affirmed that God was the woman's joy, love and peace.

The woman gained her poise at once, but sent word by her son, not to treat any longer, because she was "so happy, it wasn't respectable."

So "mortal mind" loves to hang on to its griefs and regrets.

I knew a woman who went about bragging of her troubles, so, of course, she always had something to brag about.

The old idea was if a woman did not worry about her children, she was not a good mother.

Now, we know that mother-fear is responsible for many of the diseases and accidents which come into the lives of children.

For fear pictures vividly the disease or situation feared, and these pictures objectify, if not neutralized.

Happy is the mother who can say sincerely, that she puts her child in God's hands, and knows therefore, that he is divinely protected.

For example: A woman awoke suddenly, in the night, feeling her brother was in great danger. Instead of giving in to her fears, she commenced making statements of Truth, saying, "Man is a perfect idea in Divine Mind, and is always in his right place, therefore, my brother is in his right place, and is divinely protected."

The next day she found that her brother had been in close proximity to an explosion in a mine, but had miraculously escaped.

So man is his brother's keeper (in thought) and every man should know that the thing he loves dwells in "the secret place of the most high, and abides under the shadow of the Almighty."

"There shall no evil befall thee, neither shall any plague come nigh thy dwelling."

"Perfect love casteth out fear. He that feareth is not made perfect in love," and "Love is the fulfilling of the Law."

Intuition or Guidance

"In all thy ways acknowledge Him and He shall direct thy paths."

There is nothing too great of accomplishment for the man who knows the power of his word, and who follows his intuitive leads. By the word he starts in action unseen forces and can rebuild his body or remold his affairs.

It is, therefore, of the utmost importance to choose the right words, and the student carefully selects the affirmation he wishes to catapult into the invisible.

He knows that God is his supply, that there is a supply for every demand, and that his spoken word releases this supply.

"Ask and ye shall receive."

Man must make the first move. "Draw nigh to God and He will draw nigh to you."

I have often been asked just how to make a demonstration.

I reply: "Speak the word and then do not do anything until you ge t a definite lead." Demand the lead, saying, "Infinite Spirit, reveal to me the way, let me know if there is anything for me to do."

The answer will come through intuition (or hunch); a chance remark from someone, or a passage in a book, etc., etc. The answers are sometimes quite startling in their exactness. For example: A woman desired a large sum of money. She spoke the words: "Infinite Spirit, open the way for my immediate supply, let all that is mine by divine right now reach me, in great avalanches of abundance." Then she added: "Give me a definite lead, let me know if there is anything for me to do."

The thought came quickly, "Give a certain friend" (who had helped her spiritually) "a hundred dollars." She told her friend, who said, "Wait and get another lead, before giving it." So she waited, and that day met a woman who said to her, "I gave someone a dollar today; it was just as much for me, as it would be for you to give someone a hundred."

This was indeed an unmistakable lead, so she knew she was right in giving the hundred dollars. It was a gift which proved a great investment, for shortly after that, a large sum of money came to her in a remarkable way.

Giving opens the way for receiving. In order to create activity in finances, one should give. Tithing or giving one-tenth of one's income, is an old Jewish custom, and is sure to bring increase. Many of the richest men in this country have been tithers, and I have never known it to fail as an investment.

The tenth-part goes forth and returns blessed and multiplied. But the gift or tithe must be given with love and cheerfulness, for "God loveth a cheerful giver." Bills should be paid cheerfully; all money should be sent forth fearlessly and with a blessing.

This attitude of mind makes man master of money. It is his to obey, and his spoken word then opens vast reservoirs of wealth.

Man, himself, limits his supply by his limited vision. Sometimes the student has a great realization of wealth, but is afraid to act.

The vision and action must go hand in hand, as in the case of the man who bought the fur-lined overcoat.

A woman came to me asking me to "speak the word" for a position. So I demanded: "Infinite Spirit, open the way for this woman's right position." Never ask for just "a position"; ask for the right position, the place already planned in Divine Mind, as it is the only one that will give satisfaction.

I then gave thanks that she had already received, and that it would manifest quickly. Very soon, she had three positions offered her, two in New York and one in Palm Beach, and she did not know which to choose. I said, "Ask for a definite lead."

The time was almost up and was still undecided, when one day, she telephoned, "When I woke up this morning, I could smell Palm Beach." She had been there before and knew its balmy fragrance.

I replied: "Well, if you can smell Palm Beach from here, it is certainly your lead." She accepted the position, and it proved a great success. Often one's lead comes at an unexpected time.

One day, I was walking down the street, when I suddenly felt a strong urge to go to a certain bakery, a block or two away.

The reasoning mind resisted, arguing, "There is nothing there that you want."

However, I had learned not to reason, so I went to the bakery, looked at everything, and there was certainly nothing there that I wanted, but coming out I encountered a woman I had thought of often, and who was in great need of the help which I could give her.

So often, one goes for one thing and finds another.

Intuition is a spiritual faculty and does not explain, but simply points the way.

A person often receives a lead during a "treatment." The idea that comes may seem quite irrelevant, but some of God's leadings are "mysterious."

In the class, one day, I was treating that each individual would receive a definite lead. A woman came to me afterwards, and said: "While you were treating, I got the hunch to take my furniture out of storage and get an apartment." The woman had come to be treated for health. I told her I knew in getting a home of her own, her health would improve, and I added, "I believe your trouble, which is a congestion, has come from having things stored away. Congestion of things causes congestion in the body. You have violated the law of use, and your body is paying the penalty."

So I gave thanks that "Divine order was established in her mind, body and affairs."

People little dream of how their affairs react on the body. There is a mental correspondence for every disease. A person might receive instantaneous healing through the realization of his body being a perfect idea in Divine Mind, and, therefore, whole and perfect, but if he continues his destructive thinking, hoarding, hating, fearing, condemning, the disease will return.

Jesus Christ knew that all sickness came from sin, but admonished the leper after the healing, to go and sin no more, lest a worse thing come upon him.

So man's soul (or subconscious mind) must be washed whiter than snow, for permanent healing; and the metaphysician is always delving deep for the "correspondence."

Jesus Christ said, "Condemn not lest ye also be condemned."

"Judge not, lest ye be judged."

Many people have attracted disease and unhappiness through condemnation of others.

What man condemns in others, he attracts to himself.

For example: A friend came to me in anger and distress, because her husband had deserted her for another woman. She condemned the other woman, and said continually, "She knew he was a married man, and had no right to accept his attentions."

I replied. "Stop condemning the woman, bless her, and be through with the situation, otherwise, you are attracting the same thing to yourself."

She was deaf to my words, and a year or two later, became deeply interested in a married man, herself.

Man picks up a live-wire whenever he criticises or condemns, and may expect a shock.

Indecision is a stumbling-block in many a pathway. In order to overcome it, make the statement, repeatedly, "I am always under direct inspiration; I make right decisions, quickly."

These words impress the subconscious, and soon one finds himself awake and alert, making his right moves without hesitation. I have found it destructive to look to the psychic plane for guidance, as it is the plane of many minds and not "The One Mind."

As man opens his mind to subjectivity, he becomes a target for destructive forces. The psychic plane is the result of man's mortal thought, and is on the "plane of opposites." He may receive either good or bad messages.

The science of numbers and the reading of horoscopes, keep man down on the mental (or mortal) plane, for they deal only with the Karmic path.

I know of a man who should have been dead, years ago, according to his horoscope, but he is alive and a leader of one of the biggest movements in this country for the uplift of humanity.

It takes a very strong mind to neutralize a prophecy of evil. The student should declare, "Every false prophecy shall come to naught; every plan my Father in heaven has not planned, shall be dissolved and dissipated, the divine idea now comes to pass."

However, if any good message has ever been given one, of coming happiness, or wealth, harbor and expect it, and it will manifest sooner or later, through the law of expectancy.

Man's will should be used to back the universal will. "I will that the will of God be done."

It is God's will to give every man, every righteous desire of his heart, and man's will should be used to hold the perfect vision, without wavering.

The prodigal son said: "I will arise and go to my Father."

It is, indeed, often an effort of the will to leave the husks and swine of mortal thinking. It is so much easier, for the average person, to have fear than faith; so faith is an effort of the will.

As man becomes spiritually awakened he recognizes that any external inharmony is the correspondence of mental inharmony. If he stumbles or falls, he may know he is stumbling or falling in consciousness.

One day, a student was walking along the street condemning someone in her thoughts. She was saying, mentally, "That woman is the most disagreeable woman on earth," when suddenly three boy scouts rushed around the corner and almost knocked her over. She did not condemn the boy scouts, but immediately called on the law of forgiveness, and "saluted the divinity" in the woman. Wisdom's way are ways of pleasantness and all her paths are peace.

When one has made his demands upon the Universal, he must be ready for surprises. Everything may seem to be going wrong, when in reality, it is going right.

For example: A woman was told that there was no loss in divine mind, therefore, she could not lose anything which belonged to her; anything lost, would be returned, or she would receive its equivalent.

Several years previously, she had lost two thousand dollars. She had loaned the money to a relative during her lifetime, but the relative had died, leaving no mention of it in her will. The woman was resentful and angry, and as she had no written statement of the transaction, she never received the money, so she determined to deny the loss, and collect the two thousand dollars from the Bank of the Universal. She had to begin by forgiving the woman, as resentment and unforgiveness close the doors of this wonderful bank.

She made this statement, "I deny loss, there is no loss in Divine Mind, therefore, I cannot lose the two thousand dollars, which belong to me by divine right. "As one door shuts another door opens."

She was living in an apartment house which was for sale; and in the lease was a clause, stating that if the house was sold, the tenants would be required to move out within ninety days.

Suddenly, the landlord broke the leases and raised the rent. Again, injustice was on her pathway, but this time she was undisturbed. She blessed the landlord, and said, "As the rent has been raised, it means that I'll be that much richer, for God is my supply."

New leases were made out for the advanced rent, but by some divine mistake, the ninety days clause had been forgotten. Soon after, the landlord had an opportunity to sell the house. On account of the mistake in the new leases, the tenants held possession for another year.

The agent offered each tenant two hundred dollars if he would vacate. Several families moved; three remained, including the woman. A month or two passed, and the agent again appeared. This time he said to the woman, "Will you break your lease for the sum of fifteen hundred dollars?" It flashed upon her, "Here comes the two thousand dollars." She remembered having said to friends in the house, "We will all act together if anything more is said about leaving." So her lead was to consult her friends.

These friends said: "Well, if they have offered you fifteen hundred they will certainly give two thousand." So she received a check for two thousand dollars for giving up the apartment. It was certainly a remarkable working of the law, and the apparent injustice was merely opening the way for her demonstration.

It proved that there is no loss, and when man takes his spiritual stand, he collects all that is his from this great Reservoir of Good.

"I will restore to you the years the locusts have eaten."

The locusts are the doubts, fears, resentments and regrets of mortal thinking.

These adverse thoughts, alone, rob man; for "No man gives to himself but himself, and no man takes away from himself, but himself."

Man is here to prove God and "to bear witness to the truth," and he can only prove God by bringing plenty out of lack, and justice out of injustice.

"Prove me now herewith, saith the Lord of hosts, if I will not open you the windows of heaven, and pour out a blessing, that there shall not be room enough to receive it."

Perfect Self-expression
Or
The Divine Design

"No wind can drive my bark astray nor change the tide of destiny."

There is for each man, perfect self-expression. There is a place which he is to fill and no one else can fill, something which he is to do, which no one else can do; it is his destiny!

This achievement is held, a perfect idea in Divine Mind, awaiting man's recognition. As the imaging faculty is the creative faculty, it is necessary for man to see the idea, before it can manifest.

So man's highest demand is for the Divine Design of his life.

He may not have the faintest conception of what it is, for there is, possibly, some marvelous talent, hidden deep within him.

His demand should be: "Infinite Spirit, open the way for the Divine Design of my life to manifest; let the genius within me now be released; let me see clearly the perfect plan."

The perfect plan includes health, wealth, love and perfect self-expression. This is the square of life, which brings perfect happiness. When one has made this demand, he may find great changes taking place in his life, for nearly every man has wandered far from the Divine Design.

I know, in one woman's case, it was as though a cyclone had struck her affairs, but readjustments came quickly, and new and wonderful conditions took the place of old ones.

Perfect self-expression will never be labor; but of such absorbing interest that it will seem almost like play. The student knows, also, as man comes into the world financed by God, the supply needed for his perfect self-expression will be at hand.

Many a genius has struggled for years with the problem of supply, when his spoken word, and faith, would have released quickly, the necessary funds.

For example: After the class, one day, a man came to me and handed me a cent.

He said: "I have just seven cents in the world, and I'm going to give you one; for I have faith in the power of your spoken word. I want you to speak the word for my perfect self-expression and prosperity."

I "spoke the word," and did not see him again until a year later. He came in one day, successful and happy, with a roll of yellow bills in his pocket. He said, "Immediately after you spoke the word, I had a position offered me in a distant city, and am now demonstrating health, happiness and supply."

A woman's perfect self-expression may be in becoming a perfect wife, a perfect mother, a perfect home-maker and not necessarily in having a public career.

Demand definite leads, and the way will be made easy and successful.

One should not visualize or force a mental picture. When he demands the Divine Design to come into his conscious mind, he will receive flashes of inspiration, and begin to see himself making some great accomplishment. This is the picture, or idea, he must hold without wavering.

The thing man seeks is seeking him—the telephone was seeking Bell!

Parents should never force careers and professions upon their children. With a knowledge of spiritual Truth, the Divine Plan could be spoken for, early in childhood, or prenatally.

A prenatal treatment should be: "Let the God in this child have perfect expression; let the Divine Design of his mind, body and affairs be made manifest throughout his life, throughout eternity."

God's will be done, not man's; God's pattern, not man's pattern, is the command we find running through all the scriptures, and the Bible is a book dealing with the science of the mind. It is a book telling man how to release his soul (or subconscious mind) from bondage.

The battles described are pictures of man waging war against mortal thoughts. "A man's foes shall be they of his own household." Every man is Jehoshaphat, and every man is David, who slays Goliath (mortal thinking) with the little white stone (faith).

So man must be careful that he is not the "wicked and slothful servant" who buried his talent. There is a terrible penalty to be paid for not using one's ability.

Often fear stands between man and his perfect self-expression. Stage-fright has hampered many a genius. This may be overcome by the spoken word, or treatment. The individual then loses all self-consciousness, and feels simply that he is a channel for Infinite Intelligence to express Itself through.

He is under direct inspiration, fearless, and confident; for he feels that it is the "Father within" him who does the work.

A young boy came often to my class with his mother. He asked me to "speak the word" for his coming examinations at school.

I told him to make the statement: "I am one with Infinite Intelligence. I know everything I should know on this subject." He had an excellent knowledge of history, but was not sure of his arithmetic. I saw him afterwards, and he said: "I spoke the word for my arithmetic, and passed with the highest honors; but thought I could depend on myself for history, and got a very poor mark." Man often receives a set-back when he is "too sure of himself," which means he is trusting to his personality and not the "Father within."

Another one of my students gave me an example of this. She took an extended trip abroad one summer, visiting many countries, where she was ignorant of the languages. She was calling for guidance and protection every minute, and her affairs went smoothly and miraculously. Her luggage was never delayed nor lost! Accommodations were always ready for her at the best hotels; and she had perfect service wherever she went. She returned to New York. Knowing the language, she felt God was no longer necessary, so looked after her affairs in an ordinary manner.

Everything went wrong, her trunks delayed, amid inharmony and confusion. The student must form the habit of "practicing the Presence of God" every minute. "In all thy ways acknowledge him;" nothing is too small or too great.

Sometimes an insignificant incident may be the turning point in a man's life.

Robert Fulton, watching some boiling water, simmering in a tea kettle, saw a steamboat!

I have seen a student, often, keep back his demonstration, through resistance, or pointing the way.

He pins his faith to one channel only, and dictates just the way he desires the manifestation to come, which brings things to a standstill.

"My way, not your way!" is the command of Infinite Intelligence. Like all Power, be it steam or electricity, it must have a nonresistant engine or instrument to work through, and man is that engine or instrument.

Over and over again, man is told to "stand still". "Oh Judah, fear not; but to-morrow go out against them, for the Lord will be with you. You shall not need to fight this battle; set yourselves, stand ye still, and see the salvation of the Lord with you."

We see this in the incidents of the two thousand dollars coming to the woman through the landlord when she became nonresistant and undisturbed, and the woman who won the man's love "after all suffering had ceased."

The student's goal is Poise! Poise is Power, for it gives God-Power a chance to rush through man, to "will and to do Its good pleasure."

Poised, he thinks clearly, and makes "right decisions quickly." "He never misses a trick."

Anger blurs the visions, poisons the blood, is the root of many diseases, and causes wrong decision leading to failure.

It has been named one of the worst "sins," as its reaction is so harmful. The student learns that in metaphysics sin has a much broader meaning than in the old teaching. "Whatsoever is not of faith is sin."

He finds that fear and worry are deadly sins. They are inverted faith, and through distorted mental pictures, bring to pass the thing he fears. His work is to drive out these enemies (from the subconscious mind). "When Man is fearless he is finished!" Maeterlinck says, that "Man is God afraid."

So, as we read in the previous chapters: Man can only vanquish fear by walking up to the thing he is afraid of. When Jehoshaphat and his army prepared to meet the enemy, singing "Praise the Lord, for his mercy endureth forever," they found their enemies had destroyed each other, and there was nothing to fight.

For example: A woman asked a friend to deliver a message to another friend. The woman feared to give the message, as the reasoning mind said, "Don't get mixed-up in this affair, don't give that message."

She was troubled in spirit, for she had given her promise. At last, she determined to "walk up to the lion," and call on the law of divine protection. She met the friend to whom she was to deliver the message. She opened her mouth to speak it, when her friend said, "So-and-So has left town." This made it unnecessary to give the message, as the situation depended upon the person being in town. As she was willing to do it, she was not obliged to; as she did not fear, the situation vanished.

The student often delays his demonstration through a belief in incompletion. He should make this statement:

"In Divine Mind there is only completion, therefore, my demonstration is completed. My perfect work, my perfect home, my perfect health." Whatever he demands are perfect ideas registered in Divine Mind, and must manifest, "under grace in a perfect way." He gives thanks he has already received on the invisible, and makes active preparation for receiving on the visible.

One of my students was in need of a financial demonstration. She came to me and asked why it was not completed.

I replied: "Perhaps, you are in the habit of leaving things unfinished, and the subconscious has gotten into the habit of not completing (as the without, so the within)."

She said, "You are right. I often begin things and never finish them.

"I'll go home and finish something I commenced weeks ago, and I know it will be symbolic of my demonstration."

So she sewed assiduously, and the article was soon completed. Shortly after, the money came in a most curious manner.

Her husband was paid his salary twice that month. He told the people of their mistake, and they sent word to keep it.

When man asks, believing, he must receive, for God creates His own channels!

I have been sometimes asked, "Suppose one has several talents, how is he to know which one to choose?" Demand to be shown definitely. Say: "Infinite Spirit, give me a definite lead, reveal to me my perfect self-expression, show me which talent I am to make use of now."

I have known people to suddenly enter a new line of work, and be fully equipped, with little or no training. So make the statement: "I am fully equipped for the Divine Plan of my life," and be fearless in grasping opportunities.

Some people are cheerful givers, but bad receivers. They refuse gifts through pride, or some negative reason, thereby blocking their channels, and invariably find themselves eventually with little or nothing. For example: A woman who had given away a great deal of money, had a gift offered her of several thousand dollars. She refused to take it, saying she did not need it. Shortly after that, her finances were "tied up," and she found herself in debt for that amount. Man should receive gracefully the bread returning to him upon the water—freely ye have given, freely ye shall receive.

There is always the perfect balance of giving and receiving, and though man should give without thinking of returns, he violates law if he does not accept the returns which come to him; for all gifts are from God, man being merely the channel.

A thought of lack should never be held over the giver.

For example: When the man gave me the one cent, I did not say: "Poor man, he cannot afford to give me that." I saw him rich and prosperous, with his supply pouring in. It was this thought which brought it. If one has been a bad receiver, he must become a good one, and take even a postage stamp if it is given him, and open up his channels for receiving.

The Lord loveth a cheerful receiver, as well as a cheerful giver.

I have often been asked why one man is born rich and healthy, and another poor and sick.

Where there is an effect there is always a cause; there is no such thing as chance.

This question is answered through the law of reincarnation. Man goes through many births and deaths, until he knows the truth which sets him free.

He is drawn back to the earth plane through unsatisfied desire, to pay his Karmic debts, or to "fulfill his destiny."

The man born rich and healthy has had pictures in his subconscious mind, in his past life, of health and riches; and the poor and sick man, of disease and poverty. Man manifests, on any plane, the sum total of his subconscious beliefs.

However, birth and death are man-made laws, for the "wages of sin is death"; the Adamic fall in consciousness through the belief in two powers. The real man, spiritual man, is birthless and deathless! He never was born and has never died—"As he was in the beginning, he is now, and ever shall be!"

So through the truth, man is set free from the law of Karma, sin and death, and manifests the man made in "His image and likeness." Man's freedom comes through fulfilling his destiny, bringing into manifestation the Divine Design of his life.

His lord will say unto him: "Well done thou good and faithful servant, thou hast been faithful over a few things, I will make thee ruler over many things (death itself); enter thou into the joy of thy Lord (eternal life)."

Denials and Affirmations

"Thou shalt also decree a thing, and it shall be established unto thee."

All the good that is to be made manifest in man's life is already an accomplished fact in divine mind, and is released through man's recognition, or spoken word, so he must be careful to decree that only the Divine Idea be made manifest, for often, he decrees, through his "idle words," failure or misfortune.

It is, therefore, of the utmost importance, to word one's demands correctly, as stated in a previous chapter.

If one desires a home, friend, position or any other good thing, make the demand for the "divine selection."

For example: "Infinite Spirit, open the way for my right home, my right friend, my right position. I give thanks it now manifests under grace in a perfect way."

The latter part of the statement is most important. For example: I knew a woman who demanded a thousand dollars. Her daughter was injured and they received a thousand dollars indemnity, so it did not come in a "perfect way." The demand should have been worded in this way: "Infinite Spirit, I give thanks that the one thousand dollars, which is mine by divine right, is now released, and reaches me under grace, in a perfect way."

As one grows in a financial consciousness, he should demand that the enormous sums of money, which are his by divine right, reach him under grace, in perfect ways.

It is impossible for man to release more than he thinks is possible, for one is bound by the limited expectancies of the subconscious. He must enlarge his expectancies in order to receive in a larger way.

Man so often limits himself in his demands. For example: A student made the demand for six hundred dollars, by a certain date. He did receive it, but heard afterwards, that he came very near receiving a thousand dollars, but he was given just six hundred, as the result of his spoken word.

"They limited the Holy One of Israel." Wealth is a matter of consciousness. The French have a legend giving an example of this. A poor man was walking along a road when he met a traveler, who stopped him and said: "My good friend, I see you are poor. Take this gold nugget, sell it, and you will be rich all your days."

The man was overjoyed at his good fortune, and took the nugget home. He immediately found work and became so prosperous that he did not sell the nugget. Years passed, and he became a very rich man. One day he met a poor man on the road. He stopped him and said: "My good friend, I will give you this gold nugget, which, if you sell, will make you rich for life." The mendicant took the nugget, had it valued, and found it was only brass. So we see, the first man became rich through feeling rich, thinking the nugget was gold.

Every man has within himself a gold nugget; it is his consciousness of gold, of opulence, which brings riches into his life. In making his demands, man begins at his journey's end, that is, he declares he has already received. "Before ye call I shall answer."

Continually affirming establishes the belief in the subconscious.

It would not be necessary to make an affirmation more than once if one had perfect faith! One should not plead or supplicate, but give thanks repeatedly, that he has received.

"The desert shall rejoice and blossom as the rose." This rejoicing which is yet in the desert (state of consciousness) opens the way for release. The Lord's Prayer is in the form of command and demand, "Give us this day our daily bread, and forgive us our debts as we forgive our debtors," and ends in praise, "For thine is the Kingdom and the Power and the Glory, forever. Amen." "Concerning the works of my hands, command ye me." So prayer is command and demand, praise and thanksgiving. The student's work is in making himself believe that "with God all things are possible."

This is easy enough to state in the abstract, but a little more difficult when confronted with a problem. For example: It was necessary for a woman to demonstrate a large sum of money within a stated time. She knew she must do something to get a realization (for realization is manifestation), and she demanded a "lead."

She was walking through a department store, when she saw a very beautiful pink enamel papercutter. She felt the "pull" towards it. The thought came. "I haven't a paper cutter good enough to open letters containing large cheques."

So she bought the papercutter, which the reasoning mind would have called an extravagance. When she held it in her hand, she had a flash of a picture of herself opening an envelope containing a large cheque, and in a few weeks, she received the money. The pink papercutter was her bridge of active faith.

Many stories are told of the power of the subconscious when directed in faith.

For example: A man was spending the night in a farmhouse. The windows of the room had been nailed down, and in the middle of the night he felt suffocated and made his way in the dark to the window. He could not open it, so he smashed the pane with his fist, drew in draughts of fine fresh air, and had a wonderful night's sleep.

The next morning, he found he had smashed the glass of a bookcase and the window had remained closed during the whole night. He had supplied himself with oxygen, simply by his thought of oxygen.

When a student starts out to demonstrate, he should never turn back. "Let not that man who wavers think that he shall receive anything of the Lord."

A student once made this wonderful statement, "When I ask the Father for anything, I put my foot down, and I say: Father, I'll take nothing less than I've asked for, but more!" So man should never compromise: "Having done all—Stand." This is sometimes the most difficult time of demonstrating. The temptation comes to give up, to turn back, to compromise.

"He also serves who only stands and waits."

Demonstrations often come at the eleventh hour because man then lets go, that is, stops reasoning, and Infinite Intelligence has a chance to work.

"Man's dreary desires are answered drearily, and his impatient desires, long delayed or violently fulfilled."

For example: A woman asked me why it was she was constantly losing or breaking her glasses.

We found she often said to herself and others with vexation, "I wish I could get rid of my glasses." So her impatient desire was violently fulfilled. What she should have demanded was perfect eye-sight, but what she registered in the subconscious was simply the impatient desire to be rid of her glasses; so they were continually being broken or lost.

Two attitudes of mind cause loss: depreciation, as in the case of the woman who did not appreciate her husband, or fear of loss, which makes a picture of loss in the subconscious.

When a student is able to let go of his problem (cast his burden) he will have instantaneous manifestation.

For example: A woman was out during a very stormy day and her umbrella was blown inside-out. She was about to make a call on some people whom she had never met and she did not wish to make her first appearance with a dilapidated umbrella. She could not throw it away, as it did not belong to her. So in desperation, she exclaimed: "Oh, God, you take charge of this umbrella, I don't know what to do."

A moment later, a voice behind her said: "Lady, do you want your umbrella mended?" There stood an umbrella mender.

She replied, "Indeed, I do."

The man mended the umbrella, while she went into the house to pay her call, and when she returned, she had a good umbrella. So there is always an umbrella mender at hand, on man's pathway, when one puts the umbrella (or situation) in God's Hands.

One should always follow a denial with an affirmation.

For example: I was called on the 'phone late one night to treat a man whom I had never seen. He was apparently very ill. I made the statement: "I deny this appearance of disease. It is unreal, therefore cannot register in his consciousness; this man is a perfect idea in Divine Mind, pure substance expressing perfection."

There is no time or space, in Divine Mind, therefore the word reaches instantly its destination and does not "return void." I have treated patients in Europe and have found that the result was instantaneous.

I am asked so often the difference between visualizing and visioning. Visualizing is a mental process governed by the reasoning or conscious mind; visioning is a spiritual process, governed by intuition, or the superconscious mind. The student should train his mind to receive these flashes of inspiration, and work out the "divine pictures," through definite leads. When a man can say, "I desire only that which God desires for me," his false desires fade from the consciousness, and a new set of blueprints is given him by the Master Architect, the God within. God's plan for each man transcends the limitation of the reasoning mind, and is always the square of life, containing health, wealth, love and perfect self-expression. Many a man is building for himself in imagination a bungalow when he should be building a palace.

If a student tries to force a demonstration (through the reasoning mind) he brings it to a standstill. "I will hasten it," saith the Lord. He should act only through intuition, or definite leads. "Rest in the Lord and wait patiently. Trust also in him, and he will bring it to pass."

I have seen the law work in the most astonishing manner. For example: A student stated that it was necessary for her to have a hundred dollars by the following day. It was a debt of vital importance which had to be met. I "spoke the word," declaring Spirit was "never too late" and that the supply was at hand.

That evening she 'phoned me of the miracle. She said that the thought came to her to go to her safety-deposit box at the bank to examine some papers. She looked over the papers, and at the bottom of the box, was a new one hundred dollar-bill. She was astounded, and said she knew she had never put it there, for she had gone through the papers many times. It may have been a materialization, as Jesus Christ materialized the loaves and fishes. Man will reach the stage where his "word is made flesh," or materialized, instantly. "The fields, ripe with the harvest," will manifest immediately, as in all of the miracles of Jesus Christ.

There is a tremendous power alone in the name Jesus Christ. It stands for Truth Made Manifest. He said, "Whatsoever ye ask the Father, in y name, he will give it to you."

The power of this name raises the student into the fourth dimension, where he is freed from all astral and psychic influences, and he becomes "unconditioned and absolute, as God Himself is unconditioned and absolute."

I have seen many healings accomplished by using the words, "In the name of Jesus Christ."

Christ was both person and principle; and the Christ within each man is his Redeemer and Salvation.

The Christ within, is his own fourth dimensional self, the man made in God's image and likeness. This is the self which has never failed, never known sickness or sorrow, was never born and has never died. It is the "resurrection and the life" of each man! "No man cometh to the Father save by the Son," means, that God, the Universal, working on the place of the particular, becomes the Christ in man;

and the Holy Ghost, means God-inaction. So daily, man is manifesting the Trinity of Father, Son and Holy Ghost.

Man should make an art of thinking. The Master Thinker is an artist and is careful to paint only the divine designs upon the canvas of his mind; and he paints these pictures with masterly strokes of power and decision, having perfect faith that there is no power to mar their perfection and that they shall manifest in his life the ideal made real.

All power is given man (through right thinking) to bring his heaven upon his earth, and this is the goal of the "Game of Life."

The simple rules are fearless faith, nonresistance and love!

May each reader be now freed from that thing which has held him in bondage through the ages, standing between him and his own, and "know the Truth which makes him free"—free to fulfill his destiny, to bring into manifestation the "Divine Design of his life, Health, Wealth, Love and Perfect Self-Expression." "Be ye transformed by the renewing of your mind."

Denials and Affirmations

(For Prosperity)
God is my unfailing supply, and large sums of money come to me quickly, under grace, in perfect ways.

(For Right Conditions)
Every plan my Father in heaven has not planned, shall be dissolved and dissipated, and the Divine Idea now comes to pass.

(For Right Conditions)
Only that which is true of God is true of me, for I and the Father are *One*.

(For Faith)
As I am one with God, I am one with my good, for God is both the Giver and the Gift. I cannot separate the Giver from the gift.

(For Right Conditions)
Divine Love now dissolves and dissipates every wrong condition in my mind, body and affairs. Divine Love is the most powerful chemical in the universe, and dissolves everything which is not of itself!

(For Health)
Divine Love floods my consciousness with health, and every cell in my body is filled with light.

(For the Eyesight)
My eyes are God's eyes, I see with the eyes of spirit. I see clearly the open way; there are no obstacles on my pathway. I see clearly the perfect plan.

(For Guidance)
I am divinely sensitive to my intuitive leads, and give instant obedience to Thy will.

(For the Hearing)

My ears are God's ears, I hear with the ears of spirit. I am nonresistant and am willing to be led. I hear glad tidings of great joy.

(For Right Work)
I have a perfect work
In a perfect way;
I give a perfect service
For perfect pay.

(For Freedom from all Bondage)
I cast this burden on the Christ within, and I go free!

How To Live Life And Love It
by Genevieve Behrend

Table of Contents

Foreword

The purpose of this series of personal-pointer Lessons, which are herein compiled into one volume, is to indicate in a clear, concise way "the natural principles governing the relation between the creative action of all thought-power and material things," i.e., circumstances and conditions.

If these few simple principles are carefully studied, and mastered to your satisfaction, and then put into practical, hourly application, the student will find very soon that it is possible for man to make conscious contact with the Almighty, Ever-Present, Never-Failing God; and this just naturally means individual *freedom*, freedom from every form of limitation and bondage of any nature. (Read Mark 9:23.) Then try to believe that the Spirit of Life, which is your life also, knows "How to Live Life and Love It."

All the joy Life has to give is yours right now! Let us start on the highway to unqualified success now. God is our guide.

Your loving companion,

Genevieve Behrend

Live Life And Love It!

MASTER: Let us begin this morning's lesson with the certain knowledge that every living thing really wishes to enjoy Life. Once one really has entered into the true Spirit of Life that one can not help loving to live and is certain to enjoy life.

PUPIL: That is just it. If one could get into the Spirit of Living Life, I am sure one, every one, would enjoy it. But it seems to me that the general run of humanity live in the spirit of death rather than of life. The average person I know is always wishing that he could but at the same time knowing that he can't. That does not seem like really living.

MASTER: Indeed that is not living and people who live in that form of mental action are "the living dead." Let us see if we can not find an easy, logical method of entering into the true Spirit of Life. We know that we must enter into the Spirit of a book, or a picture, or of music, else they are entirely meaningless to us. To really appreciate anything we must share the mental attitude of the creative thought and feeling which brought them into outward form.

PUPIL: Now I am wondering if getting into the spirit of a thing would be getting into the spiritual prototype of the thing we may wish to enjoy. For example, I should very much enjoy a home of my own, a husband and children. Can one really get into the spirit of these good things before one does have them, or before one can see them in form?

MASTER: I am pleased that you mention the spiritual prototype is the spiritual, or mental, purpose of a thing, and is the true place of origin of anything. So you wish a home, husband, children?

PUPIL: Yes, a home in the country, not a large house, one just large enough that we can live in every room of it.

MASTER: The house is to be the home?

PUPIL: Why yes, of course.

MASTER: I asked this, you see, because just a house may not always be a home while a mere tent may be. Your prototype for the home would be *protection, shelter, freedom.* To begin at the beginning let us get into the *feeling* of perfect protection, shelter, freedom. Let us really feel in tune with these qualities of Spirit; and they in their turn will attract unto us the ways and means for the home.

PUPIL: So far I have been jumbling everything together in my thought. Should I not take each thing separately and try to enter into the spiritual origin, or purpose, of that one thing before going on to another?

MASTER: By all means finish planting one thought securely in the mind before trying to introduce another. After you have really tuned into the feeling of *Protection, shelter, security, freedom,* then begin to mentally build your house and people it with a husband and children. Thus you are making a mental picture of the forms you wish the Creative Energy to take. Be specific and accurate in making your mental picture, remembering that the mental picture you make is the mould into which the unformed Spirit is poured for solidifying into actual, outward form. The house itself may be a bungalow, or a two-story house, or may be of brick, or stone, or wood, or what not. It may have any number of rooms, doors, windows, a fire-place, etc. In other words you must first mentally blueprint your house. When your mental picture is perfectly finished, and your *feeling* is that these things *are* yours *now,* and you *know* that your mind is in perfect tune with the Source of all things, then, and not until then, are you ready to take the next step into the attainment of your desires.

PUPIL: But the matter of the right husband, that seems very difficult for me. First, I am not in the right position to contact men and now I have only two men acquaintances, neither of which I should care to live with in my model home.

MASTER: What you say does not enter into the matter at all. All that the individual does is to place into the Originating Creative Power the *quality* one wishes to differentiate, just as one plugs into the electric current in the house when one wishes to use it. The light, the heater, the Frigidaire, the fan, the iron, or any other thing one may want to use, all are there. All of the power is already there, too. It is ready and waiting; all that is necessary is your *recognition* of it and your taking action to utilize it. Your recognition and your desire cause you to make the right contact; and the power that is there does all the rest. The ways and means of your meeting the one and only husband are not your own concern; they form themselves into line automatically as a result of your turning on the correct switch.

PUPIL: Do you mean that it is not necessary for me to do anything to try to meet people? Do I not have to go to parties, or visit friends? Sometimes when I should be much happier at home I go to such places, and do such things, because there is always a chance of meeting the right one there.

MASTER: All of that is entirely unnecessary. The power you have turned on within yourself is an *Attracting* Power, remember! To give you an example:

One time when we were in Chicago, living at the Medinah Athletic Club, a young lady came to me with much the same attitude that you express and received the same answer I give here. She was a trained nurse, a graduate of St. Luke's. She was tired of living alone, wished a home, a husband, children. After she had had ten or twelve personal interviews and lessons with me I told her, one morning as she was leaving our apartment, that it would not be necessary for her to come to see me again. She felt sure also that the contact had been made. Our apartment was on the forty-second floor; and as she caught the elevator down she said a "great wave of peace and contentment came over her."

In her heart she had the consciousness of love and protection even now. At the thirty-fourth floor the elevator stopped and a young man who was very ill got into the elevator. Almost at once he folded up on the floor, unconscious. The elevator operator knew him since he had an apartment in the building; and the nurse and operator together got the man back to his apartment, into bed, and sent for the house-physician who said that the nurse had done exactly the right thing. In about an hour the man regained consciousness and sent for his own physician who wished to assign a nurse of his own choosing to the case. But the patient insisted on having the nurse who had helped him from the elevator, and kept her in attendance on him until he was fully recovered. Just about six months later patient and nurse were married.

PUPIL: That was certainly a lucky break for her, that she should take just that elevator, at that time. That seems to me like drawing the lucky number on bank-night at the theatre. Of course someone always wins but there is no certainty about it, is there?

MASTER: Really the two positions are not at all parallel; they are not even similar. With the nurse it was not luck at all. Deliberately, consciously, in faith, she had plugged into a circuit of great power within herself, the circuit of Universal Power that we call God, or Life and which did produce a perfect reciprocity of feeling and a certain sense of security, protection, provision, companionship. In other words she deliberately "initiated a train of causation directed to her individual purpose," to quote Troward, just as you would attach the cord to your electric-iron if you wished to press clothes. There was no luck in the matter whatsoever; it was purest science manifesting, as it always will and does, in answer to a strong desire scientifically placed. Whether it is plugging in to a circuit of electric energy or tuning in with the Creative Life Principle the procedure is exactly the same.

PUPIL: I am beginning to see the light. But the case you have just told me about still seems rather spectacular and unusual.

MASTER: That is because you have not trained the objective quality of your mind to know that it can always *trust* the Intelligent Creative Spirit of Life within yourself. You are letting preconceived ideas, and shallow and false ones, take precedent in your mind over pure, scientific Principle. You do not feel that you need to know the principles of electricity before you can use your vacuum-cleaner. All we know about electricity is gleaned from what we see it *do*. The same thing applies to Life. The innermost principles of Life will always remain a profound mystery. But one can, and should, live life to the full in the self and love it.

PUPIL: I am wondering if the nurse "lived happily ever after" with her unusually-acquired husband. And did they have the home and the children she so much desired?

MASTER: The couple have lived very happily together for a number of years now and do have a comfortable home and three children. I shall explain more of that later. The secret of living life and loving this: First, your feeling towards the livingness of life in you, as well as in all life everywhere, should be to *recognize* Life as Intelligent and to know that when this Intelligence is working through you it does not change its essential nature. It has always been a *Receptive* Power, that is *amenable to suggestion*, and it is always *responsive* and *creative*. This is the basis of Troward's meaning in his words which I use for my own favorite affirmation, and which, quoted, is this:

"My mind *is* a center of *divine* operation. The divine operation is *always* for *expansion* and fuller *expression*; and this means the production of something beyond what has gone before, something entirely *new*, not included in past experience though proceeding out of it by an orderly sequence of growth. Therefore since the Divine can not change its inherent nature it must operate in the same manner in me; consequently in my own special world, of which I am the center, it will move forward to produce *new* conditions, always in advance of any that have gone before."

Once you really plug your individual consciousness into the great power of the Universe the above will be your line of thinking. You will involuntarily look to the Life-Principle in you, not only as the only Creative Energy but also as a directive Power. That is you will let God determine, through your conscious mind, the actual forms and courses which the conditions for its manifestations will always take in your own individual world. Do remember always that the Originating Spirit of Life (of *your* life, too) is forever a *Forming* Power. It is for this reason that we should use such great care in the selection of our *habitual* thoughts and feelings -for create they will, and always.

PUPIL: How may I know, for example, that my true husband is being guided to me, or I to him?

MASTER: By your feeling of *certainty*, even though outward conditions show no sign of the fact. Still you are *sure*. You feel close. You *know* you are protected. You feel the influence of love all about you. You have stimulated these special qualities of Life in your individual world by your having persistently looked to God, knowing that He does manifest in you. Your mental attitude of faith and trust and expectancy has attracted all the joys of life. You realize that all that Life has to give is present with you *now* just as all that light has to give is present wherever light is.

PUPIL: Do I understand that if I live as closely as possible in the consciousness of reciprocity of feeling, and know that love is guiding, protecting and providing for me with its abundance, I can attract these qualities of life in the form of a man?

MASTER: Yes. For the house and the home *feel* protection, shelter, perfect harmony. For the husband *feel* love and joy; then *live in the feeling of these things*. Feeling is one of the strongest elements in Life and is also the most responsive.

The Fine Art Of Giving

PUPIL: It seems to me that the pace you are setting here is going to be rather severe discipline for me. But since it is to be for only a few weeks, if I wish, I shall try it. If there is not a big change for the better, both inside and out, at the end of that time, I can stop. N'est-ce pas?

MASTER: Yes, but please do not enter lightly upon this study. And do not seek to cultivate an acquaintance with God for the sake of what you will be able to get from Him. This is a tragic mistake that many people make, and which is difficult for many of them to rectify. They seek first to get, and promise faithfully that they will then give. But in so doing they have inverted the Spirit's Law of Compensation, which is good, which is as just as it is good, and which is as immutable as it is both good and just.

PUPIL: This sounds interesting. What is this Great Law?

MASTER: The *Law* is that *first* we must *give!* And after we have given the getting automatically follows, just as day naturally comes with the rising of the sun. But the getting of anything good never precedes the giving of something of value! *true giving*, giving with love as unto God Himself, cannot possibly impoverish anyone; nor can withholding from the Spirit and its service ever truly enrich one. Verily, " 'tis more blessed to give than to receive!" *giving* as unto God opens wide the Sanctuary of Jehovah within us in which we may always find *peace. giving* makes of the giver a direct channel for the transmission of Infinite Love and Power into one's daily, hourly life. Then will adversity flee; and certain achievement of "all things whatsoever ye will" follows immediately. But, I repeat, *first* ye must *give!*

PUPIL: But what can we give to God if He already has everything?

MASTER: We can give Him the one thing of which He does not have too much, of which He can never have too much, of which we can never hope to give Him too much. The one thing that God wishes us to give Him, first, last and always, is nothing less than the greatest gift in the Universe. Now what is it?

PUPIL: I am sure that it is Love.

MASTER: Right, but just what is Love?

PUPIL: Why God is Love.

MASTER: That is correct, too. But if God is Love, what is God? And if Love is God, what is Love?

PUPIL: Is this a parable? What is Love? What is God? That's just what I would like to know, too. Tell us please!

MASTER: Just what God is, just what Love is, each person must answer for himself. For after all your own conception of God and of Love *is* God and *is* Love to you! But perhaps we can set forth a few thoughts that may prove helpful, and which will be practical. To some Love is passion, and can only be conferred upon, or come from, the opposite sex. To some Love is the tenderness of a mother for her child, or of a doting father for his brood. To others Love is the love of friends, parents, or orphans. And there are some who love themselves most of all. But *real love* is Love of God, and for God! To *love Him* is the *first* Commandment! And if one keeps this great commandment there is no need of any other commandment; for if we really *do love God*, which is the first and greatest of the commandments, we automatically keep inviolate all the others!

PUPIL: But is it enough to just love God with all of our hearts, all of our souls, and all of our minds? Must we not *do* something about it as well?

MASTER: Certainly we must do something about it. Love without the fruits of Love is dead! If we love God, we will serve Him devotedly, faithfully, happily, continuously.

PUPIL: How best may we serve Him?

MASTER: *by giving of ourselves* to our fellowman! By giving of ourselves to our neighbors as unto ourselves. A scientist, one like Doctor Walter Reed for example, who gives his very life, and lovingly and gladly, in order to benefit mankind knows the true love of God. So does the heroic nurse who ministers to afflicted mankind out of sheer love of mankind. So does the self-effacing, self-sacrificing mother, or father, or teacher, or minister. There are many ways in which one may serve. All do not possess scientific talents, nor healing talents, nor comforting talents. But all do possess something they can give! Some who feel themselves unable to serve directly give of themselves by donating money to worthy causes, and these, too, are serving God because they Love their neighbors and therefore Love Him. Let me give you an example of *true love* as I personally knew it in a wonderful woman, one of many cases that I know.

PUPIL: Yes, do give us an example. They always help to clarify things, and show us how others have done what we wish to do.

MASTER: Very well. This divine soul was reared in a home of great wealth and culture. But as a very young woman she made up her mind to go out into the world, "on the firing-line" itself, as she called it, to serve actively lovingly, there. She became a nun, and as such was assigned to a hospital as a trained nurse. As she entered upon her life-work she was filled with love for mankind, with enthusiasm for serving God by serving his suffering ones. And she did serve lovingly, happily, faithfully, tenderly eight hours a day, or even twelve hours daily. But the hospital was woefully understaffed; and Marie, as we shall call her here, was soon subject to call sixteen hours daily; and even during the eight hours when she was supposed to have her rest she was often summoned and asked to serve more. Her quarters were right on the same floor with many of the patients, and this ward was her charge day and night. Often at two or three o'clock in the morning the bell beside her bed would ring with an urgent summons. She would arise at once, go to the patient and minister to his or her wants. But in due time she became physically tired, and of course she began to resent the calls that broke into her rest, especially when it seemed to her, as it often did at these times, that the patient merely wished a drink of water, or wanted a pillow adjusted a certain way, or was merely lonely, all of which were irritating trifles to a weary nurse.

For a month or more these trials went on, seemingly from bad to worse. Marie resolved almost desperately to do something about it, and immediately. So she cast about for a way to best remedy the situation. For days she thought about the matter, asking the Spirit for guidance. At length the flash came, directly from the Infinite! She took up a little card, wrote down the new motto that had been given her, and fastened it on the wall above her bed, right by the service bell, so that she might see it and be again reminded every time the buzzer rang. On the card she had written: "*the Master calls!*" Of course her system worked from the beginning. Quite soon she was saying in immediate answer to the bell, even while sleepily fumbling for her light: "*the Master calls!*" And she would arise and go and serve, without impatience, without resentment, yes, rejoicing in the opportunity to again serve in love. As a consequence her energy was untiring; she easily and joyfully did the work of three nurses, always rested, always fresh, always efficient, always smiling, whenever called. Her patients loved her greatly. She was always cheerful, always encouraging, always aglow, as it were, with a holy Love. And to those who did not know her secret, as very few did, the patients she attended seemed to be "miraculously healed." Let your motto also be: "*the Master calls!*" And remember that the humblest service that you can render to the lowliest of your fellowmen, if rendered in *love*, is a direct service to Him!

PUPIL: This is a profoundly beautiful and powerful illustration. Is that the motto, or the principle, that you use in helping the many who come to you? If not, what is your own personal secret of serving?

MASTER: My own method, in a way, is very similar to that of Marie. Like her I wished to serve lovingly, to serve as many as possible, to help to the limit of my powers in alleviating any and all kinds of suffering, physical, mental, spiritual or other form of unhappiness. Not only do I strive always to help those who seek me out. Every person whose hand I take into mine in greeting, every person into whose eyes I look, in all places at all times, yes even the shop girl who sells me my hose, the milkman who comes to my door, the beggar on the street, everyone to whom I speak at any and all times receives the same strong spiritual impulse from me! *I intentionally see the radiant Christ in all!*

PUPIL: But I thought that you told me once you never mentally treat people unless they ask for help.

MASTER: I don't, not specifically, not specifically under any other circumstances. My secret is this: I have deliberately formed the *habit* of beholding the Christ in every soul that my eyes fall upon! I do not ever see anyone as being poor, or old, or ill, or bereaved, or lonely, or homely, or evil or imperfect in any way. I *behold each and all as only perfect! I see only the radiant Christ* in every one of them *Because the Christ is* in each of them!

The Art Of Reciprocity

MASTER: The Bible, the sages of all time, all sources of real *truth*, unite in absolute agreement concerning one great thing, namely: That God and Man are *one* and not two, that the "two" are not separated but indissolubly joined in perfect and harmonious *union*. The Invisible (Spirit) and the visible (form, or matter) actually *are* inseverably connected. Each is a complement of the other. And the whole of Truth is to be found *only* in the combination of the "two," which really are not "two" but *one* through *eternal union*!

PUPIL: I am particularly happy about this conclusion because I used to think that a person could not have both spiritual and physical blessings at one and the same time. I thought that the physical world had nothing of God in it. Yes, I thought that Spirit was utterly separated from form, or matter. Now I feel sure that the reason I did not make any real progress then was that I was trying to have an inside for Life without an outside, and an outside without any inside. In other words I was simply living in the physical world without being conscious of the fact that forever I have a direct connection with the Spiritual Realm. I am right, am I not, in believing and feeling that I must have the *realization* that each is vitally necessary to the other for the formation of a Substantial Entity.

MASTER: Yes, you are exactly right! No one can go very far on the great highway of Truth until he realizes that there never was, and never will be, an inside to anything without an outside also. While one is visible and the other invisible (to the human eye) the *only reality* is in the combination of the two. A constant awareness of this fact on our part brings us that radiant realization of *one*-ness, of *union*, that we must have if we hope to make any progress in Truth.

PUPIL: After this one basic realization what other truths must we have?

MASTER: We must *know* that underlying the totality of all things is the *source of all things*, the Great Cosmic Intelligence. We must know that no physical thing of itself only can ever create anything. The physical form is the *Instrument* that Life (God) fashioned of His own Essence in order to have something through which He could work His wonders, and give them form also. But He always *lives* in that instrument! Do not ever lose sight of this fact: The power is always greater than the form through which it manifests, just as electricity is infinitely greater than the bulb through which it manifests as light. It is through *union* of forms, positive with negative, or masculine with feminine, or Spirit with Soul, that the creation of all forms, or channels, or physical things, results. This eternal principle runs all through the Bible, is the warp and woof of it, the whole substance of it. Seek ye the answer in that Great Book!

PUPIL: But many people say that the Bible is "antiquated," that it is a "book of fables," and of "old wives' tales," etc.

MASTER: How does this concern *you*? Which is the more reliable guide, do you think, the spiritually darkened ones who criticised the Bible or thine own soul which knows light when it sees it? Are you going to do your own thinking or shall you be content to let others do it for you, and wrongly? If we must go to other people in our quest of Truth, let us resolve to go to ones who have the light of the Spirit. For instance, what does Troward say of the Bible? Let his Wisdom be our guide here. He tells us that "the Bible is the Book of the *emancipation of man!*" He adds that this means man's *complete "deliverance* from sorrow, sickness, poverty, struggle, uncertainty, from ignorance and limitation, and finally from death itself." This noble conception of Troward's is exactly what the Bible *is*. With such a wonderful Book in print one should not be surprised to learn that it has the widest circulation of any book ever published, that it is still the world's best seller. If the Bible were not Truth, it would not live through so many generations and still hold its pre-eminent position. So let us proceed on the assumption that Troward is right, that the Bible *does* contain the secret whereby the art of living a perfectly free and happy life may be attained.

PUPIL: But the Bible has never been a very interesting book to me. I have thought of it as "old world fables."

MASTER: It was uninteresting to you because you did not understand it. Nevertheless it is a most scientific Book, full of interesting facts and life-giving Truth, the finest book ever written about the greatest of all the sciences, the Science of *life*.

PUPIL: My parents were religious people, church every Sunday morning, prayers every day, and all of that. But I could never see that they were any better off, or any happier -if as happy -than the neighbors who never went to church. But I shall be glad to make an honest effort to understand and follow whatever you outline, even the Bible if you say so.

MASTER: I have spoken. And because you are honest in your desire you will be honest in your thinking; and honest thinking makes a true student. Because you truly wish to understand the art of living you shall come to know it, and when you know Life and really live it you are certain to love it. The Bible *is*, I repeat the *Book of Life*, and of Life's immutable Laws. Remember always that Life's Laws contain within themselves the solution to *every* human problem! Indeed "Wisdom is the beginning of magic." The Spirit of Christ, or Intelligent Life, within us is the *light* of each of us. It will always make the path easy, interesting and joyous *if* only we will study and understand how to use our own Divine Power, and *then really use it.* Once one has formed the habit of looking to the Bible for the answer to all problems it becomes to that one as a lantern carried on a dark night. The next steps ahead may be in total darkness, but when you approach the light you carry illuminates the path and you know exactly where to step, and just what to do. Your feeling is influenced in the right direction.

It is true that the Bible veils its most profound secrets in symbols and parables; but the Wisdom is there for the earnest and consecrated seeker! Maybe, the author, was right when he wrote: "The true artist finds that the materials for his art are ever present. But the ones who can discern the possible uses of these varied materials, and who possess the instinct, intuition and training to put them to their best uses are always few in number. The materials out of which art is made are ever present; but *the artist* appears only at intervals!" So it is with the mysterious force we call Life. Every person has it; but the ones who understand and use Life's finest possibilities, and who get out of it, consequently, its very richest growth are really very few in number. So let us put into this study of Life our very noblest personal energy.

PUPIL: It seems to me, judging from what you say here and from what you have already taught us in these lessons, that our perfecting of the art of living and loving it is based upon the training of the mind and feeling to the point where we shall find as much joy and satisfaction in self-discipline as we formerly found in self-indulgences. Am I right?

MASTER: Yes. Once one has gone that far on the path, he is then around the last turn and on the "way that is straight," the path of splendor that leads directly to conscious *union with the father!* The Bible says the art of really *living* and loving Life centers around the record of man's thoughts and feelings, his aspirations, inspirations and experiences, on his discovery of the Life-Spirit as "an ever present help in trouble." When a man has found his *real self* (the God-Self, or Christ-Radiance) within, when he has discovered the infinite possibilities and potentialities with which he is forever surrounded, when he *lives* these things and loves the life he lives he becomes the *true artist!* Then will he use the *right materials*, then will he *produce* the *results desired* in the form of the picture that he originally conceived!

PUPIL: Suppose one has never had the advantages of higher education, that one's whole life has been commonplace and restricted, would such a one be able to understand and apply these beautiful and interesting truths?

MASTER: Yes indeed! One's station in life does not make the slightest difference.

One may be a woman who is trying to cook a good meal in the one and only room that she has, on a one-burner gas-stove. One may be a man who is a shoe-salesman, and who spends his whole time every day trying to satisfy women customers who insist upon his trying to perfectly and comfortably fit dainty shoes to their large feet. One may be a king or queen or a servant or a pauper. High or low, exalted or humble, man is a spiritual being! So long as he can think he can always change the outer, or physical, effects to suit the desire of his heart. And the very first steps lie in the thought and in the feeling!

PUPIL: When one's whole environment is one of poverty, or illness, or other dark limitations, how can one have beautiful and hopeful thoughts? Is it not true that the environment influences one's thoughts and feelings? While one is forced to live in the same adverse environment I do not see how there can be much change.

MASTER: If one were perfectly satisfied with an environment such as you describe there could not, and would not, be any change. But if one were divinely dissatisfied with such conditions, and very much wished to change them, it may be done any time, as completely as one may wish, by resort to and use of the Laws of Life. Suppose, for example, that you would like a position that is more agreeable, more lucrative, shorter hours, etc. If you go forth to look for such a "job," by all means start out with the feeling that you have something valuable to *give* an employer, and not go out to see how much you can get. If you *give* the getting will automatically follow. Carry the light of God-consciousness with you in seeking betterment of your position; and when you approach your prospective employer let the light shine. Suppose too, that you wish a better, more comfortable house in which to live. The very fact that you desire this change is *proof positive* that it is for you to have *if* you will meet the requirements. Many persons try to bring harmony into a home by getting a larger and better home, or by changing companions, by moving into another community.

PUPIL: That would help, would it not?

MASTER: Temporarily it might. But it would in no sense endure. To attempt to bring happiness or freedom into one's life through outward changes only is not wisdom, is not true art. Such is misuse of the divine materials. The change must occur within, and within first! It must first be established in mind, and firmly enthroned there if it is to be other than only temporarily effective. As long as a trend of thought remains the same the result will be the same. *The Law of Life is: to change an effect the cause must be* *changed first. Cause leads; effects follow! Thought is the cause; conditions are the effects!*

PUPIL: Does one's longing for beautiful surroundings, for health and freedom, for a lovely picture in perfect balance, come from the Great Artist who has made all of Nature? Is it He painting His ideal picture for us on the canvas of our individual minds?

MASTER: Yes, God is Mind, Life, Intelligence, Power, Beauty, Love, Harmony, etc. If any of these things are desired by us, and they are, then surely the Creator of them all must have planted that thought-seed in the mind. He must have whispered into that mental ear and that spiritual heart that *the truth is yours!* God has chosen *you* as a holy instrument through which to manifest all of His beautiful and wonderful qualities of Life. It is the *divine order* and *will* that *you* should manifest that particular thing, that particular place in Life!

God-Consciousness Versus Sense-Consciousness

PUPIL: Then if our truly fine desires are the desires of God Himself trying to manifest in and through us as individuals, in some particular way, why are there so many misfits in life? Why are there so very few who are doing, really doing, just what they would like to do? Why are there so very, very few living the life they truly wish to live? Why? Why? Why? Surely God can fulfill His own desires.

MASTER: Unless *all* things are possible to God then nothing is possible to Him. God has projected each human forth from Himself, each of us possessing an individual mind, for the sole purpose of manifesting Himself and His glory through us. Verily the *mind* of man *is* the *Son* of God! The Son has been given absolute liberty. Each can always make of his life, for a time at least, whatsoever he may choose. Man already possesses everything that God had to give him! Each person can make or mar his own picture, exactly as he wishes. By nature man is free to draw from the Ever-Present Parent Mind anything, and all things, that he requires to fulfill his desires. If this is not true then God's highest creation, man, is a mere nothing, an automatic something like a clock which when once wound will run until it runs down. Man *is*, however, God's own idea in flesh. The Intelligent Life in man is man's Divine Father! Man is already perfect and complete, *is* made of the same essence as his Father (God)!

There is only one reason why every mortal does not manifest and reproduce the Life, Love and Beauty which we see brought out in such radiance and perfection in all of Nature, manifested in Nature to the extreme point where mechanical and automatic actions can bring them. But we as individuals have a Law of Being that is somewhat different in one way from that which governs the other creatures that are of the world we call Nature. For us that are human the only perfect reproduction of Life, Love, Power and Beauty that we can ever know must come from Liberty. That is to say we have freedom of choice that is commensurate with that of the Originating Life-Spirit Itself. In other words we as individuals have the *liberty* of accepting or rejecting either good or evil, exactly as we may choose them. And the choice that we make results from the state of our consciousness. If we are God-conscious, we *are* gods. But if we are sense-conscious only, then we are creatures of darkness, of illness, of poverty, of loneliness, and all other things that are undesirable. "Choose ye well, therefore, whom ye will serve!" God-consciousness or sense-consciousness, which?

PUPIL: You have given us a powerful and illuminating "dose" here. Already we have a whole lesson. But I still do not see why God's highest creation, man should ever reject any of the good things of life.

MASTER: *if* man really understood the Law of his own Being, he never should reject the good things. But there are *few* who fully understand this Law, which is a wide-open door to *absolute freedom!* Most people believe that the "law of their being" (purposely spelled without capital letters) is a law of limitation rather than a *Law of Absolute Liberty!* Man "does not expect to find the starting point of the Creative Process reproduced in himself; so he looks to the mechanical side of things for the basis of his reasoning about Life.

Consequently his reasoning leads him to the conclusion that Life is limited because he has assumed limitation as his premise; and so, logically, he can not escape from it (limitation) in his conclusion." Here in this wonderful quotation from Troward you have the *whole story* of limitation. Here Troward shows most clearly that is all a *matter of consciousness!* And so the tragedy results because man in his dense ignorance ridicules the idea of *transcending* the law of limitation, forgetting completely (if indeed he ever learned it) that *the Law* can include all of the lower laws so fully as to completely swallow them!

PUPIL: From what you say it would seem that man's only reason for knowing limitation of any kind is his own lack of understanding. Is man to blame because he does not know?

MASTER: No man is to blame for what he does not know. But surely all persons will suffer because of *not using what they do know*! And they shall keep right on suffering until, like small children, they learn from experience.

PUPIL: It seems "strange," to say the least, that each of us must learn to find his own fuller Life in his own way. Why did not God *compel* His idea (man) to understand from birth that Life is Joy, and Joy is Freedom, etc.?

MASTER: Please *think* for just a minute! Would there be *any freedom, any liberty,* in that kind of person? Such an individual should be a mere automaton with no sense of *Liberty* at all! God forbid that any of us, His children, become robots!

PUPIL: It seems to me that most people feel life is entirely made up of a constant round of prosaic and homely activities which we are obliged to follow: To the shop, or office we go. We toil and slave, and go home again, all worn out and cranky. We sleep, maybe, then arise to repeat it all again for years until in God's mercy we die. There can be no real joy in that kind of life; but to most of mankind that is all. Still this is *not* all, is it?

MASTER: Indeed that is *not* all, not even for the darkest and most limited of persons. However dark, spiritually and materially, a person may be, deep down in his soul there is a conviction that Life holds his desires fulfilled somehow, somewhere, sometime! He feels also that *if he only Knew how he could find a way!* Some feel that the real joy of *liberty* can come only after putting off the body at death. This is *not* the case, however, *Everything that life (god) has to give is here in our midst, and right now!*

As we humans advance in knowledge, either from study or experience, or both, we overcome one law of limitation after another *by finding the higher and Greater Law* of which all lower laws are but *partial* expressions. At length we see clearly before us, as our ultimate goal, this Truth: "Nothing less than the *Perfect law of liberty* -not liberty without Law, which is anarchy -but *liberty according to law!*" When man learns the Law of his own Being, he will specialize it in all of his ways and will have found his true place. Thus will he bring *into form* all of the desires of his heart; then will he know the *real art of living!*

PUPIL: Can anyone who will learn from Life, either by study or experience, that the Creative Energy, with *all* that it has to give, is an Ever-Present, Responsive Quality of Life? Then can one really materialize, really bring into outward form, his most secret and sacred desires! That would be the art of living sure enough.

MASTER: *the law of life is changeless forever!* It is always calling to you in these words, or in ones like them: "Come unto *me!* Learn about *me!* Through *me all* things are possible unto you because *we, you* and I, are eternally *one!* I am *life!* I am Creative; I am always Responsive to the thoughts and emotions with which I am impressed by you! I am *mind!* The Law of Mind is *my* law! Because this is true it is Truth also that '*as you think in your heart so are you!*' Thinking *gives form* to the *un-*formed Life!"

PUPIL: This is splendid! But again it is getting "heavy." May we have another personal illustration of the adaptation of this principle to everyday living as people live it? This will help, I am sure.

MASTER: All right; I am always happy to comply with such requests if they will really help you. I once knew a dentist, a very fine dentist and a good man. He confided to me one day that music was his very life, and not prosaic dentistry. He said that he was weary of being "down in the mouth all of the time."

"So," I asked, "you feel that you are not in your right place?"

"I know that I am not!" he replied.

"Just why aren't you in your right groove?" I queried.

"Because music will not yield me enough money to keep my family in anything like moderate comfort. I feel that marriage and a family are among Life's deepest joys and greatest blessings. But music is like politics; one has to have lots of 'pull' to get into the few places that will really pay for a good violinist."

"Are you sure of that?" I asked.

"Yes, quite!"

"Well, Mr. Dentist," I said, "I know a God who is All-Intelligent, All-Powerful, Ever-present, Ever-Responsive and Forever Creative! *he* is also the Greatest of Master Artists, the Real Maestro! He lives forever deep within your own soul. If you will try going into Him there, if you will establish Harmony there, and will know and understand the Beauty which your music must express there, and if you will be content only with perfection there and in your music, I *know* that you can and will reap all the reward that any one can wish for in music, just as in any other profession, art or business."

"Your words cause my hopes to soar," he said. "But how can one like me, one who knows very little about God, contact Him?"

"Go within yourself! Go through, or beneath, the confusing, bewildering, disheartening past experiences. Live wholly in and enjoy only the harmonious side of your nature, which is wise, beautiful and most powerful in all ways. Then practice, practice, practice putting that *inner* Beauty and Harmony into vibration through the strings of your violin."

"But I am too old to take this up now."

"Not at all! Loving music as you do, you have kept up with your practice, have you not? Then *do try what I have told you!* Try it with faith and love in your heart. Hold them there with a determination and pride which simply will not surrender."

The dentist continued to find excuses, many of them, like so many people do, tragically enough. He did not have time, nor did he feel like it, after long, hard days at the office. He should have to give some time to his family, must have some recreation, etc., etc. But I did not hear him. I kept right on singing glowing word-notes for him, tempting him to try hard, inspiring him with courage. When he stopped finding excuses, and seemed really interested, he asked for the exact method to use. I told him the following steps:

(1) First, he must thoroughly make up his mind that his love for music, his deep passion for the expression of harmony was no accident; he must know that it was nothing less than God Himself persistently, relentlessly urging for expression through him.

(2) He should go carefully over and recite to himself the Lord's prayer, quietly but with much love and feeling, not less than twice every day, each night upon retiring and each morning when he first awakened.

(3) He should faithfully *visualize* himself playing, playing, playing, joyfully, harmoniously, enthusiastically playing to large and most appreciative audiences, receiving really handsome checks for his concerts, etc.

(4) After his periods of visualizing he should faithfully use some affirmation that appealed to him, that would strengthen his faith when it sagged, that would feed his high resolve, that would fan his burning urge to a holy flame.

(5) He should practice, practice, *practice* his music, striving always with all of his heart and soul to do much better with each rendition than he had ever done before.

Within less than one year the dentist became the musician! He was making more from his "pot boiler" concerts than he had ever made at dentistry. Within another half-year he began a national concert-tour which within a few months yielded him enough to go to Europe for additional study for two years, and to have his family with him over there. Since that time he has done nothing, professionally, but play his violin. He has not, of course, accumulated a really great fortune, but he and his loved ones have all of the good things of life that they wish, and this, combined with an abiding sense of happiness, constitutes *true wealth* for any person!

PUPIL: Does this same plan apply to everyone, and the same steps?

MASTER: The *same principles* apply to all! The exact plan, and the steps that lead to its fulfillment, will vary a little, of course, with each specific case. But no matter what your big desire may be, your Father's dearest wish for you is the absolute fulfillment of that desire by you, by you in partnership with Him! He always *longs* to give you any and all good things! His *whole purpose* in having created you was that He *might express himself through you! This is exactly why he created individuals, and this is why he does live in and through them! If we would have any of his gifts as our very own we need only to lift up our fallen consciousness to this holy belief and then work in sheer joy and expectation towards the lovely vision we have in view!*

Personal Intimacy With God

PUPIL: Please tell me a definite way to get closer to God, to push the little love and understanding that I have further into the Great One-ness until my limited vision is completely absorbed in the Unlimited. Will you do this just for me?

MASTER: Gladly. Since this is your own book, you may take all the time that you require, and at such intervals as you please, to study it, then study it still some more, and to practice it until you have really mastered it and made it a part of your very self. The very best way to completely sublimate your human self, your sense self with all of its limitations, into the *infinite* is to establish within yourself a *personal intimacy with God!*

PUPIL: But can this be done? Do you mean to say that we may actually be on terms of personal intimacy with God, as with a friend or other loved one? Such a thing seems too good to be true, too strange and mysterious to believe.

MASTER: Yes, this can be done. In fact it is done in each of us at all times whether or not we are aware of it. Remember always that each of us was made by, and out of the same stuff as, the Ever-Present, Intelligent, Creative Life Itself. Each of us was fashioned out of It Itself; and each of us *is* It Itself in a physical form. This being so, it automatically follows that each of us is always in a *most personal intimacy* with God! God *is* our Maker, our very life, our body, our thoughts, our desires, our everything!

PUPIL: Then why are there any troubles at all in this world? Why is not the lot of every person peace, joy and perfection at all times?

MASTER: That question I have answered a number of times, in one form or another. But yet once again let me say that it is all a matter of each individual's own *consciousness.* Our thoughts make us what we are! The whole shape of our lives, and of what we call "conditions," take their form *from our most habitual thought and feeling!* Don't ever lose sight of this outstandingly important fact. The Originating Creative Power is *un*formed relative to your individual life *until it flows through your thought!* It is through out *constant awareness* of the truth that God *is* ever-resident within us, *is* forever flowing through us as thought, that we are lifted right out of the old, limited habits of judging everything from external appearances, or from sense-consciousness only.

PUPIL: But I still do not quite see how this awareness will change the whole life from darkness to light. Just how will it do it?

MASTER: If you are *constantly aware* of the fact that *you really are god himself* in miniature, that you *are* always on terms of personal intimacy with Him as with your own self, then you will not any longer think thoughts that are unlike Him. You will not think thoughts of limitation of any nature; you will not judge anything or anybody from the standpoint of sense-consciousness. And when you have changed your Thoughts and Feelings to the point where you are *habitually thinking only from the spiritual side of things* you will readily discover that to really *know God is to be God!* Then indeed are you in constant personal intimacy with God; and you will leave far behind you the dismal bogs of failure, lack, disease, loneliness and despair. You will emerge into, and abide securely in, the *green pastures* of the fulfillment of your every treasured desire!

Persist, persist and yet again persist, in your steady recognition of the Truth that the actual purpose of the Divine in having projected *you* into being from its own Bosom was this and this *only*: That it might *continually flow through you as consciousness*, and that it might always *specialize in you as health, wealth, peace and joy!* Through this realization you lift your thought and feeling above limitations, and this is the solution to every problem. Yes, through the radiant gate of *personal intimacy with God* we step into a *new world* in which *all is life and liberty!* Truly God *is* an *everpresent everywhere all-the-time, loving, responsive, creative power!*

PUPIL: Since you often encourage us to use the Bible as a standard and a way-shower, can you refer us to a place in the Bible in which we are given a means of establishing this conscious personal intimacy with God?

MASTER: Certainly. The Bible is replete with illustrations of this very principle. For instance, let's turn to St. Matthew, Chapter 22, verses 36, 37, 38, 39 and 40; and note what Jesus, the Greatest of all Great Teachers, says there. Let us study it and analyze it carefully. Here it is:

(a) Verse 36: "Master, what is the *great Commandment* in the Law?" This question, asked of Jesus by the lawyer, was one of vital importance; and in the answer that Jesus gave is the *golden key* that millions desire. Note the reply below:

(b) Verses 37 and 38: "Jesus said unto him: 'Thou shalt *love* the Lord thy God with *all thy heart*, and with *all thy soul*, and with *all thy mind! this* is the *first* and *great* commandment." Kindly note very carefully, and ponder deeply, the *three* steps that are united into *one* through His use of the word "*love*." The heart, the soul and the mind constitute *all* of the *spiritual being!* Hence if we really love God with *all* of our heart and soul and mind, we are in fact loving Him with *all of our all!* Is this not true? Indeed it *is!* Here then we have

Jesus' own way, His own method, of establishing within Himself *personal intimacy with god!*

(c) Verses 39 and 40 read thus: "And the second (commandment) is like unto it (like unto the first one) Thou shalt *love thy neighbor as thyself!* On these *Two* commandments hang *all* the *Law* and the prophets." Please observe here the tremendous importance that Jesus places upon loving our neighbors as we love our own selves. There are many who pay lip-service to this Divine injunction, and who profess that they really *do* love their neighbors as themselves. But when it comes to the crucial test of dividing their possessions in love with a less fortunate neighbor, or of going to any extremity of "trouble" for him, their protestations of love for the neighbors are far too often found to be only mere words, shallow and empty and vain. So remember this: in words *without deeds to support them* there is *no virtue!* It is a *Fact* that our neighbors (every last one of them) are as precious in the sight of God as we are; in truth our neighbors are an integral part of ourselves, in other forms. It is a *fact* also that we can not really love God unless we love our neighbor; and it is a still greater *truth* that if we *do* love our neighbor as we love our self we are loving God. God is *one!* Yet most of us make the tragic mistake of thinking that God is many, that our neighbor is one person and we another, etc. The *divine reality*, however, is that *all people* (yes every last one of the millions and millions on earth) are *one body unified forever in God!* This being so, it is impossible for us to help a neighbor (who is our self) without also helping ourselves. Neither can we criticize, condemn or injure a neighbor (who is our self) without doing ourselves greater harm than is done to the neighbor. In *personal intimacy with God* there is, in reality *no* "neighbor" and *no* "self," as two persons, as ones separate and apart from each other; rather each of us is also all other persons, and all other persons are our own selves! When the dwellers on earth learn this all-important lesson that Jesus taught, and when all persons are obedient to this Law, then we shall have the Millennium here in our midst -then will all of us be veritable angels of the *one divine body!*

PUPIL: This is a most beautiful and powerful illustration. In addition to studying about it and thinking about it what else should we do about it?

MASTER: The most important thing of all is to *practice* it, to *live* it! Otherwise there is no virtue in it at all. If you can accept these words of Jesus as Truth, then *ally* yourself with them in your *thought* and *feeling* and *actions*, then will your whole being be fed with spiritual *manna*. You will be given constant suggestions by the Spirit regarding the sanest and most fruitful methods of living your own personal life in *true unity with God.*

PUPIL: And will this not develop still more in us that great essential to which you gave such importance in Lesson Number One, namely a good disposition?

MASTER: Indeed it will! And no age in all of history has ever more needed to learn and practice this great lesson of *growth, development* and true *enrichment* than the people of today. Many read the Truth; few assimilate it! Many hear the Truth; few heed it! Many know the Truth; *few do it!* That is exactly why there is a real *master* only at long and rare intervals. The price of *mastery* is really easy; but it is so much contrary to sense-consciousness (out of which all selfishness is born) that *few* have the courage, the faith and the spiritual stamina, and the *love*, to try it earnestly, or to stick to it through outward confusion, until it *has been proved!*

PUPIL: Is there any other method you can think of that will help us to understand this Great Law still better? Are there any short cuts? In the study I mean, not in the practice of it?

MASTER: Yes, there are short-cuts from which a truly observant and intelligent person may find this Law actually fulfilled in beautiful harmony, and from which we humans may learn a very great deal, if we will. Perhaps the greatest of these shortcuts to *illumination* is the one that is most widely distributed, and to which every last soul has access in one form or another, and with very little "trouble" if they sincerely wish to seek it out. I mean *nature*, of course. *all* of Nature shows forth the *glory of living in constant personal intimacy with God!*

By way of example of what I mean, let us briefly study the four seasons of the year, and the reaction of Nature to each. Spring in all of Nature is the period of *immortality* expressed anew, and in wonderful splendor! It is the season of budding, of flowering, of mating, of Generation and of Re-generation, all of which are among the *holiest* of the functions of Nature. And mark well how all of Dame Nature's children are always *obedient* to the urge of Spring, to the sublime song of the Spirit! Only men are rebellious to the holy commands of the Spirit; and it appears quite obvious that only men sin. How long will it be before we who are human awaken to the *true glory* that is *our divine birthright?*

In the realm of Nature summer is the time when fruits are formed, developed and ripened in fulfillment of the Law of the Spirit. It is the season when seeds are formed within the fruits so that with the coming of another spring all of Nature may obey again the great injunction found so often in the account of Creation in Genesis, namely; "Be ye fruitful and multiply, and fill the face of the earth with fruit."

With the autumn comes the *precious harvest*, the time when the radiant *promise* that was given in the spring is *fulfilled in form*, just as every promise of the Spirit to *us* will surely be manifested in form in our lives, and with a most bountiful harvest, *if* only we humans will learn to *obey* the Spirit without question, as do the fair children of Nature, and cease our foolish rebellion that is the one and only source of all of our afflictions!

Then follows the winter and Nature *rests* from its labors of the spring, summer and fall, just as we also must have our periods of rest. But winter positively is *not* aging, or decadence, or death, not in Nature. It is the season of rest, of slumber, only. But if you want to think that winter is the symbol of "death," as some people insist upon doing, I will agree with you for a minute solely for the purpose of pointing out the *fallacy* of death, or the belief in death, as clearly revealed by Nature. In winter Nature does *appear* dead. *but is it dead?* By no means! With the first few warm days of spring the *life* which has been merely *somnolent* in Nature, (but which has *not* perished because it can *not* perish, not ever) again *responds!* The buds, animated anew by the vitality of the Spirit, swell and burst; and the leaves and flowers that were hidden from view (but *there* nevertheless) come harmoniously, joyously forth in their beauty and glory to express *immortality!* As Nature *does* so may *man do also* if he only will. *if you* would *know true illumination,* and the *power* and the *glory* that are born of it, *go thou to nature! Study Her ways and be wise! Study Her ways and really live!*

Individuality

(What Is the Truth about the Individual and His Individuality?)

MASTER: Have you ever given thought to the matter of *how* you came into existence? Are you convinced that there was, and is, a *definite purpose* in the Divine Mind to account for your being here on earth? Or do you think that you create the purpose of your life for yourself, independently of all other factors, after you come into this world?

PUPIL: You ask questions that I scarcely know how to answer. These questions have perhaps been of mild and brief interest to me in the past; but I have never given them any real thought. I have let my mind wander as concerns these points. One time I would think that the Creative Parent Mind does have a definite purpose in my being here, and that this being so there is no use in my trying to change things. But it would then occur to me that this conception of things would mean the "pre-destination" of the fundamentalists. So I would change my mind and decide that I must have some hand in determining my mental and spiritual progress. Is this right?

MASTER: Indeed you do have a hand in your self-development. You have a *very great part* in it! The life that is you as an individual came directly out of the Great Whole of Intelligent Life (God), from out of its very own sacred heart-center. Your very life is the Spirit's *gift of its own self to you!* Secondly, the Divine *did* have a specific purpose in having made you namely: That it might have a *new form*, a new center, through which it might operate as *thought* and *feeling*, and through which it might yet more fully *enjoy itself* in a particular way. This also is the Spirit's *gift of its own self to you! but* the manner in which you as an individual use these *holy gifts* is left entirely in your hands, without interference from the Spirit. You were given other holy boons; you were given *initiative* and *selection*; you were given absolute *freedom of choice*! The distance that you travel towards the goal of spiritual perfection in this earth life depends solely upon *you*, just as the degree of rapidity with which you may mentally grow is entirely up to *you!*

PUPIL: But are we not given certain divine urges, or longings at all stages of our lives which will help us to know the right way to go? Are we not given these certain desires, or impulses, or stimuli?

MASTER: Certainly. And unless one follows these Divine impulses one is never really quite satisfied, one is always restless, always feels that some essential is lacking, that his right place eludes him. Your very individuality is an *exact complement* of the Great Whole, is a specialized action of all of Life. The only difference in the Life, the Love, the Beauty or the Power of the Universal (God) and of the individual (man), as expressed through the Universal and the individual, is a difference in *scale. the quality of the two* (which in reality are but *one*) *is exactly* The *same!*

The very same Creator who made and directs the whole universe also made and will direct you, if you will let Him do so, because *he himself lives in you* as the Life of you. His infinite Creative Power and Intelligent Love are the *very same in you* that they are in all other created things. Therefore it is not just sentiment to say and feel and *know*, as did Jesus: '*the Father (God) and I are one! the Father in me, he doeth the work!*" If only we will develop a constant recognition of this most profound Truth, we shall then really *have* an abiding sense of *liberty*, of *liberty in union*, of *liberty in conscious union with all of life*! This is not just an idle but beautiful rhapsody; it is a simple, but most powerful and illuminating, *statement of fact!*

PUPIL: Am I right then in believing that if I could really think myself into an unshakeable conviction that God *is* ever-present in me, and that *all* of His Creative Power is mine to draw from at my own will and pleasure, I could accomplish *anything* and *everything* that I might wish, and could *be* and *have* whatsoever I might desire?

MASTER: Yes, you are right. The Creative Power of God in us is *un*formed with respect to what we may wish to accomplish until we ourselves give it definite direction with our thought and feeling. It is *Always responsive*, remember, to any and all of our thoughts and feelings. These things being true, and they *are* true, any person may *be, do* and *have* whatsoever that one may desire, *if*, of course, one *actively works* in a corresponding direction. It is logic, it is purest gospel, that there is no other way than the one that Life's true purpose in us is to be forever seeking to express itself through us as *freedom*! Remember always, I urge you, that our *thought*S and *feelings do become things*, and that they determine the shape that the unformed substance of the Spirit takes in its living expression in our individual lives. It is, as Troward says, like water flowing through a pipe; the water always assumes the shape and the size of the pipe through which it is sent. It is like harnessed electricity which always manifests in exact correspondence with the kind of instrument through which it passes as it works. It the light-bulb the electricity *actually becomes* light; in the doorbell it rings the bell; in the refrigerator it generates cold; in the stove it becomes heat. It is the same electricity, the same Power, in every case; and the instrument through which it passes determines what the Power is and what it does! Once a person truly grasps the real meaning of the Spirit's Principles, then one realizes fully that we as individuals are actually sent out from the very Heart of God Himself in order that we may *become* and *be* new and perfect centers through which *he* can operate in *joy*, in ever-increasing *joy*.

This and this only, is the will of God towards us! Yes, the exalted mission of each of us is that we may be new instruments for *divine expression*. If we will to become that, and will make the necessary mental and physical effort to realize this Truth, then we will *know* that we *are* filling our right place in life. We shall experience true and lasting happiness then because we *shall be doing* the things we *most enjoy doing*. There will be an ever present-sense of *growth* in our lives also. Only a very few individuals have ever reached this empyrean height in consciousness while on the earth-plane; *still it is possible to all*. Because so few attain this exalted level most people have the merest existence, one that is filled with seemingly continual and perplexing problems of one sort or another.

PUPIL: It seems to me there are many more people who are unhappy here than happy ones. So many of my personal friends feel themselves to be misfits in life, I do not think that I know even one person, including myself, who is perfectly happy. If one has health, as some do, then that one may have financial troubles. If they do not have financial worries, and no real physical woes, then they have family discord. And so on it goes until one wonders if there is such a thing as complete happiness in this phase of existence.

MASTER: You are right; and the real reason for all of this unrest is this: These individuals have not recognized that their *thoughts* and *feelings* are the *only instruments* by which the All-Creative Energy *can* manifest in their lives. It is of no avail to blame Providence, or other people, for your troubles. No matter what form chaotic conditions take in your life *you alone are responsible for them*; and *you alone can rectify them* through use of your inseverable contact with God. Once one learns through study and practice, or through experience, *to allow* the *will of God* (which is always *good*) *to have free action in and through Him*, then *all bondage to conditions is over!*

PUPIL: At the risk of appearing dull may I ask yet again just how this can be done by each of us?

MASTER: I have given you the answer a number of times in this book; but it is worth repeating in a little different form, for it is an *all-important* item. Here is the answer yet again:

(1) Mentally go deep within your inmost self, your own Divine inmost, and ask yourself: "What *does* God really mean to me?" "What must the Divine Nature in me be like?"

(2) Once you have formed a definite and positive conclusion on these points, try to reproduce this same feeling all through your whole being. *Keep trying*, and you will succeed in doing it. It is worth the effort required, a million times over.

(3) Do *not* let yourself be discouraged with this practice if you do not seem to get immediate results. Remember always that Troward says "it is the intention that counts; it is the intention which registers on the reproductive disk of Creative Life."

(4) Another powerful help, to me personally at least, is to diligently use that affirmation from Troward which begins: "My mind *is* a center of Divine operation," etc. (See "Your Invisible Power," or Troward's "Dore Lectures"). The Lord's Prayer is also an excellent aid, as I have repeatedly written herein.

(5) Try, try, try with all of your concentrated purpose to *live hourly* in the *feeling* of the affirmation, or the prayer. Do *not* let yourself slip and fall by indulgence in what you may call "justifiable impatience" for there is no such thing. Anger, or jealousy, or fear, and all like things, will cause you to slip also, for these things are unlike your idea of God, or of God's thought.

PUPIL: That is a very tall order!

MASTER: Not when you realize constantly that it is the intention that counts. The more you keep your intention right the less frequently will you slip in your practice of these principles; and soon your whole life shall have been altered until it *is* like your own conception of God.

PUPIL: Many people who seem to have a very good idea of Christian Science, Divine Science, Unity, etc., try very hard for more money, better health, higher social position. Yet they do not seem to get far. Why?

MASTER: Whether or not they are conscious of it they are looking to the outside as the source from which these things shall come to them. But the *origin of all good things is within!* All good is *within* your own Life-Stream; and this *must be recognized!* Our recognition of the *within*, the Spiritual, as the *true source* of all good things *will give them form* in the *outer* or physical, *world* in which we live. Once the contact is made *within*, and faithfully held, the things will *automatically* come to pass in the outer. The whole secret is this: We *must* know exactly *who* we are, *what* we are and *why* we are! Knowing this, our contact with the *source of all good* is never interrupted. It is our task to take care of the *inner* things; and if we do, the outer things *shall take care of themselves. Then shall we go forward, and only forward, happily, harmoniously, serenely accomplishing any and all good things that we may wish!*

Personal Pointers On Success

MASTER: No one ever slides into real success without personal effort. It takes all one has to attain unto real success, and to hold it: but by the very same law each person *has all it takes*! If we are willing to reach out for achievement, and to use all of our faculties to that end, then unqualified, constant success is surely ours. It has been said that Napoleon never blundered into a victory. He always won his battles *in his mind* before he won them on the field. This is exactly what every successful person does!

PUPIL: What is the very first step on the high road to success?

MASTER: The very first step is to *decide* definitely and positively what form of success you want. Henry Ford, for example, wished with all of his heart and soul to make *better automobiles cheaper*, cars that were within the financial reach of all persons. Thomas A. Edison wanted to provide various efficient electrical appliances at moderate prices for the convenience and comfort of the world. Jesus the Christ had one outstanding desire ever-present in His consciousness: To *show the way* for every human being to find the Father-Principle within himself, to show all how to find and know and trust that Infinite Divine Power which really will, and *does*, protect all, guide all, provide for all. Each of these men had a divine urge that burned within him, an all-consuming passion to do one thing better than it may have been done before. Because they *knew exactly what they most wished to do they did it*!

PUPIL: If one does not know exactly what line of endeavor to pursue, what is a good thing to look for in determining just what is best to do?

MASTER: Here is another most-important essential to success; this will give you your cue. The *more good* a person *can do for others* with his product, his life, his work, or whatever it may be, the *greater success* will that person have! No one ever succeeded in any very great degree whose dominant motive was that of personal gain only. If one actually helps others, many others, to live happier, better, more successful lives, one need give little thought to the gain that will accompany the success; for if one does this the gain to self can not possibly be withheld. One's chief motive then in reaching out for success is not to see how much he may help himself but to see how greatly he may help many others.

PUPIL: These two steps are most helpful to me. But before taking other steps may I ask just what pitfalls I should look out for most when first I start on the road?

MASTER: Here are two of the most common snares, I think:

(1) Never yet has success come, and never shall it come, to any person who simply wishes for it. Mere wishes are idle and utterly impotent unless the wish is great enough to *inspire one to immediate action*. Yes, *action*, not wishes, is the *big thing*.

(2) Keeping your mind centered on the big success that you "are going to be" will *never* bring it to pass. You must *know* yourself successful *now*. So long as one looks upon success as a *future* acquirement just so long will success be *postponed*, just so long will its attainment always remain *future*. From the very start one must learn to *back up* the *thought* with the *feeling*, the absolute conviction, that *I am success now!*

PUPIL: These are splendid, too. Now I am ready for another step forward.

MASTER: Since you have now firmly resolved to make a business of acquiring true success in accordance with Life's immutable Laws, you must throw your whole energy into making your mind a center for positive thoughts only, for constructive thoughts only. You are deliberately careful of the words you use. You are deliberately careful of your mental reaction to the words you may hear. For instance, if you hear people talking about a tornado you should not let your thoughts dwell upon destruction but rather upon tremendous power *positively* used. If you hear people talking about disease, you should inwardly know that while disease is a natural result of broken natural laws it is not necessarily evil, and that in Life as Life *all is good and perfect*. In a word it will be necessary for you to avoid all detours, even though they may appear easy and short.

PUPIL: What are some of these detours? How will they be marked?

MASTER: All of them should be marked with lots of red lanterns for certainly they are dangerous to one seeking success. Here are a few of them which you will recognize as questions that you have asked yourself, just as millions of other Truth-seekers; and yet they wonder why success always eludes them.

(1) "Well, *why* doesn't it come?"

(2) "*when* will it come?"

(3) "*maybe* this is the way it will come."

(4) "Perhaps it is not God's will that I have this."

Success does not come for the one who asks: "Well, why doesn't it come?" simply because he is asking *why* rather than *knowing* that *it now is!* For the one who whimpers: "When will it come?" it shall never come so long as he asks *when*. What they wish *now is* or else it never will be. And as concerns "God's will" for us His will for us is anything good we may desire.

PUPIL: Just why is it that if we wish success for ourselves only, for personal gain only, we shall not be apt to get it?

MASTER: Here is an illustration. Suppose you went to your own personal banker and asked him for a loan of one hundred thousand dollars, knowing that he had that much, and more to loan and that your worth justified a loan of that amount. No doubt his first question would be that one that bankers always ask first of anybody seeking a loan, i.e., "What do you want the money for?" Let's suppose you answered: "Oh, I wish to take a year's cruise on my yacht, doing nothing, just loafing, resting, sleeping; eating. I need the change, you see." Do you think he would let you have the money? No not a soul! No more will the Great Universal Banker (God) under like, or similar, circumstances. You must approach Him with a really good idea, one which will bring good to many, not just to yourself. I know men who have millions and who began with no money, who began only with an idea. Their basic ideas were so universal towards the production of good they were able to secure from others all the money necessary to finance the beginning of their enterprises. The great secret of individual success is the very same as that of the national success that has made America the wealthiest land on earth, and is this: Our men of affairs, of greatest success, have learned to share with all of our people through benefiting all of the people, either directly or indirectly, through dispensing higher quality goods at less cost, through sharing earnings more generously with employees, etc. They have learned that it is an absolute science that giving to and sharing with many always have getting as a natural correlative! Get your thought right; capture an idea that will prove helpful to many; then *draw in confidence* on the Unlimited Banker for all that you require. You will discover that you cannot keep money from gravitating to you. Herein lies *sure* and *continuing success!*

PUPIL: May we have here, in conclusion, the gist of this whole matter of true success, in summary form? This will facilitate ready reference by us who are students.

MASTER: Certainly you may have this. It may be said that the steps to success are seven in number; and here they are:

(1) Thoroughly make up your mind exactly what you want most right now.

(2) Be certain that your desire has in it the element of good for many. Then ask your own inmost soul for the most perfect idea, or ideas, relative to your desire, ideas that will *produce good for many*.

(3) Make a mental picture of your desire as *fulfilled now*, and *now* only, making the mental picture complete, vivid, alive with feeling. This is the meaning of Jesus' great statement to "*ask believing that you (already) have.*" In

the mental picture you *actually do have* (mentally, which is the realm of all *true* causation) your desire right now. Once you really get into the *feeling* that what you want already *is* yours (mentally) you will *soon* realize how quickly it grows into actual *form*. Keep out of your mind all fear-habits of thought. Know that fear-habits can be readily changed into *faith-habits*. Fear and faith are the same, one being one end of the stick and the other the other end of the same stick. The fear-end of the stick is a *shovel* and will surely dig the grave of success; the *faith*-end is a *jewelled crown* ready to adorn the head of any who will wear it.

(4) If necessary, *compel* yourself to implicitly believe that the same Power that give you your desire in the beginning will also *give you the Ways and means of its triumphant fulfillment.*

(5) Meditate carefully at frequent intervals on the *real purpose* of your desire. This *real purpose* of the desire, or the thing, is the *all-important spiritual prototype* for the thing you want. Also go over the Lord's Prayer very carefully several times daily, it will help you much in meditating more profoundly, and will *tune your mind in with the power* (God).

(6) Every night before going to sleep, and every morning upon first awakening, make a solemn vow to live *close* to your God every conscious hour, to see only good in all, to entertain only good and constructive thoughts about everything and everyone.

(7) Frequently mentally see yourself *already enjoying your fulfilled desire*. Do this every time you think of the desire; and especially at night and morning, just before sleeping and at once upon awakening, for at these periods the subconscious element of mind is especially amenable to suggestions. In this way you *do already have* your desire perfectly fulfilled (mentally); and if you persist in it you shall surely have it soon in its physical form right in the midst of your life. For example, the great bridge that now spans the Golden Gate at San Francisco was first pictured *completed* and *in use* by many in the *mind* of its designer before it became an actual reality. But by mentally picturing the bridge as *already completed* and *serving many people well* the designer *drew* from the *whole universe* the power necessary to have it actually built.

These *seven* points are the keys, or steps, to the attainment of real success in any line of endeavor, *mark them well*, and above all other things *use them!* They are *truth! they work!*

Instantaneous Healing

MASTER: It seems strange to one who has made real progress along God's great highway of Truth just how many mortals who are on the same journey will make detours that are altogether unnecessary, or will even turn and go in the opposite direction from their desired goal. For example, nearly everyone, it seems, is very much interested in a newly discovered disease, or in just disease as such, while the thing that all of us wish to know most about is *perfect health* and how to reach that rich experience that is spoken of in the Apocrypha, Ecc. 30:15-16, which reads: "Health and a good estate of body are above all gold: and a strong body above infinite wealth!" Of course we all know that it is impossible to find the Truth about *health* by holding our interest and attention on disease.

PUPIL: But we know that there is disease. Must we not reckon with this fact?

MASTER: One who recognizes disease as a reality has thus made his own law about it, and for him disease is inevitable. If disease is what you think and believe then disease is a fact for you. All bodily inharmony is first a thought and a belief; consequently its *cure* is from the mental side also. It has been said that "the Absolute (Spirit) is like the air which carries odors, both good and bad, but which remains forever untainted by them." In the Absolute all is health and harmony; it may carry the beliefs of mortals in disease about with it yet it is never tainted by them!

PUPIL: But since the belief in disease is so widely prevalent is it not well for us to know how to handle disease, or belief in disease, from the spiritual standpoint?

MASTER: It would be more scientific to know how to handle *health*; and we shall devote this lesson to Healing, to living in conscious harmony with Life's laws. We shall start with the fine art of giving an effective spiritual treatment, or mental treatment. There are a number of most important points for the healer, or practitioner, to always remember and always practice in this respect.

PUPIL: Which point is the most important of them all?

MASTER: That is difficult to answer since all of them are vitally important; but one of them is this: The practitioner should have firmly fixed in mind the *fact* that there is but *one mind* and but *one expression* of this one Mind although it fills all space with its numberless manifestations. This awareness removes the line of demarcation between patient and healer. Another vital essential is this: If one hopes to be of any help to a patient one must *not* give treatment for disease. That would surely *intensify* the disease! In giving a spiritual treatment the practitioner should utterly dismiss all thoughts of disease and of personality from the mind. To hold the thought on disease would mean *more* disease. Rather the healer should mentally see Life *whole, free, at peace* and *in harmony* through the power of the Radiant Christ within.

PUPIL: But suppose the patient is right there in front of you at the time of the treatment, that he is ill and in great pain. How can the practitioner avoid seeing the ill condition?

MASTER: If one is not sufficiently disciplined in mind to see through, or beyond, the condition one should not attempt to be a healer; or else such a one should confine his efforts exclusively to absent mental treatments. To see, or to believe in, any condition that a patient may seem to have disarms a practitioner immediately and renders his efforts impotent in behalf of the patient.

PUPIL: Are the absent mental treatments always just as effective as ones given face to face? Does not the distance of the patient from the source of treatment raise a barrier to the effectiveness of the treatments?

MASTER: A well trained and experienced practitioner is able to treat just as effectively absently as presently; and there are some who do better work absently. In Spirit there is neither *time* nor *space*, and the distance of the patient from the healer makes no difference at all. You see the first mental step that the practitioner takes is that of clearing his or her mind of the presence of anything except the *one God-spirit*. Thought is unbelievably fast in its transmission and can span the earth instantly; and it does not lose any of its power in the transmission! In giving an absent treatment the healer should be *positive* that the thought sent forth reaches the recipient *now* and with *infinite power*.

PUPIL: Why is it so vitally important to know that the Truth for the patient is his now? If he is ill it does not seem quite reasonable to me that he could be made whole right now.

MASTER: Nevertheless it is either now or never! In the Absolute the *only* time there is the *eternal now*. To it there is no past; nor is there any future. To it there is *only* the *present*. If the practitioner holds the thought that the patient "will be all right," it will always be "will be" for the patient because the healer is *postponing* the healing until some future time, and there is no future known to the Spirit, as I have said. Did Jesus ever say to any of those who were healed by Him: "You will be healed. Arise and go"? No, not ever. Always He spoke to them in the *present* tense; always He told them something to this effect: "You *are whole!* Go in Peace!"

PUPIL: Just what are the mechanics of giving a mental treatment for one who is present personally with the practitioner?

MASTER: The steps in giving a successful treatment under such circumstances are these:

(1) Have the patient *relax* physically as completely as possible, all over, toes, ankles, knees, spine, shoulders, arms, hands and even the eye-lids (for the eyes should be closed in the silence). The whole body of the patient should be as limp as possible. The greater the physical relaxation you may induce on the part of the patient the greater his *receptivity* to the mental treatment will be.

(2) Have the patient "empty" his conscious mind as completely as is possible, trying to think of nothing at all insofar as this can be done; have him try to make a vacuum of his mind, as it were. This complete *relaxation* of the conscious mind also induces a much greater *receptivity*.

(3) The healer *must* completely remove the line of demarcation between the patient and self. There are not two persons present, not really, not patient and practitioner. The two are *one*, and the establishment of this *fact* firmly in the mind of the healer is of untold importance. *Remember* that Mrs. Jones, practitioner, is *not* giving Mrs. Smith, patient, a mental treatment. As long as the one treating is aware of any sense of separation, or distinction, between patient and self there will be little if any results achieved.

(4) Once all sense of separation is really removed from the practitioner's consciousness, the actual treatment is given. The patient is now in a passive, or receptive attitude, both mentally and physically. The healer is in an active, or generating, position. Yet the "two" are one, the one person being the negative pole, the other the positive, and between them the healing current of Life may now freely pass.

Into the Absolute the practitioner now projects a steady stream of positive, constructive, powerful thought-energy, at the beginning of which process the patient's name is either silently or audibly called in order that the flow of Spirit may be given *definite direction*. The receptive attitude of the patient picks up the flow of power and so it is made his own. The affirmation the healer uses at the beginning of the silence may be said aloud once or twice although this is not necessary. Into the Bosom of the Spirit, into the Fruitful Silence, the practitioner thinks and dwells with intense concentration and feeling, yet without any sense of strain whatsoever.

PUPIL: Upon what thought does the healer dwell in the silence?

MASTER: Upon the *spiritual prototype* for the organ that may seem to be diseased, or for the thing or condition that may be desired. This *spiritual prototype* is yet another thing that is of *vital* importance. To dwell in thought upon anything physical, anything which has form, is to be on the plane of *limitation*, of *secondary causation*, of *effect. but* to think steadily upon the *spiritual prototype* is to *mentally be* in the realm of the *absolute* which is the *infinite*, which is *first cause* or *primary causation*, which is the *cause itself* and *not* the effect.

PUPIL: To me this spiritual prototype, important though I am sure it is, is the hardest thing in all of this study "to get hold of" mentally, the most difficult point to really understand. May I have some helpful pointers on this matter?

MASTER: That is true of many, in fact for nearly all "beginners" in this study. Perhaps the spiritual prototype is difficult for you because it is *formless,* Then, too, it may seem hard to understand because it is a new idea to you, one with which you are unfamiliar, of which you are not accustomed to thinking. Yet it is quite *simple*, once you know its nature. Here are some good rules to follow in this matter:

(1) The spiritual prototype of anything is the thing itself in its most incipient state, is the actual origin of the thing in the Universal Mind.

(2) To find the spiritual prototype for anything it is only necessary to determine in your own mind the *purpose* of the thing, whatever it may be. This is an *infallible* rule. Suppose, for example, one wished a good automobile and would like to know the spiritual prototype for it. One would mentally ask: "Exactly what is the *purpose* of an automobile? What is it for? What does it do? What do I really want with a car" The automobile is, of course, an instrument, a means of *progress*, of rapid, pleasant, harmonious *progress*. This being so, then the spiritual prototype for an automobile is *progress*. At least this is what a car means to me; but in selecting a spiritual prototype for anything each one should think out for himself just what the *purpose* of the thing is *to you.*

PUPIL: Will you please give us a few other prototypes, and show us how they are arrived at? With still a few more examples to serve as guides, I am sure that I shall then know how to form my own prototypes for any particular thing desired or required.

MASTER: Very well; here are a few more. Let us take the head, for example, supposing that one had a belief in a violent headache. The head is the house of the brain; and the brain is the instrument of the mind, but in no sense the mind itself. What is the purpose of the mind? It is *to know, to know* God, the *capacity to know* God! Can a *capacity to know* ever really ache, or hurt, it being a *formless thing?* No it can not! The spiritual prototype for the head then, as I see it, is the *capacity to know God*. Now for a minute let us consider the eyes. What is the purpose of the physical eye? It is the instrument of *discernment*, which is a purely spiritual factor, *discernment* as such having no form of its own. The *capacity of discernment* is the spiritual prototype for the eyes, to me. Here are a few other spiritual prototypes for you; and in these that now follow I shall not explain for you just how I arrived at the conclusion. I shall name the particular organ, or part, of the body and the prototype for it, as I see it, and give you the benefit of thinking out for yourself just why I have chosen this particular prototype for each specific thing.

Teeth -Capacity to analyze and dissect God's ideas;

Lungs -Capacity to *know life* as *life*;

Heart -Capacity of *love*;

Stomach -Capacity of *understanding*;

Liver -Capacity of *faith*;

Kidneys -Capacity of *purity* and *cleanliness*.

The spiritual prototype, please remember always, is the purpose of the thing. Every physical thing has a purpose; consequently it has a *spiritual correspondence*. By letting your thoughts dwell upon the purpose of any physical organ, or thing, you make direct and most powerful *contact* with the *source of all things*, with the *first cause* which projected forth from itself all concentrated things; for as Troward told me, "*matter is only spirit* slowed *down to a point of visibility*."

PUPIL: These examples will help me very much, I am sure. But now I am wondering just what is the best way to help ourselves, and others, forget human weaknesses, aches and pains, etc. It seems to me that most of us have the habit of dwelling too much in thought upon such negative things.

MASTER: I find that the very best way to get away from negative thoughts and feelings is this: *to deliberately train the thought and feeling to travel along the road of our blessings!* Our every conscious moment *does have* a blessing in it, if only one will look carefully for it, recognize it and be happy because of it. In looking for our blessings it will help greatly to recall to mind the many joys we have experienced, as well as those we hope to experience. In these ways we are able to forget the negative things of which the human side of us is so prone to accuse us.

PUPIL: May we have an illustration of this point, please? Something out of your own experience?

MASTER: Yes. Here is an actual experience in which I had a part. In Los Angeles several years ago a lady came to me with the problem of cancer, with which inharmony she had been told that she was grievously afflicted. Her whole attention, it seemed to me, was rigidly held on the limitation the cancerous condition was causing her, or should soon cause her to know. She owned and operated a restaurant, and was doing much of the work herself. Several doctors, she said, had told her there was no cure for her, that the disease had spread until an operation was not to be considered, that she must stay off her feet and spend most of her time, such as remained to her, in bed, etc. This, she said, meant that she must go out of business, of course, and when she did that she would be in dire want, in fact an object of charity. With her mind filled with these negative thoughts of illness and lack, which were certain to come unless she could be healed, she came to see me.

When I had talked the matter over with her I asked her to let me think things over for three days before giving her my decision about accepting her case for mental treatment. I asked for this delay in order that I might thoroughly check to see how much time I could allot to her, to see if I could arrange for all the time she would require. After two days of changing some appointments, and postponing some others which were not really urgent, I told the lady to come. My first question to her was this:

"Do you absolutely *believe* what Jesus told His disciples, as recorded in Mark 10:27, and which reads as follows: 'With man it is impossible, but not with God; *for with God all things are possible!*' ?"

She assured me positively that she *did believe* just that; but said that she found her own mind too untrained and chaotic to keep her thought and feeling *off* what seemed to be the inevitable and hold it *on the fact* that God *is* the *only power* there is, that *he* is *forever present, always amenable to suggestion, eternally responsive and always creative*. Hence she wished the help of the Spirit through me.

I told her that I should ask her to know with me *hourly*, continually, that her relation to God is always I-AM, and that whenever she thought or said "I-AM" to remember that she was thinking or saying, in reality, "*God is.*" I told her also that God created her out of Himself, for Himself, and that to Him and in Him she was forever complete, whole, perfect. "God is love!" I told her; and I asked her to always try to feel His Great Love surging through her. I quoted I John 4:16-18 to her: "God is love; and he that *dwelleth in love dwelleth in God* and *God in him!*" I also asked her to know that God is *life*, Intelligent, Loving, Harmonious, Creative Life, and asked her to *hold her conscious thought and feeling* on these things.

"But," she protested, "you have not given me any affirmation for *my* cancer!"

"Did you say 'My cancer'?" I asked her with much feeling and emphasis. "Do you really want cancer, my dear? Are you determined to have it? If not, then why *are you claiming it for your own* by saying 'my cancer'? Remember thoughts are things!"

"Oh, no!" she exclaimed. "I see what you mean. Just listen to me. I must conquer this negative habit of thought."

I assured her yet again that she *was* a Divine Child, that all of her needs were forever supplied *through her recognition* of them. I then told her to try to constantly keep in her consciousness thoughts which contained some quality of the following:

Belief Confidence Conviction Credit Honesty Patience Reliance Sincerity .and other ideas in which there was some of the *essence of faith*. I stressed the fact that by keeping these things in mind her *thought* and *feeling* would have the *essence* of *faith* in them; and that she should soon form the *habit* of thinking in that way. It was my endeavor to get her to keep her mind *off herself* and *on the things of the spirit*. I knew that if I could get her to do this *habitually* God should take care of the rest of the matter.

This lady assured me that she would try to do exactly as I had asked although it seemed more plausible to doubt than to believe that she could be in perfect health again after so much suffering, and the opinions of several doctors that she was doomed.

Still again I told her most positively that it is written: "*God is with you to save you!*" I asked her to remember that *faith is alive* and that it *leads to more life* which doubt is dead and leads nowhere. The leading characteristic of faith is that it constantly flows and burns with constantly increasing brightness and expectancy. Faith always travels in the one direction of understanding. Doubt is a blight upon every effort towards Truth.

This patient came to see me regularly every day for some two weeks; and her condition began to improve from the very start. Then she had only absent treatment at frequent intervals, with an occasional visit in person, for another six weeks. At the end of two months she was entirely free from any evidences of cancer, free in body, in mind and in affairs. Immediately she began to build up physically and when I last saw her, some two of three years after she first came to me, she was in robust health, prospering in business and sure of her contact with the Spirit.

PUPIL: This illustration clears up in my mind, when I go back over it point by point, a number of ideas which were very hazy and uncertain to me. Thank you. I do know that doubts make one wretched from morning until night.

MASTER: Exactly so. And it would seem that after a while people who indulge in them would learn this fact and make an "about face" and a "forward march" in the direction of faith. Faith is a brightly-glowing light and lives within us. It has its source in the fountain-head of *intuition*. Its radiance is seen in the long shafts of splendor that lead one forever upward into the kingdom of the beautiful, the true, and the good.

PUPIL: If one does not have any faith, how does one get it?

MASTER: One does *not* get faith. *every soul already has it!* It has been yours forever; it is as much a part of you, of your Divine Being, as is your heart, your lungs, your mind: It is a gift as precious as Life itself, and is born of Life itself, forever innate in every living soul. It is true that some are less aware of faith than others through having neglected it, through having blighted it with doubts, fears, anxiety, etc. But the quality *is* still there, and by cultivation it will spring into fullness again. All that is required is this: *that you exercise the faith that you already have* for just a few weeks. Deliberately look for it! Insist on seeing it! *Persist in using it!*

Is Desire A Divine Impulse?

MASTER: Is desire a Divine Impulse? One hears this question asked in as many different forms, it seems, as there are humans. So frequently is it propounded and discussed it seems to me that it will be helpful to answer it from Troward's standpoint; after you have studied and meditated upon it from his views you will arrive at your own satisfactory conclusion.

PUPIL: I am glad that you have brought this up for us. I have often wished I knew just what God wanted me to do when I have been undecided about some move, perhaps a momentous decision.

MASTER: The only way anyone can fully understand Life's law of attraction is through seeing what it does under certain given conditions. In a tree it is growth; in an animal it is development; in all of nature it is evolution. From the lowest to the highest forms all growth is prompted by the organized creature pushing forth in its own accomplishment. One can not do otherwise than believe in the law of unfoldment which is the hallowed desire of the All-Originating Life to see *itself* more and more fully manifested. Since we as humans are branches of the one and only tree of Life this fact is also true of us.

PUPIL: May I ask a question, please?

MASTER: Certainly, any time.

PUPIL: Do you mean that all growth is a result of a *desire* for self-expression, that all evolution is within the great Creative Mind?

MASTER: Just so; and each of us is a direct result of that desire. Therefore we should learn to *trust our desires*! There is but the *one great desire* and practically all of our individual desires are reflections of that one. Man's desire, his *real* desire, is for *good*. No rational person would desire anything else for himself or another.

PUPIL: But many philosophies teach that we must conquer, must overcome, must rise above all desire in order to be perfected. How do you answer this?

MASTER: I stand fast in what has already been said herein. I hold fast to the firm conviction that our desires *are divine impulses* which stimulate us to *growth* and *constant development*. Without desires we should be mere automatons, should have no wish to progress and grow. It is impossible for one to crush out all desires without *ruining* self, spirituality, physically, morally and mentally. The desires, the longings, we have are *stimuli*, are *urges* for *expression*, from the holy citadel of God within ourselves!

PUPIL: Is it true then that if we would draw into us any particular benefit we have only to impress the desire for it firmly upon the subconscious phase of mind and hold it unwaveringly? Should we do this just as an impression of sound is made upon a phonograph disk before being reproduced? Should we do this knowing that said desire is instantly transmitted into the One Great Creative Energy which is always responsive, and that is sure to be manifested in our own physical world?

MASTER: That is just what I mean. Let me give you another illustration. I know a very fine and very wise lady in Los Angles who after returning from marketing found that she had misplaced her car keys; and she had an urgent appointment awaiting her downtown within a little while. She had taken her groceries from the car into the kitchen. After looking around for the keys in every place that she could logically think of she had still failed to find them. So she told herself (her subconscious phase of mind); "I want those car keys. I must have them. Now where are they? *you know*!" Almost immediately she had the desire to empty the bag of potatoes into the kitchen sink. But she ridiculed that idea, and repeated her desire to find the keys. She did this two or three times, meanwhile keeping up her search for the keys; and every time she received back the feeling that she should empty the potato-bag. It was her habit to let her maid empty the bags and put the purchases away; and the idea of emptying the potato-bag seemed foolish anyway. But the impulse remained urgently with her although she could not see how her car keys could possibly be in the potato-bag. So she did empty the bag into the sink and almost instantly she heard a metallic sound. She looked and, behold, there were the missing keys!

PUPIL: Her deep desire to find the keys brought her the answer? It seems very simple.

MASTER: And it *is* very simple once you know the responsiveness of the law of subjective mind. This lady knew that law.

PUPIL: If she really knew the law why did she not recognize the answer to her desires the very first time she was impressed to empty the potato-bag?

MASTER: The lady to whom I refer is a very highly-educated woman, a keen student of logic. While she truly does believe in the intuitive power of the mind to capture an idea from the Infinite the old race-habit of giving *reason* first place had not been entirely uprooted from her consciousness. When intuition told her plainly to empty the bag reason set up an argument and told her that the impulse was foolish. The controversy between reason and intuition continued within her for several minutes. Then because of her study of Truth, and her application of it, she was reminded that *intuition*, and not logic, *is the true key of life!* So she was impelled to do as she was bidden. When she did so her desire had fulfillment as its correlative. Always *desire* and *fulfillment* are bound together as *cause* and *effect* through the universal law of attraction!

PUPIL: It still seems to me that a true student of Truth should have thoughts, feelings and desires so trained in the right direction that logic could not go wrong in its conclusions.

MASTER: One does not change life-long habits of reasoning overnight. Like everything else, complete change is a matter of growth. The fact that she did obey the still small voice within, and that thus was her problem solved, are all that really mattered. In time this lady, like all of us, will learn to instantly recognize the voice of intuition when it speaks and will no longer question, nor reason, will *only obey.* When we all reach that point, as we can and shall through faithful study and practice, there will be *no problem in all of human experience that will fail to yield its answer!* There is a lot of truth in the old saying: "Take care of the heart and the head will take care of itself."

PUPIL: But is not the road to the attainment of true wisdom a long, hard one?

MASTER: It is long alright, being Infinite in scope; but it is *not* hard. It is like the story of the two men who are walking to Rome. One asked the other why he had chosen a road that was so full of stones. His companion replied that he had not been aware of any stones in the road, and suggested that they sit down by the roadside and take off their shoes. This they did; and the one who had been complaining found *a pebble in his shoe.* But there was nothing wrong with the road itself.

PUPIL: The road is then what each one makes of it for himself? Is that your idea?

MASTER: That is right. The broad highway of Truth is in fact, to me at least, the most interesting road in all of life. It takes times and interesting, happy effort to establish an unbroken consciousness of the *perfect reciprocal action* between the desire for expression as it exists in the Creative Energy and in the individual mind. It is true that by *rightly establishing* our relation to the Great Parent Mind we can gradually grow into any condition that we may desire, provided of course that we first make of ourselves, through our habitual mental attitude, the *person who corresponds* to those conditions. One can never get away from the Law of Correspondences. This *science* of Correspondence, or of *cause* and *effect*, is as infallible as is mathematics; and as in mathematics its principles must be mastered before one can habitual feel: "My Father and I are *one!*" Yes, our *desires* are our own *immortal selves* *seeking fuller expression*; and one may soon prove to the doubting, bewildered self that one *can absolutely trust the desires*.

PUPIL: Somehow it is still a little difficult for me to accept the feeling that my desires are Divine impulses, or the Divine Nature Itself seeking expression through me. It seems to me that desire is selfish and often wrong, even bad for one.

MASTER: Did not Jesus say; "Seek and ye shall find!" Just why would anybody seek a thing?

PUPIL: Because he wanted that for which he was seeking.

MASTER: Very good. Are not wants and *desires* the same? Jesus also said: "*ask* believing that you have and ye shall have!" Why would one ask for a thing?

PUPIL: Because he desires it and feels it would be good for him.

MASTER: Correct. Yet again the Master said: "Except ye become as a little child ye shall in no wise enter the kingdom of heaven." If one desires to grow into the *new life of liberty* and *joy*, indeed one must become as a little child.

PUPIL: And just what did Jesus mean by that?

MASTER: Just what He said. Observe a child, any child, rich or poor. Its very impulse is desire, is to want something. All children are simply one continual incarnation of "gimme" and "want to." Naturally the child's wants are but the forerunner of the man and his wants; and in the adult desires are as natural as in the child.

PUPIL: This desire idea is truly a new one to me. But I like it.

MASTER: You will learn to love and trust your desires as your spiritual understanding expands. Vitality, which is Life, is born of desire, is the child of Love. You will be amazed at the rapid progress you will make once you have really made up your own mind to trust your desires. The more you learn to trust your wants the greater will be your flow of faith.

PUPIL: But must there not be a check somewhere on desires? A sorting of the good and the bad? All desires are not holy, are they?

MASTER: One must be rational, of course. Troward writes in his "Edinburgh Lectures" that "there is nothing wrong with the evidences of a health*Y* mind in a *healthy body*." This study presupposes that a sincere student of Truth will not harbor evil desires, that his or her mentality is normal, the behavior normal. This being so the desires of such a one should also be only natural, rational, good; and if this is so then the desires of that one are Divine impulses. Let me suggest that you read the personal letter that Troward wrote to me, an exact copy of which is found in my book, "Attaining Your Desires". Then you will see yet more clearly why you should *trust your desires*, recognizing as you do that *desires are divine impulses*!

Supreme Self-Freedom

PUPIL: So, *supreme self-freedom* is our very wonderful subject for today, is it? I am sure that you shall prove to us that supreme self-freedom can be ours, that *mind does rule the world.*

MASTER: You may always be quite certain that *your mind rules your world;* and you may always know that your individual world is a branch of the Universal World. Your mind makes of your world a thing of *beauty, peace* and *absolute freedom,* if only you so will.

PUPIL: I am convinced that this is true *if* only one could truly control one's mind, thoughts and feelings at all times. I know that others have attained this mastery, this self control; but somehow it does not seem to be for me, as much as I desire it.

MASTER: At one time in our lives each of us thought this same thing about the multiplication-tables. How difficult they seemed to us as children; yet each of us mastered them by *persistent effort.* It is like that with *absolute selffreedom.* It is dormant within each soul, waiting only for us to call upon it, to arouse it, to recognize it, to give it our attention, our concentrated observation, in our every thought, our every feeling, every act. It is not difficult to have if we make it *first* in our lives just as a great scientist puts his science *before everything else!* In theory at least all of us realize that we get only what we *reach for* and *reach for steadily.*

PUPIL: Is not Annette Kellerman, the great swimmer, an example of this? Was she not a cripple as a child, and considered hopelessly crippled?

MASTER: Yes, she was. But through insistent, persistent, determined, steady effort she became the physically-perfect woman, a model for the women of the world. Her science was the science of health, the science of physical beauty and perfection. There are many sciences; and each of us may select the one with which we are most in tune and pursue it to a dazzling goal.

PUPIL: But has not science boasted that it has Disproved the Holy Bible?

MASTER: It may be that some scientists make this boast. But it is not true. The fact of the matter is that *science has confirmed the truth of the bible!* It might be said that science has written a new Bible for the *thinking* mind merely by clarifying the old one. Science has made of the Bible the Book supreme for those who are determined to live *here* and *now.* Science has proved that *"the word"* of Life, of the Spirit, *is a living word of power!* Truly "the heavens do declare the glory of God, and the firmament sheweth His handiwork."

In reading your Bible always substitute the word "Subconscious Mind" for the word "Lord." Try this faithfully for awhile and see what an astonishing growth you will make. Try this with such passages as Isaiah 40:31, Mark 29:30, Luke 18:29-30 and a host of others. Look about you; look at the results achieved by those who have learned to *love*, to *use* and to *trust* the *mind.* Strength, power, beauty, television, wire-photography, microscope, telescope, spectroscope, all of these, yes *all* of *all things*, are *results* from the Great Creative Energy whose progress, harmony; telephone, wireless, airplanes, chief attributes are these:

1. It is *ever-present, everywhere*;
2. It is always *amenable* to suggestion;
3. It is *forever responsive*;
4. It is *eternally creative.*

This *God-energy, remember,* manifests in the *mind of man,* in fact *is* the mind of man. The three Bible-references given above, and many others, teach us that if one puts the *development* of the *divine spark within first,* over all else, the *divine* in return will make that one *first* with it! Truly then the *bets* Life has to give is the possession of that one!

PUPIL: Am I right in believing that the precious promises of the Bible all hinge upon our making intelligent decisions, Loving Life (God) *first* in everything? And if I do is *everything* I may desire sure to be mine?

MASTER: That is right, *if you make God first,* if you really *do* make Him *first.* That is to say we should make it our *first* effort to *know* life's laws and *to live them!* tn this connection please read over and over again, or better still *memorize* letter perfect, the 22nd Chapter of Job, beginning at verse 21 and continuing to the end of the Chapter. The promises given there, the power, the freedom, the plenty, *are* yours, exactly as promised, if you will take the time, the effort, to become *acquainted* with the *loving parent-power* which is always *able,* and ever *more than willing* to do these things *in you, through you.* As you read be sure to bear in mind constantly that the 21st verse is the *key* to all of the others that follow it. The gist of this whole passage in Job is this: *we get out of life exactly what we put into it, plus much increase as interest on our faith!* Some state this in a more homely way by saying that "we get what we pay for, and no more."

PUPIL: I have often wondered about this in connection with tithing. Is it true that tithing is a very old Law which has the greatest power back of it?

MASTER: Indeed tithing *is a law* which has *much power* in it! I have tithed for twenty-five years, religiously so. The practice of tithing is a divine-habit-forming virtue. People tithe because they recognize God and wish to *develop* their recognition and expectancy. Regular, systematic tithers are those who have formed the *habit* of *counting their blessings*. As a result their *Blessings constantly increase*! Did not Abraham give a tenth of his *all* to Melchizedek as a *token* of acknowledgment that his *successes were from God?* And when Jesus sent His disciples forth into the cities of Israel He expressly forbade them to take with them any money or provisions. Why? Because He wished the people of those cities to recognize God in His servants, and to support them with their tithes. As Saint Paul said: "The people who receive spiritual instruction shall administer some of their *good* to him who gives the instruction." *it is a fact* abundantly *proved* that the *habit of tithing is a sure road to supreme self-freedom!*

PUPIL: Am I to understand that the habit of tithing would give me a consciousness of an *abiding partnership with God?* Because my tithing is to God and His servants? Is this correct? Does one tithe to God's cause in recognition, in loving recognition, of Divine guidance? Does one necessarily have to tithe to churches only?

MASTER: No, one need not tithe to churches only. Some people tithe regularly to missionary organizations, some to charities, and many tithe to individuals who work in God's vineyards, irrespective of organizations or affiliations. The value of tithing lies in the *establishment of the feeling of constant divine partnership.* Tithing brings one into the *high* and *fruitful consciousness* of *God and company, unlimited!* If one keeps in *conscious* touch with the Ever-Present, Responsive Substance of Life by regularly returning to it some of the substance (funds) which it has placed in his stewardship, this constitutes a practical acknowledgment of blessings and thus *increases the blessings manyfold.* The ancient Israelites *proved* this fact consistently; and for centuries the Jews have practiced tithing, as they do today. The Mormons of today prove this Law constantly also. When I was lecturing in Salt Lake City during the "Depression" there was not a *single mormon,* or *mormon family on relief!* The reason is obvious. *they tithe!*

PUPIL: I did not realize that tithing was so very great a stimulant for the steady inflow of supply; but now it seems to me that it would give one the same sense of security one has when the taxes are paid in full.

MASTER: That is right. After all your money is yourself; You are God's, your money is His also. Humanity exchanges its abilities, integrity, labor, etc., for money. In my thirty-five years as a practitioner I have had thousands of people come to me for spiritual help for increased supply; *but* in all of that time I have *never had a solitary tither* seek my help for financial increase! In fact I have had very few tithers, ones who religiously follow the practice, ever seek my help for *any kind of inharmony!* Tithing *does* carry with it a *wealth of* *blessings. Giving is worship!* If one *really* worships God, and considers Him one's *bets* business partner, one acknowledges His help by giving to His cause *first.* The average person gives a mere pittance to God, *after* they have paid everything else. That is *not* tithing in any sense. A tithe is not a tithe unless it is ten percent. The tithe should be paid first, from the gross profit; and it should be tendered in genuine love, thanksgiving and joy, if not in sheer abandon.

PUPIL: Is tithing required by the Intelligent, Creative Power in Life? Surely God does not need the money, or lands, or cattle.

MASTER: Tithing is voluntary. Yet it *is required* if one wishes a continual increase of blessings. It is a great joy to recognize God as a partner. To me a partner means one of whom we are fond, with whom we labor for a common good, and with whom we happily *share* in love. In order to receive benefits from tithing there *must* be *joy in giving.* To tithe grudgingly yields no blessings, or few at best. "He who gives *himself* with his gifts feeds three, himself, his hungering neighbor and *me!*" Tithing brings with it an *abiding sense of security,* has within its loving bosom an abundance of *success-ideas* which when adopted bring health, wealth and happiness. This is the *Law of Tithing.*

PUPIL: Thank you for this lesson on tithing. I should like to hear much more about it. But are you going to tell us today how to reason ourselves into certainty?

MASTER: This is hardly what I meant when we were discussing reasoning out an affirmation before trying to absorb it. For example let us consider freedom. Freedom is joy; joy is freedom. But it seems there are few who have either freedom or joy to any great extent. Many seem to be bound by miseries; their every day is full of discord. To them work, all kinds of work, is disagreeable. To them most people are unbearable; things that happen are awful. The weather is abominable; it rains when it shouldn't; when it should rain it doesn't. They buy things, then regret it. They sell things and then are hurt because they didn't receive more money. If they don't go places they feel slighted; if they do go places they feel sure they were snubbed. If they don't have things they are despondent; if they do have things they are not what they want, etc., etc., etc.

PUPIL: Heavens, is this the average person you are describing?

MASTER: No. I am just giving you an intimate glimpse of a person in bondage, of ones who have not trained their minds to *hold only thoughts of absolute freedom.* Perfect joy and freedom are yours *now. Take* them and make them *yours.*

PUPIL: How may one enter upon these joy thoughts at will?

MASTER: That is the place for the affirmation. Take, for example, the thought: *"the very bets life has to give is mine now!"* Reason about this for a minute. Why is it true? Because Life (God) made me out of Himself and *lives in me.* The very life of me is God. Life is happy; life is free; life is health; life is wealth; Life is *all good.*

PUPIL: I can see this *but* suppose that when you have satisfied yourself this is true some member of the family, or some friend, jabs you with a very unkind remark? What then? Are you supposed to laugh that off?

MASTER: If you *really are conscious* that the *bets* Life has to give is yours, you will instantly realize at all times that you are not supposed to try to live for another. You have all you can do to keep the stream of joy flowing through your own consciousness. When I first began my study with Troward he cautioned me every day: "Watch your *thoughts* and *feelings!* They *do take form,* you know!" And he really got that great Truth across to my consciousness. When I went to Ruan Manor to study with him, I had been accustomed to a personal maid all of my life. I took my maid with me when I went to Troward. There was not one modern convenience where I lived in Ruan Manor; and none could be obtained thereabouts. We had been there just a month when Marie came to me in tears and told me she was heartbroken to leave me but she could not stay in that awful place any longer; she just must go back to Paris. She was too lonely, etc. Of course my first thoughts were: "If Marie goes, what shall I do? Here we are miles from anywhere, with no conveniences of any kind.

What does this mean? Why should this disaster come to me now, of all times, when I really am trying to know God?" Just when my thoughts reached that station, and were gathering momentum, Troward's warning: *"watch your thoughts!"* came to my mind and I stopped right there. I began to use the will exercise he had taught me. I also used affirmations he had given me, to hold my thoughts where the Creative Power in *thoughts and feelings* could produce what I wanted. What I wanted most was *freedom to continue with my study.* I deliberately held my thoughts in the *right* place.

Only two days later the lady from whom I rented our rooms came to me and said she believed that Marie had been trying to tell her that she was leaving me (Marie was French and spoke no English) and that she wished she could find me another good personal maid before she went to Paris. I told the lady this was the case. She said that her daughter was coming home from London in just a few days, that her daughter had worked there for several years as a good personal maid, and that she felt sure the girl would be happy to work for me in that capacity. Marie left after teaching the other girl just how I wished things done; and the new maid was as satisfactory as the first.

In this episode I had my first good lesson in knowing that I must *watch my thoughts*, that *they do become things*!

PUPIL: You have said that your favorite affirmation is the Lord's Prayer. Please show us how you would reason this out in order to better understand it before using it, part of it at least.

MASTER: Very well. The first two words of that prayer carry a tremendous power, if they are thought over, or spoken, with much feeling. What does "Our Father" suggest? Our Father, our very own Father? When you were a child what was your idea of your father? Your idea of him may have been exaggerated but you *believed* him to be rich beyond all words, influential, kind, loving, good, always ready to give, to help, to comfort, to make you happy and to see that you had everything that your little heart could desire. Then try to feel yourself as a child of God, with all the enthusiasm of a child. Know that you are so like *him* that He adores you, guides you, shields you, protects you, gives you everything He has to give in generous quantity, that you are, and that you have, *his all*.

Do this with the whole prayer. Think about it all, understand and assimilate it all; then *use it all*! If you will do your part you will find that the Father-Principle in life *is always responsive*! Your objective quality of mind may not know what is best for you because it can only realize the objective and limited side of Life. But *the Father in you, he knows*! Ask Him, be guided by Him. Your real desires are but reflections from Him which shine through and register in your mind.

PUPIL: Would it not be a good idea for us to frequently refer back to the lesson on "Desire, a Divine Impulse" when there is any confusion of mind about desires?

MASTER: Yes, that is recommended; in fact I trust that you will frequently review all of the Lessons of this Course. And I devoutly wish that you would earnestly *try to make God first* in your heart, and mind, and soul, and daily and hourly life. If you will, it will mean for you a life of *supreme self-freedom* and truly you will *make of yourself* a reflection of God's *own idea* who is the *perfected* you. To this end I recommend the following, all of which I urge you to memorize, letter perfect. I also *urge* you to *use* and *use* and yet again *use* these points and affirmations, faithfully and regularly. Here they are:

For *daily*, Systematic, Loving Use:

Your hourly effort should be that of fully realizing your true place in the Great Plan of Life.

Just what is this *true* place for each individual? It is, as Troward taught me, the following three things:

1. *Worship* of God Alone;
2. The absolute *equality* of all individuals;

3. Complete *control* of all else.

Affirmations:

1. *I am* intelligent, Loving Spirit, *living* in Creative Love and Power! In Him do I *live* and *move* and have my *whole being*!

2. *I am* a specialized *part of* God's own Self-Manifestation! God *is* specialized in me; therefore *I am* perfect Harmony!

3. *I am* direct knowledge of *all* Truth! *I am* perfect Intuition! *I am* Spiritual perception at its fullness! There is but *one* Wisdom; therefore *I am* Perfect Wisdom!

4. My mind *is* a center of *divine* operation; therefore *I am* always thinking good thoughts, speaking only constructive words! Time is Eternal; God is the *only* Giver! His Loving Intelligence is continually working *in* and *through* me; hence *I am* ever working correctly. *I am* thinking the *right* thoughts, in the *right* way, at the *right* time, towards the *right* result! God's work *in* and *through* me is always *well* done!

5. *I am* Specialized Spirit! *I am* always receiving rich, powerful inspirations from the Great, Universal, Parent Spirit. Divine Intelligence is always thinking *new, fresh, clear* ideas through me, ones far beyond any I have ever known before. My prayers are the outflow of the Great Oversoul of the Universe. They go forth in His Name; and *always* they *accomplish* that for which I send them. *God is glorifying himself in and through me now*!

Exercises For Health

1. Breathing, Bathing and Short, Easy, Profitable Exercises for Health:

Note: (These exercises are given as a stimulant to your capacity, both mental and physical. Mind and body are one. When both body and mind are strong happiness and success usually follow, especially if one adds to them mental and bodily efficiency.)

Correct breathing is one of Nature's most powerful methods of building a powerful body, a perfect body. Let us begin now to breathe correctly and profitably. If these exercises are taken as intended there will not be any strain. The first exercise is this:

Upon arising in the morning first drink two or three glasses of water. The effect will be better if you will take the water just as hot as you can bear to drink it, with the juice of one-half a lemon in it. Then stand erect, or else lie flat on the floor. Exhale completely. Whether standing or lying on floor bend knees slightly. As you exhale contract both the chest and the diaphragm, pushing the latter *out* and *down* as far as possible without causing strain. Naturally this will extend the abdomen. Then without lifting your chest pull abdomen *in* as far as you can. Then without any attempt at correct breathing push abdomen *out* and *in* rapidly at least twelve times.

After you have mastered the above exercise for the abdomen and diaphragm, take the next exercise -for not more than two minutes each time. This exercise is: Stand erect, or lie flat on the back. Exhale completely, contracting chest. Then slowly inhale through the nostrils, trying not to allow chest to move. Let the diaphragm push the abdomen down, then hold the breath for three or four seconds. Exhale slowly. Then forget all about abdomen and diaphragm and inhale deeply, letting breath lift chest walls up and out to their fullest capacity. Hold breath a few seconds and exhale all the breath.

If you will practice these two simple exercises each morning for ten days, you will note a great improvement in physical condition and vitality, the head and mind will be clearer and you will have a real zest for work.

No doubt you know that the right kind of bath is a splendid nerve-tonic, as well as a most important point in attaining physical and mental perfection. When bathing for cleanliness the water should be of blood temperature, never hot or cold. After the cleansing bath, fill the wash-basin with cold water. Scoop up two handfuls and apply to the forehead, and rub up and down the face. Dip hands in cold water again and shake off all surplus water, then rub off balance behind the ears. Repeat process on back of neck. These things soothe and strengthen the nerves.

2. A certain way of relief for constipation is this: First, meditate on the perfect and harmonious action of Life. In Nature one does not find either inaction or over-action. Think over how the Life in your body regulates the flow of blood, the action of the muscles, both voluntary and involuntary, and how all of these things are done in perfect harmony. For a regulatory exercise in relieving constipation the following is splendid. First, as soon as you arise in the morning, drink two glasses of hot water. Then stand, or lie on the back on floor.

Breathe deeply. As you inhale extend the abdomen and contract it as you exhale, contracting it all you possibly can. Do this without letting chest rise at all. Do the exercise rapidly, vigorously, always inhaling through the nostrils and exhaling through the mouth. Take about eight seconds for each complete breath. Do this for a minute or two then use another minute to recover normal breathing. A second exercise is recommended; and it is better if taken in connection with the one just given. It is this: Again stand erect or lie on the back, preferably the latter. Draw first the right knee and then the left up to the chest as snug as possible.

Inhale deeply as you put foot down to floor and exhale as you draw knee down to chest. Do this exercise rapidly, vigorously for one minute. After the exercise try to get into the feeling of gratitude that you *are* able to *consciously* tune in with the harmonious action of Life. If you keep thinking deeply on the fact that *all* of the qualities of Life must be present anywhere and everywhere that Life is, the feeling of *one*-ness will come and you will enjoy the thrill of it. The very best there is is yours now and the perfect movement is manifesting *now*.

3. How to Retain Youth and to Banish Gray Hairs and Wrinkles if They Offend You:

Think, know, feel, be thankful for the fact that Life as Life has *no* age and yet is ageless. Give this fact a little profound thought every day. Soon you will get the deep and abiding awareness of it. In your mind's eye, and in memory, try to recall how you felt about certain things when you were twenty, how you looked then, and acted, and bubbled over with energy. Ask yourself if your point of view about Life in general has changed radically, or if you have simply forgotten how to Live Life and Love it, as you did then. The emotions, the fine understanding, the zest for activity, as you had them in youth have not glided off without leaving a trace in the development of your advancing years.

Try to give yourself a careful going over mentally each day, and *live* for a while each day the experiences of your youth, bringing them back into your *feeling*. Perhaps you say: "Oh, but youth is so foolish!" That may be so; but remember always that it *does things!* Try to weed out and destroy the doubts of your advancing years; try to prune out of yourself, out of your thought and feeling, your tendency towards being over-conservative. Old age is only an *ossified Idea!* Being over-conservative and opposed to progress and change are the things that make one old, and usually impotent. Your youth was all right; *live it again!* Live it in *feeling* and keep the feeling bolstered temporarily by making mental pictures of your happy, cocksure self as you were at twenty. *see* your face, figure and hair as they were then.

And each day do the following exercise for the banishment of gray hair. Vigorously *rub* the whole scalp, from the nape of the neck up over the crown to the hair-line on the forehead, using Glover's Mange Cure. This liquid is not for dogs only, but is also an excellent tonic and stimulant for human hair. Rub the liquid well into the scalp. The gray hair may fall out for a while after you have done this exercise faithfully for several days but keep it up and new hair will come in with the natural color of the hair of your youth. Yes, mentally go back to twenty and balance its vitality with your present wisdom! *know* with all of your heart and soul, and all of your emotional self, that Life as Life *is* manifesting in you in a particular way in order that it may find new avenues for expressing itself as the *joy* of living.

Make an hourly effort to keep in your consciousness your *joys* only. *Make them register!* Deliberately *be happy* and your body will respond to it in every way. It will also help, particularly for the ladies, to sit in front of the vanity a half-hour each day, seeing yourself *not* as you are now (if aged) but *as you were* in youth. Do this with deep concentration, deepest feeling, affirming something like this: "*I am* Life. *I am youth*, eternal *youth!*" The important thing, however, is to *see* yourself as youth, to *feel* youth, to know that you *are* youth. Soon you will find a decided improvement setting in. Thought *is* always creative!

Soon you will look younger; soon you will feel younger; soon you will be younger, not in years of course but years do not make aging. Some are old at twenty-five; others are young at eighty. It is flexibility of mind, a keen enjoyment of living, that make for elasticity of muscle and for youth.

4. A Method of Attracting Money:

Meditate on the *riches* of Life as it really is. All that we can see or think of in Nature shows us only *abundance*. Every growing thing is amply provided for. The grass and tress, and other growing things, do not know poverty. In the soil, in the air, in the sunshine, there is an abundance of nourishment for all. *think* about this great fundamental Truth because it applies to *you* also. Wherever you may be, whatever your station in life may be, the Creator of all Life *has* just as amply provided for you as He has for the grass, the birds, all of Nature. It is not His fault that all do not express or manifest this bounty; people are as poor, or will soon be as rich, as they *accept* for themselves in the *consciousness.* Everything that your individual nature may require has *already been provided* for you by the Creator. One has only to *accept* it, first in consciousness then in fact. Your *steady recognition* of this fact forms a veritable magnet in the mind which will attract every requirement to you, not as money that will drop in your lap without effort but as ideas, which when *acted upon,* will yield an abundant harvest.

Try this. Begin right now to take the time, two or three times daily, to focus your thought at the base of the brain: "Spirit of God (Life), *I am grateful* to you for the *abundance* that *is* mine now!" Any other good affirmation that may appeal to you, one that you compose for yourself perhaps, will do provided the use of it *lifts* your thought and feeling into *certainty* that abundance *is* yours now. The more completely you can flood your mind, your *consciousness,* with the recognition of Life's abundance, for you as well as for all, the more quickly your thought and feeling will manifest in *form.* Rich ideas will come to you intuitively, particularly if you impress the *riches* that *are* yours *now* upon your mind just before going to sleep. Any good idea if acted upon with wisdom and energy will yield great abundance for any one who apprehends it and works in *faith* towards its fulfillment.

5. The Value of Sleep and a New Method of Inducing It:

Sleep is Nature's restorative for tired tissues and often is found to be the only effective refreshener of the body machine. The exact amount of sleep required varies with different individuals, much depending upon how fatigued a person is when retiring. If one feels the need of relaxation and sleep, and yet cannot easily go to sleep, try the following method, which you may have read in my book, "The Healing Power is Life." It is this: Sit nude on the edge of your bathtub, feet outside the tub. Take a fountain syringe and fill it with water that is blood-warm (*not* hot). Place the end of the tube at nape of neck and let the warm water trickle down your spine until you begin to feel relaxed; then go to bed quickly, comfortable, warm and relaxed.

Another aid towards relaxation (and relaxation, if complete, is sure to induce sleep in a weary person) is this: Lying in bed, on the back, deliberately send the message down to your toes, firmly, "Relax!" Continue sending the message until the toes do spread and relax. Then relax ankles in same manner, also knees, then base of spine, and the spine itself to base of head, also hands and arms. As a rule one will never get this far with the relaxation-exercise; almost invariably one will slip off into deep, restful sleep before having consciously relaxed more than half the body. Upon awakening if you feel recuperated, don't force yourself to remain in bed, whatever the hour.

Get up and do something that you are interested in doing. Be sure the room you sleep in is always well ventilated; almost all people breathe more deeply when sleeping than when awake, unless exercising quite freely. Do not eat a big meal just before retiring.

If you will give this method of inducing sleep a fair trial, you will find it very effective in inducing refreshing sleep that will have a real recuperative value.

"How To Live Life And Love It!"

MASTER: If you are anxious and uncertain about the future because of the fast-moving and extremely chaotic changes now going on all about you, here is a lesson that will help you find your true self and to stay at peace. Once we really find the true self we are in tune with Life as it is. Then we can live life and love it! Life really is glorious once one knows how to live it. Try to imagine for a few minutes that you know a secret which opens all of the closed doors of seeming limitation and that you can then step into a new world in which all is Life and Liberty. In order to enter this fair paradise of freedom the mind must be trained to choose carefully the emotional trend of thinking.

PUPIL: Do you mean that only those who have developed their different mental faculties through study and practice of Truth can enter this kingdom?

MASTER: That is exactly what I mean, since thoughts alone are creative. Those who have leaned the value of the trained will, imagination, intuition, and who live accordingly, can really feel secure. The tendency of thought, the habits of thought, determine with precision one's outward affairs. So as you start to travel this road which leads to absolute liberty in all things it is necessary to leave behind all excess baggage such as self pity, intolerance, criticism, fear, despondency, feelings of superiority, and all other negative and destructive occupants of your mental house. Take all these and put them in a secure bag; then tie a string of resolute determination tightly around them and dump them on a trash-pile. Cover the worthless bag of destructive evils with oil and set it on fire. Then are you really ready to start on your journey.

PUPIL: It would seem that one is only able to "go places" on this road by developing self-control. Is that so necessary?

MASTER: Yes, vitally necessary. However true and powerful a truth may be there must be a method of application of the principle to the individual. The best and surest method of manifesting the truth that God and man are one, and that God lives in and thinks through each of us, is to deliberately cultivate self-control with its consequent serenity of mind. In your endeavor to use this great Power for your individual purpose in the affairs of your hourly life you must be able to catch your thought the minute it begins to wander into doubts, fears, condemnations, criticisms, etc. and turn it in the direction you *do* wish to go. Thus will you build certainty into your soul and body and the possession of certainty within means certainty and all things good in the affairs.

PUPIL: You make it seem that my disposition and self-control need much of my attention. I will admit that I am not patient; and of course I am intolerant, but only with those who deserve it -only with those who do not seem to try to do their part do I lose my temper.

MASTER: It is not my intention to be personal about your disposition. But I do say earnestly that every person who wishes to enjoy the blessings of true freedom *must* learn careful thought-selection, which means absolute thought-control, or self-control. In this way you will very soon entertain only the thought-guests you admire and enjoy. The uncouth, the grouchy, the selfish, the condemnatory, the suspicious, the tramp thoughts, all of whom will try to make a convenience of your mental domain, must be turned out of your mind. The best way to do this is put your whole feeling into an affirmation, whatever one appeals to you at the moment. Hold steadily to that thought and feeling until everything unlike it is out of your mind. Then lock your mental doors and use your will to keep out thoughts you have dismissed from your presence.

PUPIL: This making my mind do my new will is not going to be easy. I will practically have to make over completely my habitual mental processes.

MASTER: No, it will not be easy. But the goal the discipline will lead you to is worth a thousand times the effort required, however much effort that may be. If you will mentally stick tight to your resolve to make your mind a conscious center of divine operation, even for one week, seeing yourself growing steadily into what you wish to become, you will be amazed at your own growth and the genuine interest you have in everything around you.

Also you will discover many, many wonderful things about yourself that you never knew before. Once you focus your attention and your intention on the Intelligent Life within you, and try to reproduce it in your own self, you will begin to get results that will seem almost phenomenal to you, and at once. Keep your consciousness focused on the fact that the Spirit of Life has no fears, no anxiety, and soon your feeling will correspond with It. Just try this, say for two weeks, without slipping; then ask yourself if you would go back to your old estate, if you could.

PUPIL: Is one apt to be "hypnotized," and thus hindered in progress, by the thoughts of others about one? Sometimes I seem to be making real progress when suddenly, and for no apparent reason, there is an almost uncontrollable impulse and feeling of "oh what is the use!" I am like a ship without a rudder, trying to plow through some invisible, and invincible, force, and "getting nowhere fast," as the saying is. At best these experiences are long, long detours off the main road. What causes these episodes?

MASTER: You gave it its right name in the beginning. It is hypnotism; but as a rule it is self-hypnotism, almost unconsciously done because of the old habits of thought; and it comes as the result of your letting things other than your aim hold your attention. Your efforts to control your thoughts should be steady, continuous, with no unguarded moments. Mere spasmodic efforts, however strongly indulged in at the times of their occurrence to you, will never take you very far on the road to the new goal you have set. Before you study any further in these lessons, yes right now, make up your mind positively that you are entering upon the study to win, and that you will make an earnest, steady, continuous effort to do so.

My own personal remedy for overcoming any tendency to slip back into the old rut of wrong thinking, and I assure you that I have always found it a most potent and sure panacea, is, believe it or not, that wonderful thing, derisively called "old-fashioned and out of date" by some, -The Lord's Prayer. Go carefully over the Lord's Prayer every day. If you do not already know it thoroughly, memorize it, so that you can repeat it anywhere, anytime, silently if you like. Us it, repeat it carefully, slowly, and with much depth of feeling, as often as there is the least tendency to slip off your path.

After you have finished with your reading, or repetition of the Prayer, then take up your mental picture again, mentally seeing, feeling, believing, knowing that you are already in possession of whatever it is that you want.

This is what Jesus meant when He said for us to always, "ask believing that ye already have and ye *shall have!*" If you will do these things, very soon you will find that you *are* on the road to Freedom and Joy, and it will constantly grow easier for you to stay on the highway, without so many detours.

PUPIL: Just now I should like very much to have more money. In fact I must have it. Do you mean that I can attract the money I need by living with the Lord's Prayer for, say half an hour every morning and every night, just "precipitate" the money right out of the very air? That seems incredible!

MASTER: What you ask is incredible! And you are not getting my real meaning. The finest statement of the Law of Life ever uttered is, in my opinion, that wonderful, wonderful statement of Jesus, namely: "Seek ye *first* the kingdom of God and His righteousness (right-use-ness) and (then) all things will be added unto you." But please note that *first* you must seek the kingdom, must make an honest effort to make your mind a center of divine operation only, and for its own sake and not from any ulterior motive.

Then will all things be added unto you. What happens to you through the steady, persistent use of the Lord's Prayer, as we were discussing it, is this: With the constant change in your mental attitude as you progress you are developing more and more strength and spiritual power. This self-mastery you are steadily developing is the growth of Divine Wisdom, Power and Beauty within you. Naturally then your whole outside world will gradually change to correspond to your new inside world because your most habitual thought takes outward form. Delightful changes will come into the circle of your individual world. Your thought and feeling will attract corresponding shapes; and you will feel much encouraged to go on and on and on into more and more joy and freedom.

Imagination and Intuition

MASTER: Today we shall discuss that great power we call imagination.

PUPIL: May I ask just what imagination is. I have heard you often speak of it as our "spiritual aeroplane," and say that "it wings us." But just what is it?

MASTER: No mortal can possibly answer that question. With all of our scientific research no one has found any rational clue as to the source of this great power, outside of God or Spirit. Nor has anyone been able to determine how far the use of imagination is able to carry one. It is Infinite. It is the mystery of mysteries; and it might be compared to electricity in this respect. Yet we know it does exist and that its power for good is inconceivable, if used constructively, correctly. What we should do is to inquire into its usefulness to us. Every normal person is equipped with it to some degree; and like the will the imagination can be developed. If rightly understood and correctly used it will perform seeming miracles.

PUPIL: But why do you call imagination the "spiritual aeroplane?"

MASTER: Because imagination, correctly used, can and will lift one, as if on wings, above and beyond all limitation, above one's low, narrow views of life, into a cloudless domain of true perspective. Imagination gives one clear vision of possibilities in your life which you have never been able to see before. Then while you realize that it takes determination and effort to achieve success; you also know that you can, with the imagination, tap the source of unlimited possibilities and Intelligent Energy. In a flash that mysterious, winged thing called imagination shows you where all the riches of Life are to be found.

PUPIL: Suppose one feels weak, obscure, poor, that you know your ideas are good but that you lack the money or health to carry them into effect. What can imagination do about these things?

MASTER: Imagination will reveal that strength and power and means are to be found within your Divine self and that a better and better acquaintance with, and a more frequent use of, the God-powers within is certain to lead to success on any line.

PUPIL: Can imagination lift one to great spiritual heights? Or does it pertain more to material success?

MASTER: Jesus, the Nazarene, lifted himself to the exalted Christhood through understanding and using his powers of imagination. Is that not reaching the heights spiritually?

PUPIL: Is it the imagination that opens the door for limitless good to enter?

MASTER: No, not correctly speaking. It is intuition, a feminine, or soul, quality which first captures an idea from the Infinite and passes it on to the imagination. Imagination raises one to a place in consciousness where all things are not only possible but are present, spiritual facts. Look all about at the ones who have risen above every conceivable handicap to very great success. Let us take Louis Pasteur, for example. He did not have any better mentality, or more strength, or more money, than any other ordinary Frenchman; and he was just as obscure as the lowest of them. His mental tools, by nature, were no sharper than yours are. But that strange and mysterious thing called imagination was very active in him and soared far beyond his scant equipment and early hardships into new realms of wisdom.

Many times he was not sure; but he imagined; and because he imagined he discovered; and because he discovered he wrought miraculous cures and to this day his wisdom prevents disease and death in countless millions. Truly Pasteur was a saint. The same is true of Paracelsus. People said he was lucky. Envious and lazy people always say this of anyone that succeeds. But the cures of Paracelsus were not luck; they were the result of his imagination and industry. Jesus intimately acquainted himself with God through the use of his fertile imagination; and through use of the same mystic power he was able to enter into other lives. His success easily can be attributed to his ability to see God (which is Perfection) in every person he contacted, however tragic, lonely, hopeless or vicious that one seemed. Through his recognition of God in all men he helped men to see God in themselves. This was the source of his great power!

PUPIL: Then imagination is a veritable dynamo and not just a means of trivial, idle day-dreaming?

MASTER: Yes. Recognize your imagination as a dynamo of limitless power. Use all of it that you possess whenever you need it. Understanding of it, and experience in using it, will readily prove it to be the most powerful force in your mental equipment. Used correctly it will carry your light up among the brightest stars of highest heaven. It is not enough to dream and idly desire, not any more than it is enough to start an aeroplane's motor just to watch the propeller go round and round. You must fuel your imagination with knowledge and purpose. You must take your bearings and hold your course. Risks, hardships, will be only still greater opportunities to use your imagination in your journey through the clouds.

PUPIL: All of this sounds very interesting and inspiring. But when I look about me and see the people who are succeeding, and who have so much more in life than I have, it is confusing. They do not seem to know, or care, a thing about God. How about that?

MASTER: If I were you I would try attending to my own knitting and start at once to develop my own power; also I would stop envying others their success.

PUPIL: Oh I am not envying anybody anything. I simply do not understand.

MASTER: It would help if you would try to avoid a tailspin of self-pity. As soon as you observe someone who is getting on better than you are you must project yourself into his life critically. Try doing this same thing constructively. Explore his tactics, his tastes, his imagination and industry; and then ask yourself if you might not get along better and faster if you adopted some of the means he employs.

PUPIL: How can I know how another does his work to succeed? And I did not realize that I have been feeling sorry for myself. How would it be to try to see myself as others see me?

MASTER: It would help very much if you will turn your imagination on yourself without any excuses or alibis. Your imagination will show you your true self if you have the courage to use it and trust it. And let you intuition help you also.

Husbands, Wives, Children

(Children, How to Bring Them Forth If You Wish Them, Home, Husbands, Wives, if You Desire Them.)

PUPIL: It seems to me that many of my married friends would be perfectly happy if only children would come to them. It seems strange they can not have any.

MASTER: No, it is not strange. It is all according to Law. "Principle is not governed by precedent." Children are the result of knowing, feeling, living that Law consciously or unconsciously; they are the birth of new ideas, something different. Every baby is a new idea, a new form in which Life lives. Get into the habit of developing new ideas and you will find these very ideas taking the form of children. It need not matter what the new ideas are about so long as you fully develop them. Then mentally picture as many children as you would like to have. When about to give birth to the new idea in form (a baby) I would suggest the daily help of a really good Mental Science practitioner, also at the time of birth. With proper understanding the birth of the child will be as natural as the spiritual idea which preceded the form.

PUPIL: All of this sounds very wonderful and convincing while I talk with you. At the risk of your thinking my mind a sieve may I ask you to put all three steps, husband, home, children, into concise, separate form.

MASTER: Very well. The idea of concentration is not a leaky one and I shall be happy to present them in the order you name. But first what, exactly what, does the word husband mean to you? What characteristics do you wish the husband to manifest? What should his disposition be in order to be in tune with yours? These are your very first steps along the way.

PUPIL: To me husband symbolizes certain characteristics I would like to attract to myself from the masculine side of Life, or quality of Life, a type of man I admire. His main qualities should be, for me, understanding and love. With these two attributes well-developed in both of us I believe happiness would be certain to follow.

MASTER: With love and understanding well developed in husband and wife happiness is certain to follow. The one certain way to attract this type of husband is to develop love and understanding in your self. It is a very great truth that like attracts like! So first think over carefully just the type of man you feel could be happy with you.

PUPIL: Oh, I thought I was to think of the qualities my husband should have to make me happy.

MASTER: That method would help to develop self-centeredness, selfishness. But the other way is a reaching out to *give* what you have and has a very great attracting power. When you have determined the type of man whom you feel would be happy with you, then take for yourself an early morning-hour and through reading and meditation think yourself into the quality of Life you wish to attract and hold the feeling. Herein lies the real value of holding your thought and feeling into place, just like plugging into the light socket when you want light. If you keep pulling the plug you will not get much light. The secret is: *make* your contact in thought and feeling and *hold it*, with a happy, expectant attitude. Of course this ability to hold an idea is arrived at by developing the will.

PUPIL: It seems to me that visualizing will not work unless the mental pictures made are held in place in mind. Is that right?

MASTER: That is exactly right. They must be held in place, again just like the electric contact for lights must be held in place if you are to benefit by the light which will then stay on. Your magnet of thought and feeling draws from out of the whole Universe such qualities as Love, Understanding, Protection, Provision, husband, children, whatever it is you have visualized.

PUPIL: It is like a postage-stamp then; it only has value if it sticks. Am I right about this: that what I really AM that I *attract?* Might this not be the meaning of Jesus' statement in Matthew 13:20 when he said "For whomsoever hath to him shall be given and he shall have more abundance; but whosoever hath not from him shall be taken away even that which he hath?" When one really *has* a husband in feeling and mentally pictures him one really does *have* that husband; and he is *sure* to appear in form as a human being: Is this not having more abundance? How slowly I grow. First I wanted my husband to have understanding; now I see that he *is* understanding.

MASTER: That is it. Every conceivable thing that the human mind and heart can desire *is* already in existence. Like the electricity it has always been there; and as soon as one realizes it and tunes the desire in with that quality of Life which it is the current begins to flow in that direction. Then one has real abundance through continually having the recognition that whatsoever he may want he already has it.

PUPIL: Is the process the same if one wants several children?

MASTER: Yes, fundamentally it is the same. If we wish to manifest our new ideas of Life in the form of children, it is necessary to make the desire known to God, the Great, Ever-Present, Formative, Responsive, Creative, Intelligent Power. It being Responsive and Creative it manifests in form, as children.

PUPIL: Just what should one first begin to think and feel?

MASTER: First, let us suppose that your desire for children is in perfect accord with the Divine Plan to bring into earth existence a continual advancement of the human race. So your idea of the new birth is that you may be a means, or a channel, through which the All-Creating Principle of Intelligent, Beautiful, Perfect Life may reproduce Itself in a new form, one capable of recognizing itself as an individualized action of Pure Spirit. Then by reading good articles or books or by meditating on an affirmation that appeals to you, you tune your thought and feeling in with the very highest rate of vibration.

Stay with the thought and feeling until you are certain that you *have* made your contact with the Divine Intelligence, just as you are certain that you shall turn on the light when you plug into a light-socket. You know, under the latter circumstance, that the contact *is* made because the room is flooded with light. And in the mental instance you know your contact *is* made because your whole feeling *is* flooded with certainty and a sense of security in God's Love and Power as they manifest in and through you.

PUPIL: It seems to me that one would have to keep constantly in mind the thought of begetting perfect ideas relative to every act.

MASTER: Jesus said: "Watch and pray lest you enter into temptation." You feel towards God (Life) in the same way your child feels toward you. If you obey the Laws of Life because you love your Father (Life) your child will do the same.

PUPIL: Is it necessary that both father and mother should desire the children? Should they take their meditations together? Should they discuss the hope of children?

MASTER: If both father and mother desire children the new idea will be a more perfect idea of God. It is not necessary to take the meditations together, in fact, I personally prefer to have all of my meditations alone. And it seems to me the less one discusses a desire with anyone the more quickly and perfectly the desire manifests. If one talks about a thing usually it is put in the future and is rarely discussed as a *present fact*; hence the manifestation is delayed indefinitely because of the habit of looking upon it as a future manifestation, as something that "will be" rather than something that *is*.

PUPIL: How is this for a method of bringing children of your own into one's personal life? First, study and think over the fundamental Law of Life as always giving expression to its highest ideals and ideas in human form. Man is God's highest ideal and the children of men are specialized ideas of the One

Great Creative Source of all things. Are not our children the results of God's ideas of giving birth to our highest desires?

MASTER: You have the right idea. Try to really feel that God, Life, Love, Wisdom, is giving birth to a particular idea through you. Plant that idea, that thought-seed, in the garden of your individual subconscious mind. By using your individual subconscious quality of mind in this way you are doing your part to let all the Creative Energy in the Universe act in and through you without limit.

Thus you are a bridge between the two extremes in the scale of Nature, one of which is the innermost Creative Spirit of Life and the other the particular, external form of a child. Your objective quality of thought-power mentally sees your perfect child, then passes the thought and the picture into the creative power of your individual quality of subconscious mind which in turn transfers the thought-seed into *all* of the growing power there is in Life, thus bridging the two extremes of Nature. Your thought-seed will grow into perfect externalization just as a kernel of corn will when planted under the proper conditions.

PUPIL: This idea of a thought-seed clears up the whole Idea that my individual subconscious mind is the bridge between myself and the whole vast sea of Life.

MASTER: If you plant a kernel of corn you first make sure the soil and the climate is the proper kind to grow corn.

PUPIL: Does that mean I should look into my own character and physical condition, and so forth, to determine if I really am the type of woman to bear perfect children?

MASTER: You are right. It is vitally important to know these things. Once you have found out that these are clear, and you and your husband are sure in your minds that you wish to create in form your highest ideal of Love, as children, then proceed. Remember that the seed you plant, having all the vitality, all the vital essence, necessary to draw to itself from out of All Life every element necessary to cause it to grow into a perfect outward reproduction, a perfect child.

Every parent, or parent-tobe, should be an enlightened parent, of course, and should do all within the power to bring forth, cherish, nurture and rear, the finest children possible. It will help those who are, or who desire to be, parents if they will inform themselves fully along the most scientific lines on this question. This they may do in numerous ways, through the reading of good books on the subject, ones that are written by specialists, also by taking courses on the subject that are offered almost continually through university-extension plans, also in many places by city and state departments; and lastly to seek the advice and care of the best physicians from conception forward.

Life, Love, Beauty

MASTER: In his wonderful books Judge Troward stresses often that the Spirit of Life also is one of Love and Beauty, and that where the One is the others will be found, too, as a matter of necessity. Where Life is Love is. One is the correlative of the other. Where Life and Love are Beauty must be.

PUPIL: May we have another illustration to clarify this?

MASTER: Certainly. All persons have an appreciation of art. The ancient Greeks were supreme in the arts for many centuries. To this day many of their works have never been equaled. I have never seen that fact more compellingly illustrated than it was one day last summer at our home on The Esplanade, Redondo Beach, California. A gentleman friend of Mr. Smith's (Worth Smith, my husband) who, like Mr. Smith, has been a student of the Great Pyramid for many years, called on us. He brought a wonderful book and showed us many lovely pictures of exquisite Greek vases. Alongside each photograph was a sketch of the same vase with the basic design highlighted in geometry, many lines drawn to salient features of the sketch.

Of all the grace and beauty and absolute perfection of symmetry I have ever seen, or hope to, those pictures and sketches had it, without a solitary flaw in any of them. Each was purest harmony, so much so that one marveled and it seemed that music itself flowed from them. Each vase was an expression of God and His laws of Life, Love, Beauty and Harmony, executed to perfection by artists in whom His Love, Beauty, Harmony *lived*. Because of their adoration of Beauty, and its Source in the Father, they were able to conceive Beauty in the mind when planning the designs of the vases. No doubt they sketched the designs as shown in the book, by employment of the geometry in which they excelled. With the model before them they then fashioned the works of superb Harmony to glorify the earth. Wherever perfect Harmony is there you will find perfect Love for they are twin blessings!

PUPIL: But all of us can not make such masterpieces, you know, for all of us do not have such artistic talents. Do we?

MASTER: All of us have some talent within us. Unfortunately, many seem to never realize it and never do anything about it. Even so any person of intelligence can put into whatever task that one may have to do the Spirit of Life, Love, Beauty and Harmony, *if* only one will, and can make of the fruits of the task many things of Beauty. Some housewives, for example, make of housekeeping and rearing children a thing of drudgery as a result of their lack of illumination about the true divinity of housekeeping. Others put Love, Beauty, Harmony, Order and Joy into the same task and make a glory of it. It is a matter of the spiritual consciousness one has, or acquires through study if it is not there innately .

PUPIL: Will you please cite an example from the Bible which features this matter of consciousness of our divinity as being the root of all blessings?

MASTER: Gladly indeed. Study carefully St. Matthew, chapter 13, verse 12. Jesus uttered those golden words to teach mankind that like does attract like, *invariably* and *infallibly*. That passage states the law of attraction at its best, including an unshakable faith, visualizing by means of which one *has* spiritually, or in the mind, even that which is sought, and which serves as a magnet of infinite power to draw to one the glad fulfillment in form, or physical reality, provided only one also *works* confidently and happily to carry out the ideas the Father gives one, through intuition, as steps in the path to the shining goal.

Now let us directly quote the passage, then strip it bare of all the "mystery" so many claim it contains for them. Unfortunately, to many that verse remains a riddle for life unless they are sufficiently interested to seek until they find the key to its solution. The passage reads:

"For whosoever *hath*, to him shall be given, and he shall have more abundance: but whosoever hath *not* from him shall be taken away even that he hath."

The big question is: "For whosoever hath" what? Does it mean the one who has wealth of money, or property, or other earthly possessions? No, although the one who has the thing that is meant is certain to acquire financial independence and retain it. It means simply that "whosoever hath" the *consciousness* of the Father within, who has that exalted awareness as an abiding conviction, who has implicit faith in it, and who actively carries on in the work that one does, whatever it may be, the ideas of Life, Love, Beauty and Harmony the Father gives that one in an *unending* stream, to that one will be *given all* he may ever require, and to spare. But the person who "hath not" the high consciousness is subject to all the sorrows, lacks and other inharmonies circumstances and conditions can bring to bear upon him, even to the point of losing all he has gained through habitual employment of secondary causation. . . for since he has not the awareness he is, or shall be, "under the rule of an iron destiny," to quote Troward, and dwells in anxiety and fear, knowing not that "the eternal God is our refuge and a very present help in trouble."

PUPIL: Can that Love, Beauty and Harmony be caused to flow from one person, a practitioner let us say, into and through another so that the second party will be aware of the spiritual uplift, and receive corresponding benefits?

MASTER: Yes, indeed, that is done easily. That is the mission of the practitioner, for he or she does these things for others many hours a day. I well recall an incident that occurred not long ago in the beautiful home of a dearly beloved friend and student in Denver. I was sitting with her privately in her lovely living-room, holding her left hand in my right, thus completing a circuit exactly as an electric circuit is made, positive pole in contact with the negative pole. With my mind I made contact with the Love, Beauty and Harmony the Spirit is. From the Universal Spirit of Life those qualities flowed into me, and through me into my dear friend, and through her back into the Universal. For minutes we kept the contact and both of us were aware of the surge of tremendous power flowing through us. I have this friend's kind permission to mention her name. She is Grace N. Northcutt. It is she whose gracious generosity accounts for the new edition of this book you are now reading.

PUPIL: Then it is true that as one makes of it a habit to consciously recognize God in one's daily, hourly, even minute-by-minute living in that degree one will get good results?

MASTER: Yes. The correspondence is exact! As we apply the laws of electricity we are certain to get results that correspond to those laws only. It is folly to apply one set of creative laws to a problem and expect to get results that correspond to a different code. So it is that if we set in motion through concentrated and consecrated thinking the laws of Harmony then only Harmony will manifest in and through us, and in our affairs!

Again I give you the golden key which will unlock any door of bondage and which will never disappoint you if you persist in the use of it in wisdom. It is, I repeat, that twelfth verse of the thirteen chapter of Matthew.

PUPIL: How is it obtained? What price does one have to pay for the key?

MASTER: The price is given in the fifteenth chapter of John and is, as Jesus said: *"abide in me!"* That will put you in an entirely new relationship to your Father and to your environment, will open up many new possibilities hitherto undreamed of, all by an orderly sequence of creative laws that result from your new mental attitude. Thought is the energy by which the law of attraction is brought into operation. It is by thought that we keep the sap of life flowing from the trunk into the branches. The statement Jesus made in Matthew 13:12 is so important that He made it repeatedly, worded a bit differently, yet containing the self-same law He expressed therein.

PUPIL: May we have a schedule, and some affirmations, for daily use? If we have one before us, in print, it should help a lot, it seems to me, in our follow-through.

MASTER: First I shall give you two affirmations I have found very effective and powerful when consistently used with profound feeling.

1. "Father, I thank Thee for the conscious knowledge that all my good comes from Thee only, and that I no longer look to man as the source of my supply!"

2. "God *is* my ever-present supply and large sums of money come to me quickly, under grace and in perfect ways, so to bountifully supply my every need, and to spare!"

Moreover a careful study of these three references will be a great aid, i.e., Mark 5:36 and 9:23, John 20:29.

Lastly, I am happy to give you an excellent routine for daily use that Troward himself gave to me. I have used it faithfully for thirty-five years now and it is a powerful help indeed.

It is this:

Monday. . . Watch your words!

Tuesday. . . Watch your feeling!

Wednesday. . . Watch your acts!

Thursday. . . Watch your receiving!

Friday. . . Watch your giving!

Saturday. . . Look for the Spirit of Life and Love in everybody and in everything!

Sunday. . . Let the Lord's Prayer abide with you continually!

Life Power and How to Use It
by Elizabeth Towne

Table of Contents

Methuselah and the Sun

To see the beauty of the world, and hear
The rising harmony of growth, whose shade
Of undertone is harmonized decay;
To know that love is life—that blood is one
And rushes to the union—that the heart
Is like a cup athirst for wine of love;
Who sees and feels this meaning utterly,
The wrong of law, the right of man, the natural truth,
Partaking not of selfish aims, withholding not
The word that strengthens and the hand that helps!
Who wants and sympathizes with the pettiest life,
And loves all things,
And reaches up to God
With thanks and blessing—
He alone is living. —John Boyle O'Reilly

The sun gives forth to us heat and light rays, without which this old world could never be. Glory to warmth and light, which are power and wisdom shed upon us.

But there is likewise a third kind of ray shed by old Sol, whose mission we may not so readily bless. The sun's actinic rays are death-dealing. They cause disintegration, decomposition.

There are people who declare that time was when a great canopy of vapor hung over the earth and revolved with it, as Jupiter's vapory canopies now do; and that this vapory canopy kept off almost completely the actinic rays, while it admitted light and heat rays. Thus they account for Adam's and Methuselah's great ages. And they say that, unless this vapory canopy is again formed around our earth, to ward off these death-dealing rays, we shall never attain immortality in the flesh. They claim that as heat and light rays are power and wisdom, so the actinic rays are the Devil of the Bible, the Destroyer. And they believe that before man can be saved the Destroyer must be cast into outer darkness—shut out by that sheltering canopy of vapor.

An interesting and apparently plausible theory, is it not? But there are facts yet to be reckoned with. It is true that if a great watery veil spread itself over the earth to-day there might be no more death.

But neither could there be growth. Every form of life would continue as it is, wrinkles, gray hair and all. Why? Because there must be dissolution of old forms before there can be new ones made with that material. Take a photo plate as an instance: Here is a glass surface covered with a delicate gelatine; expose it in a dark-room under a red light and you can see just what it looks like; hold it there as long as you please and it still looks the same.

Now shut it into the black camera and sally forth on pleasure bent. The delicate film is undisturbed. But you come to a beautiful bit of woodland you want to "snap." You turn your focus upon it, and one little snap of a second's duration transforms that gelatine surface. Just for one instant of time you let in those actinic rays, and then all was darkness again inside the camera.

Now back you go into the dark-room and turn up the red light, by which you see again your beautiful bit of woodland, reproduced on that delicate gelatine surface. If you let in a bit of daylight your picture would be gone in a wink—the delicate gelatine would be "pied" in an attempt to reproduce whatever it faced. But you don't let in the light of day; you "fix" your bit of beautiful woodland by dipping the plate in a solution which hardens the particles of gelatine to the glass.

Henceforth the light cannot affect that gelatine; the picture you have, but life, progress, change, possibilities, are gone from the delicate gelatine forever.

But if you could live forever under a red light you would not need to "fix" your negative; it would forever retain that picture. And if you continued to live under the red light you might as well throw away your camera and plates—you could never take another picture. And you wouldn't need such amusement either—not for long. A few days in the red light and you would be sick, and a few more days and you would go mad. Finally nature would "fix" you, and there would be no more change. (I wonder if scientists have ever tried keeping a dead form hermetically sealed under red glass. The cutting off of the actinic rays ought to arrest decay and facial change.)

You see, the actinic rays, the devil or destroying rays of the sun, are absolutely essential to all change in the photo plate. Probably the actinic rays soften and separate the atoms of the gelatine, which are immediately polarized into the form of the scene it faces in the light and heat rays. Without the softening action of the actinic rays the gelatine could not take the form of the scene it faces; and without the light and heat rays it could not "see" and "feel" the scene, even if the actinic rays were present. It takes the trinity of rays, light, heat and actinic, to produce a photograph negative.

It is said that all inventions are but clumsy copies of mechanisms found in the human body and brain; that man contains on a microscopic scale all the inventions ever thought of, or that ever will be thought of. This is another way of saying that man is the microcosm, the universe the macrocosm. Victor Hugo expresses the same truth when he says "man is an infinite little copy of God."

The entire photographing process goes on in body and brain. Not a thought or sight but is photographed upon some tiny cell. Not a cell but may be cleaned of that impression, resensitized and given another impression.

Perhaps cells are immortal, as science claims. If so every cell must have undergone this cleaning, resensitizing and re-photographing process countless billions of times—with countless possibilities ahead.

And in every one of these picturings and repicturings the actinic rays are utterly indispensable. So, I cannot believe that the immortality of anything but a marble statue is dependent upon the cutting off of the sun's actinic rays. To be sure the actinic rays cause dissolution; but dissolution merely precedes resolution; dissolution gives light and heat (wisdom and love-power) a chance to produce yet higher forms.

Blessed be the destroying rays—blessed be nature's Devil; for he but clears the way for God himself, and cleans up and rearranges the rubbish after God has passed.

But when the race was in its childhood it looked upon the work done by these actinic rays, and fear was born. It saw things die; it saw destruction in the path of the wind; and like any child it imagined evil things. It personified the destroying power as Diablos, the Devil—which means destroyer.

It saw also the building, growing principle in nature and imagined a Builder.

But being a child it drew the childish conclusion that Destroyer and Builder worked eternally against each other, that they were enemies.

You see that was before the race had conceived the idea that two could work together; it was every man-savage for himself and the devil take the hindmost.

So the baby race began to love the Builder, God, and dislike and fear the Destroyer; and in its ignorance it personified both.

But here and there a clear-seer arose who glimpsed the truth. God spoke through Isaiah saying, "Behold, I make peace and I create evil; I, the Lord, do all these things." Solomon said the Lord "creates evil for the day of evil." And every seer of every Bible has tried to make clear the oneness, the all-wisdom all-power, all-presence of God.

All life is one. The sun is God manifest. The Destroyer belongs to the trinity and can no more be dispensed with than can the other two members, wisdom and love-power. And you may rest assured the Destroyer touches only that which needs dissolution that it may be transmuted.

Has anything gone out of your life? Have you lost that which you esteemed dear? Grieve not. It has been destroyed or taken away to make place for yet higher things.

God gives and God takes away in answer to your own highest desires. The Destroyer is but cleaning the plate for a more beautiful picture.

Be still and know that all things are working for the manifestation of your deepest desires. Work with things, not against them.

Three-Fold Being

Man is a three-strata being, instead of a two-strata one as Thomson J. Hudson theorizes. The obvious stratum is commonly called conscious or objective mind. This is the surface mind, the everyday mind, the mind we use in our waking hours.

Then there is the sub-conscious mind. The sub-conscious or subjective mind is the stratum of mind which receives the knowledge and wisdom which has passed through the conscious mind. The sub-conscious stratum of mind holds the habits and instincts formed at some time and place in and by the conscious mind. "Sub" means under; the sub-conscious mind lies under the conscious mind, as the depths of the lake lie under the surface.

But there is a third layer of mind which lies within and beyond both conscious and sub-conscious mind, and whose workings Hudson confounds with those of the sub-conscious mind. This may be called, for the lack of a better name, the super-conscious mind—the mind above conscious mind—the mind above consciousness.

This super-conscious mind is what we call God, out of which comes all wisdom.

Conscious mind is the point of contact between what we have already learned in this and previous states of existence, and the limitless reservoir of truth yet to be learned. Conscious mind is like unto the surface of a lake; sub-conscious mind is like the depths of the lake, every drop of which has at some time been on the surface, and is liable at any time to be recalled there; but super-conscious mind is like the rains of heaven and the streams from snow clad heights, whence the lake is perpetually replenished.

That which we already know, which we do by instinct, rests in the sub-conscious mind, ever ready to be recalled to the conscious mind. The conscious mind has to do with that which we are now learning. Super- conscious mind contains all wisdom, knowledge and power. In it we live and move and have our being and from it we are able to call, by aspiration and inspiration whatsoever we would know.

The visible universe as it is, is the sub-conscious and conscious mind of God; it represents what has been thought out of the universal reservoir of truth. But it is only a taste of the wonderful supplies still awaiting our aspiration and inspiration.

Think of all the wonderful discoveries and inventions of the last sixty years—all thought out of that great universal reservoir; and eye hath not seen nor ear heard the glories that yet await us in the great superconscious realm.

Mrs. Boehme illustrates individuality and solidarity by a star-shaped diagram. Each point of the star represents a person, a formed character; in other words, it represents the sub-conscious or habit self, the "nature" of the person. The center of the star represents God, the universal mind, with which every person is one on the unseen side. Looking at the points alone there is diversity, separateness; but looking from the center outward toward the points we see that points and center are all one, with no separating lines.

Now imagine a line cutting each point off from the center—an imaginary line, not a real one—and you will have a fair illustration of the conscious mind. The conscious mind lies between the personality and the universality of each of us; between the human and the divine of each; between what has been realized, and that limitless reservoir of beauties waiting to be realized.

Look at the star from the center and you will see that each point is simply a little bay projecting outward from the center; so each individuality is an inlet of God, each individual mind an inlet of divine mind.

And conscious mind is the imaginary line where personal mind and divine mind meet. You can readily see that one's conscious mind, then, would be filled with personality or divinity according as he looks down and is occupied with the "physical" being, or looks up and aspires toward the universal part of himself, the God part.

Now imagine the center of the star as being fluid, ever living and always free; and think of the points as being nearly solid, partially fixed. Imagine the points as containing water of life so muddy with false beliefs that it continually deposits along its edges layers of mud, ever hardening; with the water growing thicker and the beaches ever widening. Thus will you perceive the difference between personality and universality.

Now imagine the conscious mind endowed with will; note that when it turns toward the point of the star, toward the "material" part of itself, it becomes tense with anxiety and thus shuts off the point from the center, preventing a free play of the currents of life through the star-point, the personality. So the personality dries up, literally. This is the process by which we grow old.

Then imagine the conscious mind turned in faith and love toward the center of life—think, with this broader vision and knowledge of life, how lightly it would hold the things of personality, of that little point of personality; knowing that the personality is only a little inlet of divinity, and that the broad opening between the two is always open, that personality exists as a result of ever-flowing currents of divinity, and. that only his own grasping and straining can hinder the currents;—knowing all this, conscious mind turns away from the already realized personality and throws wide the opening into the great center of all life.

Thus conscious mind looks up, not down; and comes into his kingdom of love, wisdom, power. This is inspiration and aspiration. Yes, you may receive what you will, provided you call upon the super-conscious mind, the One mind over all. Whatsoever you can ask this mind believing you receive, you shall have.

When you can't ask in faith it is usually because you have not dwelt enough with the thought of God, the divine self of all creation. When we dwell much in the thought of personality, things, "materiality," then God seems faint and far away and impotent, and we can't believe we shall receive what we ask.

We need daily periods for withdrawing from the physical life and dwelling upon the thought of our oneness with omniscience, omnipotence, omnipresence, and our oneness with each other. Thus does faith grow, aspiration and inspiration become our mental habit, and the waters of life flow freely through us.

The One Spirit will guide you in all the affairs of life, and you are "safe" only when following its promptings.

If you would know the spirit's leadings, measure your impulses by the Golden Rule; for the spirit is Love to All.

Soul, Mind, and Body

If there is an individual soul that leaves the body at death, as most of us suppose, then this individual soul must be an organization of cell souls, just as the body is an organization of cells.

The body is referred to as the "shell," the "husk," the "house we live in," the "temple." In leaving the body, then, only the coarser elements are sloughed off and left as "dead," while the soul of every cell ascends, still organized in the individual soul; and the body cells disintegrate because the soul no longer holds them together.

This agrees with the statement of Theosophy that there is an "astral body" within the material body, which is like the material body but more beautiful. Many persons claim to have seen this astral body leave its "temple." Perhaps Paul meant this when he spoke of two bodies.

It seems reasonable to suppose that this spiritual body carries within it all knowledge gained in this state of being, and that in a new generation the older experiences are "forgotten," just as a thousand things are forgotten every day of our lives—things which at some future time we may recall. The thing was there, in our sub-consciousness, all the time; it simply did not affect us strongly enough to make us think about it.

A child's interest in this generation keeps in the background of sub-consciousness its memories of past generations. If it wanted to hard enough, and thought about it enough, it could recall incidents in previous generations just as it can recall an incident of yesterday or last year which it has temporarily forgotten.

Many people claim to have recalled past states of existence by desire and concentration, and many claim to have flashes of remembrance without any special desire or intention. And the Society for Psychical Research has on record many strange cases of dual or many-sided personality, etc., which seem to confirm this conception of soul and body.

It seems to me that the soul is the naked life force which is one with spirit; that material experiences are the matrices by which the life force, or soul force, is formed and organized into individuality; and that we shed the "material" parts of the body as fast as we can—just as in the lower forms of life shells are discarded when backbones appear; the shell protecting and moulding the life-form until it is sufficiently formed and organized to do without the shell.

When the physical body becomes too stiff and un- yielding a form for the growing mind or soul, then it is discarded. And it looks as if the soul, through growth and attraction, steps into a new generation where the material at hand will afford it a better matrix.

As long as the body is alive and yielding, responding readily to the developing organization of the individual, the soul keeps changing in its matrix, its body, day by day as needed; but a stiff, too-rigid and old-style matrix or body has to be discarded in whole, for a new one. "From the soul the bodye forme doth take," and when the body becomes inadequate to express the soul growth it is sloughed off altogether.

The body, astral and material, is the storage of the past experiences and the wisdom organized through those experiences.

The "objective mind," in the brain, is the surface of this storage, the doorway by which all this wisdom and knowledge entered into individual organization. The brain is the switchboard by which we are able to use this store of wisdom and knowledge at will.

The "objective mind" governs and directs not only the switchboard, but all the sub-stores with which it connects.

The "objective mind" also connects with the universal storehouse of wisdom, upon which it draws by what we call "intuition." It is through this connection with the universal that we are enabled to "rise higher than our source" of sub-conscious wisdom and knowledge gained in previous generations. In order to grow we need the super-conscious wisdom which is All.

Just as by desire and concentration we can recall the knowledge and wisdom gained in previous generations, so by desire and concentration directed toward the Universal, the Infinite, we call to us yet greater wisdom and knowledge than any yet realized.

The body which disintegrates after death is a mere collection of cell-cocoons from which the organized cell- souls have flown to new states of being. With its soul the body loses its feeling, the atoms disintegrating, each becoming what it was before, simply a bit of "dead matter" which is not dead at all.

The atoms of matter are just the same after death as before; but the organizing and in-forming spirit and soul, spirit or soul (for there is no dividing line between them), has departed, leaving each atom to live its little life again without relation to other atoms Without this organizing spirit to draw and hold the atoms together they fall apart—"ashes to ashes."

The cell is the unit organization of the body, each cell clothed with many atoms. The soul of the cell leaves it, just as the soul leaves the body as a whole.

That the astral body is an organization of cell souls, just as the physical body is an organization of cells, I have no present doubt.

And it looks reasonable to me to suppose that the soul, or astral body, carries within it all the records of all the individual's experiences since the beginning of time. That with every generation and experience this astral grows in wisdom and knowledge and beauty of character, I see no reason to doubt.

And by the power of universal attraction it is drawn in each new generation, to the exact parentage and condition it needs to help its growth in grace.

How to Aim

To Life, the force behind the Man, intellect is a necessity, because without it he blunders into death. Just as Life, after ages of struggle, evolved that wonderful bodily organ, the eye, so that the living organism could see where it was going and what was coming to help or threaten it, and thus avoid a thousand dangers that formerly slew it, so it is evolving today a mind's eye that shall see, not the physical world, but the purpose of Life, and thereby enable the individual to work for that purpose instead of thwarting and baffling it by setting up shortsighted personal aims as at present.

Even as it is, only one sort of man has ever been happy, has ever been universally respected among all the conflicts of interests and illusions …
I sing, not arms and the hero, but the philosophic man; he who seeks in contemplation to discover the inner will of the world, in invention to discover the means of fulfilling that will, and in action to do that will by the so-discovered means. —Bernard Shaw.

Without definiteness of aim nothing can be accomplished.

With too definite an aim very little can be accomplished.

This is the paradox of all accomplishment. It looks hard, but is in reality very easy—so easy that a child lives it.

The key to the problem is this: No man liveth unto himself and none dieth unto himself; we are all members one of another; all creation moves to "one far-off divine event," the definite details of which no human being has yet grasped. Perhaps none ever will grasp it. For how can the hand or the foot conceive the structure and purposes of the whole body?

There is a Universal Aim which includes and impels all individual aims. There is one great intelligence, one spirit, one purpose actuating every human being. The "Plan of Salvation" is not a mere superstitious myth. There certainly is a "plan," a "divine event," which we are all working at, whether we know it or not.

There is a Divine Ideal beckoning us every one. Glimpses of it are caught even by the fool who hath said in his heart there is no God, no oneness of life and purpose.

As our bodies are all members of God's body, so our ideals are members of the Universal Ideal; our aims are members of the Universal Aim.

Your hand may understand and define its impulse to grasp or release; but can it understand and define your aim and purpose, which gave it the impulse?

We can imagine the hand understanding its own movements, but can it understand your movements and purposes? The hand says, "I want to grasp this"; but can it in any sense understand your purpose, which made it want to grasp?

So you say, "I want to paint pictures." or "I want to make money," or "I want to teach school," or "I want to be a home-keeper and mother," or "I want to build bridges." But can you tell why you want to do these things or others?

Can you define the Great I *want* of which your I want is but an outcropping? Can you see the Universal Ideal of which your ideal is a detail? No; you can see your individual I want, but the Universal I *want* is too large for you to take in from your point of view.

Did you ever say to yourself, "I want to be a bridge builder"; then after you had become a successful bridge builder did you find yourself rather disgusted with the bridge business? Did you find yourself saying, "I want to be a painter instead of a bridge builder"? And you couldn't imagine why your wants wouldn't stay satisfied with bridge building.

Can you imagine the hand being disgusted because after it had grasped the book awhile it found itself wanting to let go? Of course. The hand would not understand why it could not remain "constant" to its first desire: it would not see the reason for letting go.

So with us members of the "Stupendous Whole."

Universal purpose and desire play through us. We know we "want" this and we "don't want" that. When we are on the "animal" plane we simply gratify our wants when we can, and are satisfied until another want impels us. By and by we begin to reason about our wants. We call some of them "good," and gratify them if we can. We call some of them "bad" and fight them with all our puny might—and are correspondingly unhappy. In both cases we fail to see why we want what we want.

When after we have learned to build bridges we find ourselves wanting to paint pictures we resist the desire and keep on building bridges. Then, if the Universal Purpose really wants us to stop building bridges and make pictures it keeps on impelling us in the new direction until we finally find a way to get at the painting. If we are too stubborn the Universal I *want* gets us out of the way and raises up our sons and daughters to paint the pictures.

It is like this: In response to the Universal I *want* you have taught your good right hand to thread needles and sew, until it can almost do it in the dark. All the nerves and brains and muscles in your finger tips have learned that little trick. Now, in response to a new Universal I *want*, you decide that that good right hand of yours is to learn to run scales on the piano.

You sit down at the piano, place your hand in position and impel it to strike the notes. But this sort of thing is entirely new to your fingers! Every little muscle is stiff, every nerve and every tiny bit of finger-brain protests that it can't run scales!—it doesn't know how!—its work is sewing—it can't, so there! You say to yourself, "How stiff my fingers are, and how rebellious —they won't mind me at all!"

But you keep on sending your want, your will into them. You "practice" long hours every day. And by and by you find your fingers have learned the new trick and can do it without special thought and will from you. You kept pouring your want into that hand until it became the hand's want and will. From working against your want the hand has come to work with it and by it.

Why did you do it? Because the Universal I *want* kept pouring itself into you until you took up the practice; just as you poured the I *want* on into your hands until they, too, wanted to do it, and did it.

Were your fingers extra rebellious? Did they fight, and get tangled up, and imitate each other's movements? Then what did you do with them?

You kept them at it; and you kept them at it a great deal longer time than you would if they had been more obedient fingers; you kept them practicing until they learned to do the work willingly, with interest, artistically. Then you gave them beautiful things to play with, instead of hard things to work at.

Of course the beautiful things to play with are all made up of the very same sort of things your fingers have been working hard at. But the monotony of repetition is all gone from the beautiful play. It is joy to play. It is "hard work" to practice scales.

But without all those scales there can never be a satisfying play. In practice we learn by repetition to do well and gracefully one thing at a time. In play we string all these movements together in a satisfying play of joy and praise.

We hope for the perfection of action which alone makes satisfying play possible; therefore we keep practicing. The harder our fingers rebel, the longer and more persistently we keep them at it—that is all.

Now the Universal I *want* keeps us at things in precisely the same way. The Universal is working out a glorious Ideal of perfect play, wherein every member of itself shall be shining, obedient, supple enough to play with grace and full joy the "music of the spheres."

You and I being more or less stiff and disobedient and dense have to be kept at our practices until we learn to do them right. We say, "Oh, if I could only get into my right niche; but I seem to be held here in spite of all I can do!" We say we "don't like" the sort of "drudgery" we are "condemned" to—there must be something "wrong" with the universe, or with economic or family conditions, or we would not have to drudge at one kind of thing when we are "fitted" for something else, or want to do something else.

Our fingers cry out in the same way when we keep them at the scales—"Oh," they cry, "why are we compelled to this dreary commonplace repetition when our souls long for beautiful harmonies?"

You see, it never occurs to them that they are "compelled" to this commonplace scale practice because they long for beautiful harmonies and happy play.

And it doesn't occur readily to you and to me that we are held to our dish washing, our business routine, our bridge building because our souls long for greater things.

But it is so. The perfection of large ideals can never be attained except through perfection of detail; and through the dish washing, business routine, bridge building, we are perfecting the details of self-command, of body and brain control which will enable us to play the great harmonies our souls already feel.

The great things we feel and desire without being able to express them, comprise the Universal Ideal at which every soul is aiming, whether or not he knows it.

The perfection of this great Ideal we see as through smoked glass, darkly. We get all sorts of half-views of it, and spend a lot of time squabbling about it. But not one of us really knows even a tiny part of the glory and beauty and joy of that Universal Ideal, which includes and actuates all our personal ideals. "It doth not yet appear what we shall be." But we know that when the Great Ideal does appear we shall all have our places in the joy of its beauty, for every one of us will have had his place and done his part in working out that ideal.

The Universal Ideal is gently urging us on to ineffable good. But none of us can conceive the details of the good which is yet to appear. We are all hoping and working for this "Indeterminate Good," as Hanford Henderson calls it.

It constitutes our large Ideal, which includes all our lesser, fleeting ideals and even our passing wishes and longings.

It is with our large ideals that definiteness of aim is a mistake- An "indeterminate good" necessitates a general aim. It will not do to say "I know exactly where the blossoms will appear when the earth blossoms as a rose, and I know exactly the day they will appear; therefore will I till only those exact spots and get my ascension robes ready for that exact hour."

The man who is so dead sure of his great aim will sooner or later, like "Perkins" in "Quincy Adams Sawyer," find himself perched on the ridgepole with his white robes flapping in the cold night and his goods in somebody else's possession. When one is too sure of the "far-off divine event" he muddles the present opportunity for hastening that event.

"Wisdom is before him that hath understanding; but the eyes of a fool are in the ends of the earth." The man who is too sure of the "indeterminate good" misses the present good. The man who aims at the Great Good which he cannot hit, misses the little Goods, near at hand, which need to be hit.

What should we think of a hunter who aimed only at big game beyond his gun's reach, while small game gamboled at his feet? We'd think him a fool who deserved to starve to death. Of course.

We miss our chances by straining after the big game beyond our reach.

The great ideal should have our faith, rather than our aim.

Aim only at that which is within reach, and trust the big things to time and the spirit.

You stand in the Now. Keep your aim for the things of the Now. Thus will your aim gain accuracy and you will be ready for the Great Things when they shall at last appear in the Now.

Where are you Now? Are you building bridges? Then aim to build this one better than any other was ever built. Aim to improve your work now.

Aim to enjoy it all; for only as joy brightens you can you see how to better your work and methods.

And proficiency at bridge building means freedom to follow your next ideal. The greater your proficiency the nearer the top you get, and the more money you get for your work; and the more money you have the more time you can take for working out your next ideal.

In proportion as you are progressively proficient at your work your money stream will increase. In proportion as you enjoy your work you will grow in efficiency and money. The drudge is held to his work because he does not put into it the love and interest and joy necessary to make him progressively proficient.

He says "lack of money keeps him from getting into a new line of work." That is it exactly—the Universal Spirit which urges us on keeps the money away from us until we have gained in this thing the proficiency needed to fit us for other work.

Are you building bridges and at the same time aiming to paint pictures? And are you too poor to drop the bridge building and devote all your time to painting pictures?

Then I say unto you have faith in your desire to paint pictures, for your desire is an outcropping of Universal Desire and is certain to find its satisfaction. Your desire is the desire of Omnipotence, Omniscience, which will in no wise disappoint itself. All desires shall be fulfilled in the fullness of time.

Would you hasten the time? Then have faith in your desire; but aim at the bridge building. Do better and better the work you find to do until the way opens to a new line of work.

And do every detail of your bridge building as if it were the painting of the greatest picture. Think you that accuracy of observation, delicacy of touch, harmony of thought and power of expression are gained only by dabbling paint on a canvas with a camel's-hair brush? No. Bridge building has its place in training a great painter. Put your soul into it while you are held to it, and give it its full chance to do the work.

Have faith in your desire to paint pictures, but aim your energies at the bridge you are building now. Keep your faith high, your aim true, and verily in an hour when you least expect it the way will open from bridge building to picture painting.

The Substance of Things

Where are the cowards who bow down to environment—
Who think they are made of what they eat, and must conform to the bed that they lie in?
I am not wax,—I am energy!
Like the whirlwind and waterspout, I twist my environment into my form, whether it will or not.
What is it that transmutes electricity into auroras, and sunlight into rainbows, and soft flakes of snow into stars, and adamant into crystals, and makes solar systems of nebulae?
Whatever it is, I am its cousin-german.
I, too, have my ideas to work out, and the universe is given me for raw material.
I am a signet, and I will put my stamp upon the molten stuff before it hardens.
What allegiance do I owe to environment? I shed environments for others as a snake sheds its skin.
The world must come my way,—slowly, if it will,—but still my way.
I am a vortex launched in chaos to suck it into shape.
    —Ernest Crosby.

.

"To a certain extent I have been benefited by these teachings. In some ways they do not appear to have a very practical result. It is possible to concentrate and obtain small things, but any real change of surroundings seems to be quite dependent upon circumstances entirely outside my own will." H. B.

Thus writes a shortsighted and faithless one—faithless because of her shortsightedness. Another woman who has observed the same things writes thus: "If I see no great results now I know it is because I am working for large things."

Life "concentrates" on a mushroom and grows it in a night; but an oak requires twenty years of "concentration." A woman "concentrates" on a good dinner, a bit of sewing, the control of her tongue for an hour, $5.00 for a new hat, the cure of a headache, and success crowns each effort. These are little things, the mushrooms of an hour, used shortly and soon forgotten.

The same woman "concentrates" for a complete change in disposition or environment, for anything in fact which seems a long way off from present conditions. Now, if she is a shortsighted woman she has little or no faith in anything which she cannot see, hear, taste, smell or feel. She can see, taste and smell a mushroom, so she believes in it. She could see an oak and believe in that. But she cannot see the acorn growing underground; therefore she has no faith that there is an oak growing. And if there is already a little oak in sight she cannot see it grow, no matter how steadily she looks at it; therefore she "fears" the oak is not growing.

But the far-seeing woman is different. She sees through things. She feels the intangible. She hears, smells, and tastes that which moves upon the face of the deep and brings forth things. She touches the true substance (that which stands under) of things which are to be.

Her faith rests in invisible life; the other woman's faith rests only in the visible things which life has made.

To say that H. B. has no faith would be an untruth. Every living being is full of faith, or he could not live.

Faith is in the atmosphere and we live by using it, just as a fish lives by using the water. Faith springs eternal in every human breast, fed from the universal source. To talk of one's little faith or one's much faith is like talking of the earth's squareness.

Every soul lives by faith and plenty of it. But he lives by faith in what? There's the rub.

Until we emerge from a sense of materiality—and no one has as yet got more than his nose above these muddy waters— we live by faith in things seen, smelt, tasted, heard and felt. These are the only things we are familiar with; to them we pin our faith, and pride ourselves upon our good sense, reason and lack of "superstition."

"I can't believe in anything unless I can see it" is our self-satisfied cry; "you can't fool me with your religious hocus-pocus, nor with your rabbit's foot and horseshoe and four-leaved clover; I can see no connection between a rabbit's foot and your good luck, therefore I know no connection exists; I can see no big God on a great white throne, consequently I know none exists; show me your God; show me the string which connects the four-leaved clover to your good luck and I'll put my faith in it."

The material one reckons without his Unseen Host. By and by the Unseen begins to juggle with him. His beautiful plans, every step of which he could plainly see, are blown awry. He can't see why! The things in which he had such faith begin to totter and tumble about his ears. He can't see why! Reluctantly he begins to see that there are mighty forces he can't see. His whole beautiful material world begins to dance to strings he can't see!

Ah, so there are things he can't see, hear, smell, taste or feel! They may be a fearful and chaotic jumble; they seem to be; but they are there, after all his certainty that he could see, smell, hear, taste and feel The Whole Thing.

And he begins to reach out toward these unseen things. He peers and peers into the darkness and stillness. And as he peers his faiths gradually loosen their hold upon the old visible things and begin to reach out into the darkness and silence.

He sends his faiths groping, groping, feeling their way through the Invisible, always seeking the strings to which visible things have been dancing and tumbling.

At first all is darkness; but by and by faith gets its tentacles around Something Unseen;—ah, there is Something which disposes what man proposes—an unseen, un-tasted, unheard, un-smelt, unfelt Something.

A terrible Something it may be, but still a Something, all-powerful, all-present. He has sent his feelers into the Invisible and touched God, the soul, the life-principle, which makes and unmakes, gives and takes away all those little things to which he was wont to pin his faiths.

The next thing is to find out the nature of this mighty Something whose home is in the Invisible. But how find out the nature of the Unseen? Not by touch, taste, smell, sight or hearing—not at first anyway. But by its fruits you may know a tree to be good or bad.

By its fruits you may know the invisible powers to be beneficent or malefic. And the material one is familiar with fruits, with things. He built such beautiful things himself, so he ought to be a judge of the fruits of labor. The fruits of his labor were all good, he knows they were. If only the great Unseen had not spoiled them all! Oh, the labors of the Unseen brought his own good efforts to naught—the Unseen must be a terrible and evil power; its fruits are destruction of his own good buildings. He fears this Great Unseen Power to which his faiths are beginning to pin themselves.

But wait: Good is beginning to rise from the ashes of his ruins. This so terrible calamity is turning out a blessing! New and greater things are forming, to take the places of the lost fruits! And they are good.

Oh, this Great Unseen works in terrifying mystery but its fruits are good.

Now he is ready to "come unto God." He begins to see the un-seeable things, and his faiths tendril them.

Those who would "come unto Him must believe that He is, and that He is a rewarder of them that diligently seek Him."

Those who would understand and feel and use the invisible forces must believe that they are, and that they reward those who diligently seek to understand and use them.

The Unseen things move the visible world. The material one being pinned by his faiths to the things of the world is moved as the world is moved. He is a mere puppet in the hands of the Unseen powers.

As he looses the faiths which bound him to the world rack, and sends his faith tendrils into the Unseen, he becomes one with the powers which pull the world-strings.

"Faith is the sub-stance (the underlying and creating principle) of things hoped for, the evidence of things not seen."

The material one's faith is pinned to things already seen; therefore, his creative principle is poured into the thing already created.

Then Life juggles and tumbles things until the material one's faiths are torn loose from their material moorings, and go feeling out into the Unseen for new things to cling to. When the whole bunch of visible things has failed us; when houses, lands, money, friends, and even fathers and mothers and brothers and sisters have gone back on us, what is there left to pin our faiths to? And without something to have faith in how could we live at all?

We couldn't live without faiths to steady us; witness the suicides and the deaths from broken hearts.

And if all visible things have failed us, if our faiths are broken loose from fathers, mothers, brothers, friends, houses and lands, where else can our faiths take hold again except in the region of the Unseen?—the region where "the wind bloweth whither it listeth and thou canst hear the sound thereof but canst not tell whence it cometh nor whither it goeth;" the region of substance, of creative power.

It seems very terrible to have our faiths broken loose from fathers, mothers, brothers, friends, houses and lands; but it is good for us, as time always proves.

Broken loose from the effects of creative energy, our faiths reach out into the Unseen and tendril the very energy itself. From a state of oneness with things we evolve a new being at one with the creative power within things.

What are the unseen things to which our torn faiths begin to attach themselves? Our faith itself is unseen, the sub-stance of things hoped for, the substantial evidence of things not yet seen.

What do we hope for that we have not yet seen?

First of all we hope for peace—another of the substantial unseen things. We hope for love, the most substantial of unseen things. Oh, if we had but peace and love we could count all else well lost! And behold, by unseen faith tendrils our bruised faiths attach themselves to the unseen substance of peace and love.

Wisdom is an unseen substance—our unseen faiths attach themselves to the unseen source of wisdom. Thought is unseen; our faiths, torn loose from things, begin to reach out into the unseen realm of thought. Ideals are unseen things. Our faiths, torn loose from the already-realized, begin to tendril the unseen ideals, the race's ideals, the family ideals, and lastly our individual ideals.

Our unseen faiths become one with these unseen ideals; and through these little faith tendrils we begin literally to draw the ideal down into our physical being and out into the visible world.

Through our faith tendrils the ideal is literally ex-pressed, pressed out into visibility.

When our faiths were attached to material things, the material things (being negative to us) sucked us dry. Now our faith tendrils reach upward to the unseen ideal realm of real substance (to which we are negative) and by the same law of dynamics it is we who draw the life; draw it from the unseen realm of real life substance.

Of ourselves we could do nothing—the things to which our faiths attached us sucked us dry of power, and the unseen powers finally tore us loose; but now that we are tendriled by our faiths to the Unseen, "the Father" in us and through us doeth the works of rightness that bring peace.

And behold, we are filled with the unseen power, and through our faith in the Unseen we pass on the fruits of the spirit, which are "love, joy, peace, longsuffering, gentleness, meekness, faith, temperance."

And being filled with the power of the Unseen we pass on the fruits of the spirit to fathers, mothers, brothers, friends, houses, lands; pass it on in every act of life and in every breath we take.

We breathe out that which, through our faith-tendrils, the Great Unseen breathes into us.

Then, behold, that which is written comes to pass: "Ye shall have an hundredfold more houses and lands and fathers and mothers and brothers in this present time." You shall have them to use at will.

While you were attached by your faiths to things they used you; now you use them.

Pin your faiths to the Unseen things and let patience have her perfect work. So shall you realize your heart's full desire. Let things rock as they will; let facts be stubborn and conditions hard if need be. Never mind them. To mind them is to pin your faiths to them.

Mind the Unseen things. Pin your faiths to your ideals.

Flout facts and hard conditions! Believe in the Unseen.

Train your faiths upward.

"Whatsoever ye desire believe that ye receive," and you shall surely have it.

If it is a mushroom expect it in a night. If you desire a great oak give it time to grow. In due time, perhaps in an hour when you least expect it, it will surely appear.

The one thing needful is to pin your little faiths to the Unseen Source of all things.

Believe in the great unseen part of yourself and the universal.

To Get at the Substance

All desirable and as-yet-unexpressed things are in the silence waiting to be drawn into expression through aspiration and inspiration.

Of course one can aspire and inspire anywhere and under almost any conditions. I remember one great aspiration of mine which was satisfied whilst I was sitting in a crowded street car with folks standing in front of me and others clinging to the running board.

The Things of the Silence are everywhere present, permeating solid things as the X-rays do. All creation cannot hinder a man communing with the Unseen at any time and in any place—all creation cannot hinder him except as he lets it.

But that is the trouble—he lets it interfere unless he is in almost agonizing earnest about the unseen things. That momentous hour on the crowded street car came after weeks of most earnest "seeking,'" after weeks of almost constant "concentrating" on this one thing I wanted to receive from the Unseen. I was so absorbed in that one subject that the crowds were as nothing to me.

In order to get anything—wisdom, power, love—from the silence one's whole interest must be absorbed in the matter.

Your interest is like the plate in a camera; it receives impressions only from that upon which it is turned. And the camera must be held steadily in one position until the impression is received.

The human camera receives impressions from the unseen in exactly the same way that it receives impressions from the seen world.

But it takes a longer time to receive a complete impression from the unseen, just as it takes a longer time to get a good negative in the dark.

The unseen is the dark to us; hence the long time it often takes to get a complete impression of anything we desire to receive in the silence. It takes a longer "exposure" to get the impression.

"Concentration" is merely the steady "exposure" of the attention, the interest, to the thing we desire to realize, to make tangible.

Now the busy person, the person who is interested in a thousand things, keeps his interest so busy taking instantaneous photographs that he has no time to get impressions from the unseen. His mind is constantly flitting from one thing to another. When it happens to turn toward the unseen it simply sweeps the dark quickly and comes back to earth again without an impression.

Instead of a steady aspiration toward the ideal there is a constant perspiration toward the real.

As there is nothing new under the sun the only progress made is around and around the same old things.

The only real relief from things as they are lies in the unseen.

The only way to get at the relief is to "concentrate" on the unseen things. In order to do this the attention must be called away from seen things. The mind must be "set on things above," and kept set until the "renewing" is complete.

People who are not yet satisfied that the visible world does not and cannot satisfy, will see no need of going into the silence on set occasions. And there is another class who are apt to see no need of it—the class whose "concentration" on the invisible is so constant that material things assume the subordinate relation. These are people who have "got the truth" by coming up through great tribulation; who have run the gamut of things and found the principle behind things.

And almost invariably, if not always (I have never heard of an exception), these are people who have tried nearly every method of spiritual culture extant, have practiced fasting and prayer, breath exercises, denials and affirmations, and treatments and concentrations of every conceivable kind.

Martin Luther was one of these; and at last, when he had tried everything else and was crawling up the church steps on all fours, he "found the truth." Immediately he arose, repudiated all his good works as unavailing, and went about praising and preaching that not by works but by faith we are healed.

Eight or ten years ago I heard Paul Militz, who had worked for years at all manner of spiritual, mental and breath exercising, repudiate it all as "unnecessary." "Not any of these things avails you," he said. And others who have "found the truth" reiterate the same statement.

And yet every one of them has "found the truth" through those very practices.

If Martin Luther had stopped short of crawling up those church steps as his own seeking spirit bade him, he would never have "found the truth." If Militz, Shelton, Burnell, et al., had left out one of their practices they would still be "seeking."

The spirit in every man bids him do things and refrain from doing other things, in order to "save" him self from something or other. Is this universal urge only a lie? No.

These concentration exercises are kindergarten methods by which we learn to use ourselves. When by practice we have learned how, we discard the kindergarten methods. What was gained by self-conscious effort becomes habit. We turn intuitively to the unseen, whereas we used to turn to it only by conscious effort, by special practices.

But why repudiate the practices? Why tell others who are trying to learn how, that their efforts are all useless? By practices we found the way; why discourage practice?

There are people who as yet are wrapped up in the material. There are those who are wrapped up in the unseen. Neither of these are in present need of set times for "concentrating" upon the unseen, the ideal side of life.

But there is a third great "middle class" who are not absorbed in the already manifest world, and who want to be one with the unseen world of causation. To these I say, follow the example of all the "adepts" of all the ages; practice "concentration."

To all who want to accomplish something I say, Go into the silence regularly for power and wisdom to accomplish.

To those whose interests are mainly in the material world, but who want to understand and be deeply interested in the unseen world—from whence come all things,—to those I say, Go into the silence at regular periods every day.

To all humanity who are longing for Something, I say. All things are in the Silence; be still and know.

The Spirit and the Individual

"I was washing my breakfast dishes one morning when it occurred to me to go to visit a friend who lived several miles away. I did my work and started to dress for my journey, when there came over me such a feeling of depression, or despondency, or gloom, that I could not understand. I kept on getting ready, all the time trying to reason away the feeling. But it would not go. Finally I got my hat on and one glove and started for the door, when such a heaviness came over me that I turned back into my room and sat down saying, 'God, I want to know what the meaning is of all this.'

The answer came loud, strong and firm, 'Stay at home.' I stayed, and taking off my hat, gloves and cape I felt so light I seemed to walk on air. At the time I supposed the voice (I call it voice for want of a more definite term) had told me to stay at home because some one was coming to me for help. This was my first year as a teacher and healer. But not a soul came that day, nor that night, and the thought flitted through my mind that perhaps it was all nonsense after all and I might as well have gone.

Well, the outcome was that the train I would have taken met with a fearful accident in which many were killed or badly injured. This is only one of many similar experiences I have had. I do not stop to reason out things. The world has tried for 1900 years to follow reason, and look at the outcome I follow my intuition and it never fails me."
—Flora P. Howard, Los Angeles, Cal.

One's reason is not a thing to be belittled and denied. It is his crowning glory, created for use.

But it is not all the wisdom a man has access to, nor is it the greatest. The man who exalts his understanding above the wisdom of the rest of creation, and un-creation, is a fool and sure to come to grief.

But he who rejoices in his personal understanding or reason as the means by which he taps the source of all wisdom, is in a fair way to profit by his own intelligence and the universal intelligence besides.

Everybody knows his foresight is not so good as his hindsight. He has demonstrated the fact many a time, by as many little tumbles off his high horse. Really, it seems as if he might have learned by this time not to be quite so sure about his reason.

After Mrs. Howard knew that the train she meant to go on had been wrecked she saw, plainly, why it was unwise for her to go on that particular train. Her reason had been enlightened, her hindsight perfected.

By what? By universal intelligence.

Suppose New York City should set itself up as the center of all wisdom—suppose she were to say, "What I cannot reason out is not worth knowing." Suppose she continued to send out decrees into all the world, but turned up her nose at the messages sent in to her. What do you suppose would happen? She would go to smash in a week. It is by her reception of all those messages as to outside doings, that she is enabled to reason out her business problems and send out messages that move the world. To exalt New York knowledge and reason, and despise outside knowledge and reason, would quickly ruin her.

Intuition is the wireless line by which we receive directions from every other station in the universe. After Mrs. Howard had received and obeyed her message from the universal—some days after—she knew why she had been so directed.

He who is puffed up in his own conceit is eternally despising his intuitions, following his back-number reasons, and getting into the "accidents." Then he wonders why he is so abused.

You see, we have none of us ever passed this way before. This day is a new day; this bit of road has never been traveled before. Nobody can know by reason what we shall run into just around the bend there. He may make a rough guess at it, but he cannot know.

But—there is Something which, whether it knows or does not know consciously, what is, or will be, around that corner there—there is Something which can and does send us by the wireless line a message to keep away, or to go to it, as the case may be.

Now Mrs. Howard was a woman with no desire to be in such a smash, and she believed her intuitions would keep her warned away from them.

Now next door to Mrs. Howard there may have lived another woman, just as "good" as Mrs. Howard, just as devoted to her intuitions, who received a message to go on that train. At the same moment Mrs. Howard's heart grew heavy and she heard the message, "Stay at home," this other woman's heart grew light and she heard the message, "Go." So she went blithely forth to the train. She mounted the steps and walked into the car and along past several vacant seats before she felt the impression to sit down. She sat down and gazed happily out of the window.

By and by, as they were bowling swiftly along there came a sudden crash, and shrieks, and hiss of steam. Then there was work to do.

This woman neighbor of Mrs. Howard's, beyond a little shaking up from which she almost instantly recovered, was entirely uninjured. There were dead and dying in front and behind her, but she was safe. There was work to do and she was there to do it.

You see, this woman was a physician and surgeon, and the only one on the train. She had been years preparing for such work, and she believed her intuitions would lead her, strong and well herself, into just such opportunities as this. So the message which depressed Mrs. Howard brought light to the soul of this woman.

Each received and interpreted the message according to her own particular character.

And what about the injured and killed? They too were "led by the spirit." Each by his own self-built character related himself to his particular "fate." I wouldn't wonder if a good many of them did it by filling up on the accident and criminal columns of the daily papers. The man who thinks in terms of accident is pretty sure to meet them.

But probably more of the "victims" were drawn through their false religion. The man who thinks himself (who really thinks it, "in his heart")—who thinks himself a "vile worm" and a great sinner deserving of a "bad end," and yet who has not "repented," is daily relating himself more closely to all sorts of violent and horrible things.

And everywhere and at all times the violent man, the strenuous man, no matter how "good" he may be, is preparing himself to be led into whatever catastrophe fits him.

There is no hit and miss about our "fates"—we get just what we are fitted for.

And through all ages we have been fitting ourselves; and we are still at it. He who is not busy fitting himself for the best is relating himself to the less good.

He who fits himself to die with his boots on will die so. He who fits himself for "accidents" will die by an accident. He who fits himself for life may perchance never again see death.

When the bubonic plague is about to appear in a place all the birds fly away. What warned them? Oh, that was only "instinct"—something common, that we wise beings never use.

Before Mt. Pelee spit destruction, all the wild animals (not one of which could have had any personal knowledge, or any record of volcano lore) fled from the vicinity. The tame animals whimpered and cowered and those which could ran away. Then the people's hearts began to sink and the most ignorant of them ran after the animals. As Mt. Pelee grew more emphatic in her prophecies all hearts grew heavier and heavier and all souls heard the message "Go."

Then there was hurried preparation for a hasty exodus. But no; the wise, educated, sensible men put their heads together and decided that they would not and others should not be guided by any such common thing as "instinct," or by their own sinking hearts. No! Even though their hearts fell into their shoes and their knees knocked and their teeth chattered they would be sensible, they would; they'd use their divine reason, they would—Mt. Pelee had never destroyed them before and it wouldn't now.

So the wise reasoners corralled the poor fools. And they were well corralled. Only one ever got away.

Now just what this spirit is like that tries to lead us into all truth, is a thing I don't know. But that there is such a spirit that pervades and would save all creatures from harm I do know, both by intuition (the spirit's witness with my spirit) and by actual and repeated experiences of both kinds. I have been led of the spirit into ways of pleasantness, peace and plenty; and before that I turned up my nose at the spirit and went my own way into all sorts of troubles.

And I have a theory, based on the spirit's witness with mine, as to what this spirit is and how it acts.

The spirit is the universal intelligence which fills this universe so full there is not room for anything else. There are just little eddies and whirls and currents and cross-currents in this great ocean of intelligence. And you are one eddy in it, and I another; and each of us sets up little swirls and currents that move us about and move other things to us. And when a leaf floats by it is drawn into our eddy, but when we swirl by a rock, the rock in unmoved and so are we. We are not related to the rock.

When gold is placed beside a horseshoe magnet it stays put. The magnet and gold are not interested in each other. But that does not prove that the magnet is stupid and dead. No, there is a great current of longing in that magnet. If it had means of locomotion it would go about the world seeking, seeking—perhaps never knowing just what it was seeking, but still seeking. And by and by it would begin to feel a definite inclination to go in a certain direction.

Now if it is just a fool magnet without great pride in its brains it will follow that definite inclination. And as it journeys the drawing power will grow, and it will journey faster, and behold, it will fly into the arms of its affinity, a steel bar. And it will cling and cling, and the bar will cling, and joy will be born.

It takes two, and an exchange of intelligence, to bring joy into being.

Or perhaps our magnet will stay at home and long, long, until it draws to it steel filings.

This is not so fanciful as you may suppose. All things are intelligent. All things are putting their little compulsions on all creation for satisfaction. And in due time all compulsions will be met. The great sea is seething with intelligence, and affinities are coming together.

It is the attraction of the magnet for the steel that constitutes what I call the spirit. That attraction is intelligence.

When in doubt as to the meaning of your solar center feelings, do nothing. Come back as Mrs. Howard did, sit down; be still; ask for the meaning; and obey.

By Crooked Paths

The Rev. R. F. Horton tells a little story of a remarkable answer to prayer.

He was with a party of tourists in Norway. In exploring some wild and marshy country one of the ladies lost one of her "goloshes." The overshoe could not be replaced short of Bergen, at the end of their tour, and it was out of the question to attempt to explore that wild country without rubbers. The golosh must be found, or the tour curtailed.

As you may imagine, every member of the party set diligently to work to find the missing rubber. Over and over they hunted the miles of glades and mountain sides they had traversed At last they gave it up and returned to the hotel.

But in the afternoon a thought came to Dr. Horton—why not pray that they find the shoe? So he prayed. And they rowed back up the fjord to the landing of the morning, and he got out and walked directly to the overshoe, in a spot he would have sworn he had before searched repeatedly.

I remember a similar experience of my own. There were four of us riding bicycles along a rather sandy road some distance from town. Two were spinning along on a tandem some distance ahead of us, on a down grade, when a rivet flew out and the chain dropped. The tandem ran for a quarter of a mile on down the hill and slowed up on the rise beyond, so that our friends were able to dismount without injury.

By this time we had overtaken them, having ridden in their track, and learned for the first time the cause of their halt. Of course everybody's immediate thought was, "Oh, we can never find that tiny gray rivet in this gray dust—probably the other bicycles ran over it— and home is three miles off!" But we all retraced our steps, diligently searching.

Two of the party are crack shots with the rifle, with very quick eyesight. I thought one of these two might find the rivet. But we all walked slowly back, far beyond the point where they became conscious of their loss, and no one spied the rivet.

Then it occurred to me that the high spirit within had not been called to our assistance. Immediately I said to myself, "Spirit, you know where the rivet is!—please show it to me!"

I thought of the spirit as the Law of Love or Attraction, which is the principle of all creation, and instantly the idea came that the little rivet could attract the eye's attention if the eye were willing to be attracted. These words floated into my mind, "Rivet, rivet, rivet my eye!"

By this time I had fallen behind the others. So I walked leisurely, calmly along, eyes willing, and those words saying themselves over and over in my mind.

And the rivet riveted my eye! I, who considered myself very slow of sight, found the rivet. And I know it was because I turned to the universal self, to God, to the Law of Attraction for the help needed, for the knowledge which not one of us had in consciousness, but which was certainly present in the universal mind in which we live and move and have our being.

Just the other day I had a little experience which illustrates the "man's extremity is God's opportunity" idea. For years I have said I could never find ready made garments to fit me. Have tried many times; waists all too short and narrow in front, sleeves skimpy. But I keep trying, every year; for everything is evolving you know, even clothes and tailors.

I wanted a new white lawn shirt waist and wondered if I couldn't find one ready made. I tried the biggest suit house in Springfield; no good.

Then one day I had an impulse to try the best places in Holyoke. I found one or two "almosts," but nothing that would quite do. So I gave it up.

Then I had another impulse to try a store of which I have always said, "I never found there anything I wanted." I nearly passed the store, saying to myself, "No use to try there, and it is late anyway." But there came the thought, or rather impression, that the spirit impelled me and I would better go.

"We'll see if it is the spirit," I said to myself—"I believe it is." It was. I found the [shirt] waist I wanted, and I found a pretty white lawn suit besides! And it was found in the most unlikely corner in the vicinity, according to my judgment and experience.

There is a little law in here that I want you to notice. The spirit leads us through impressions or attractions; and it is limited in its revelations by our mental makeup, which is the conscious and ruling part of us.

Why did not the spirit impress me in the first place to go to that store, where that [shirt] waist and dress had been waiting for me since spring? And I had wanted them since spring. The spirit did impress me about it, but when the spirit said "shirt waist" to me I said, "Springfield—if they haven't a fit there they won't have it anywhere; and anyway I know I'll never find it." But I tried—without faith. That shut the spirit up for the time.

But at the very first opportunity, on the first afternoon when I wasn't too busy to even think about such things, the spirit whispered "shirt waist" to me again. And I didn't let the spirit get any farther with its impressions; instead of asking the spirit where to go for a shirt waist I said, "Oh, yes, shirt waist—of course—I'll go to A.'s and B.'s and C.'s, where I generally get other things that suit me."

You see, my habit mind, preconceived opinions, again settled the matter. It was not until I had given up finding anything at these places, and was going right by the door of the other store, that the spirit had a chance even to whisper its name to me. The spirit had to lead me around all my prejudices in the matter, before it could get me to think of that place.

My mind was open to the thought of the shirt waist, but it was closed hard and fast against the idea of that particular store. At least the direct mental route to that store was closed. So the spirit had to lead me around by back-alley brain connections. But now the direct route is open.

The spirit always goes shopping with me, and nearly always the direct mental routes are open, so I have lots of fun shopping, never waste a lot of time at it, and I nearly always get just what I want, many times at bargain prices, though I almost never look at bargain ads in the papers. But many, many times have I gone into a store to buy a certain thing and found a big special sale on, of that very item.

Do you think these are very trivial things to be bothering the spirit about? I don't. The spirit is all-wise, all-powerful, everywhere present, and its chief end and joy is to direct folks aright.

The spirit is a sort of universal floor-walker to straighten out the snarls between supply and demand in all departments of life. And I think it is a pretty heedless or foolish individual who won't consult it in every little dilemma.

And I notice that, in spite of this thought, I find myself ignoring the spirit—thinking I know of course where I'd better go for a shirt waist.

It seems hard to remember that Life's store is always growing and changing, so that we can always save time, money and needless meandering, by asking the spirit.

Herein lies the secret of all our little experiences when it looks as if our leading of the spirit was all wrong and our prayers, longing and desires all unanswered: The spirit never fails us. It is we who grow weary following the spirit; which must lead us to the desired goal by way of our own mental paths.

You see, it is a matter of cutting new streets in our mental domain, so it won't be necessary for the spirit to take us by such roundabout ways. It is a matter of clearing out our rocky prejudices so we'll not have to travel around them.

And here the spirit helps us again. As soon as the spirit succeeded in getting me around all my prejudices and into that store I wiped away the prejudice. So there is a straight mental street now where none existed before. The next time the spirit says "shirt waist," to me it can send me straight to D.'s if it wants to.

Yes, the spirit "moves in a mysterious way its wonders to perform." It looks mysterious to us until we are led back by the straight way. Then it is so simple, so easy, we can hardly believe the spirit would condescend to it!

Ah, but it does! Nothing is too small, or too great, for the spirit's attention—if we believe. When we don't believe we are to be pitied—and the spirit keeps discreetly mum.

Spirit the Breath of Life

"My healer teaches that I must depend alone upon Spirit; that breathing exercises, foods, sunshine and air must not be made the dependence for health. He says, 'Why, you can't help breathing.'"

That is tommyrot. Sunshine and air are spirit, and the plain truth of the matter is that if you don't use them all your "dependence on spirit" will avail simply nothing. Try living in a north room with the windows shut, and see.

You "can't help breathing," but your breathing avails nothing unless by it you take in good fresh live spirit in the way of pure air and sunshine.

If we all lived under the sun and slept under the stars that healer's advice might be good enough. But we don't. We live in tight, dark rooms whence the spirit of life has fled, leaving only its cast off effluvia. We "can't help breathing," but what do we breathe? We breathe the dead air of close rooms.

Spirit is *life*, and we live by breathing it. Spirit is in fresh air; fresh air is in spirit; fresh air and spirit are one. Dead air is air minus spirit, or life.

What good will it do you to say you depend upon spirit when you don't; when you shut yourself away from the spirit of life and breathe death?

Pure air and sunshine are spirit specially prepared for your use. What good will it do you to pretend that you depend upon spirit when you shut yourself into rooms whence the spirit has flown?

If you live in close rooms you may "affirm" your dependence upon spirit until you are black in the face, and you may be "treated" every hour of the day by this healer and 10,000 more like him, and the result will be only sickness and death.

I know in my heart and soul and mind that this is true. And I have seen the truth of it demonstrated by hundreds of cases of people who failed to get well on "treatments" of any sort, and who afterward did get well on sunshine, fresh air and full breathing, along with mental treatment.

The Gospel of Fresh Air is more needed by human beings than even the Gospel of New Thought. If we understood and applied the Gospel of Fresh Air we should think right without trying.

It is in gloomy, unaired corners that evil thoughts breed—because the spirit of life is not present there in such form that it can be appropriated by human beings. They get therein the Breath of Death, and generate thoughts to match—distorted thoughts of death and evil and despair.

Come into the sunshine and breathe the Breath of Life, which generates in you the New Thought of Life, Love, Wisdom, Truth, Health, Happiness, and Success.

New Thought will not save you unless you live it, and a little observation and experimenting will prove to you that you can't live it without breathing plenty of fresh air.

If "all is spirit" why does this healer tell you that to regulate your breathing, exercise, food, etc., is to depend upon something outside spirit?

The fact of the matter is this: He fails to realize that all is spirit. He is still tangled up with good and evil, spirit and not-spirit, God and devil. He does not see spirit in everything and everything in spirit; so he puts the Keep-Off-the-Grass sign wherever he does not see spirit. This will not prevent his pointing you to the spirit where he does recognize it. None of us are wise enough as yet always to see God in all his works.

It is spirit which makes us breathe. When we shut ourselves away from the pure breath of life we shut away the power that makes us breathe.

And when we are too interested in doing indoor work the spirit finds it pretty hard work to make us breathe enough to keep us in good condition for growing. Close rooms and sedentary work defeat the spirit's will to make us breathe.

So we, by working against the spirit, form a habit of breathing too little, thus robbing ourselves of the life, health, wisdom, power, joy which the spirit is trying to give us with every breath.

Now we find ourselves hampered by self-imposed habits which need breaking. So we set ourselves to work with the Spirit of Life. We throw open the window and let in the Spirit of Life.

We go outdoors and revel in the Spirit of Sunshine. We run and jump to make ourselves inbreathe the Spirit of Life.

Being too busy to spend hours every day outdoors we do stunts in our nightdresses to make us inbreathe more of the Spirit of Life.

And always, night and day, winter and summer, we take pains to leave our windows well open that the Spirit of Life be not shut away from us for one single moment.

We are learning to depend wholly upon the Spirit.

We used to remember the Spirit only on the Sabbath day; now we remember it every day and all day and all night—we remember to breathe it and eat it as well as think it.

And verily we are blessed.

Affirmation and Wheels

Mere repetition of "I Am Success" statements will avail little. One must think the thing he desires, and he must put his shoulder to the wheel.

But the person who is full of the sense of failure and defeat is more apt than not to put his shoulder to the wrong side of the wheel. He is so discouraged and preoccupied and worried that he thinks it doesn't matter much where he puts his shoulder, the thing won't budge anyway. So he goes stupidly along drudging away with his shoulder in the same old spot—the wrong spot.

But let that man make up his mind that there is a way to budge that wheel and he will find it; and you will see things move. That man will walk around that wagon a time or two, take in the lay of the land, pat his horses into willing humor, maybe back 'em up a bit, ring out a cheerful "Gid ap," and settle his shoulder to the right spot at the right moment—and away they go. Or another team will pass just at the right time to give him a lift out.

The man who believes himself equal to any emergency which arises will be strong mentally and physically. His mind will be alert, full of expedients. Instead of pushing like a blind mule at one spot until he drops in his tracks, he will use his gumption and find another way. He will conjure up a lever of some sort to budge that load. If he can't do it alone somebody else will come along in the nick o' time to give him the lift he needs. He believes he will work it somehow, and he does.

The "I Am a Failure" man never has anybody come along in the nick o' time. "Just my luck," he whines, and keeps on putting his shoulder to the wrong part of the wheel, or tugging hopelessly and half-heartedly, or—with inward rage that takes more energy than the tug—keeps on until he has to give it up for the time.

To affirm "I Am Success" will not pull the load out of the mire except as it awakes energy to intelligent effort. All affirmations and all going into the silence are useful in waking mental and physical energy to intelligent action.

All chronic failures are such because they believe in failure and opposition and "malicious animal magnetism" and general all-around the-world-is-against-me-ness. This belief in failure fills the individual with an affinity for undesirable things.

The infallible cure, the only cure, for failure, is belief in success, belief in one's own power to turn even defeat to good advantage. The man who "doesn't know when he is beaten" will never be beaten. The "lunkhead" who "didn't know he was a lunkhead" went to the top, while the lunkhead who knew he was a lunkhead stayed at the lunkhead end of the class.

One of our big pork packers once tramped across the continent because he hadn't money to pay his way. After he arrived at his destination he said he saw on his tramp hundreds of places where he could have started in without a cent and in time made piles of money—opportunities just crying to be developed. Only the thought of a bigger chance at the end of the route kept him from stopping in the very first town on his route!

But that boy had success in him and was on the alert for opportunities. He believed in himself and the world. The failure believes only in "bad luck" and his eye is out for "soft snaps," which he is certain he'll never get a chance at.

When a man is looking for trouble and defeat he finds them.

"As a man thinketh in his heart so is he." That does not mean that a man may make a few affirmations of success, or profess new thought, and immediately become a success.

The heart of man is the emotional center of his habits or instinct, the center from which radiate his instincts, his habits, as the nerves radiate from the solar plexus.

Instincts are habit thoughts, heart thoughts. And every instinct came into being through conscious thought and effort.

Follow your internal experiences while learning to play the piano and you will gain a clear idea of how instinct comes into being. At first your fingers are stiff and every movement is a voluntary one, every movement has to be thought about, directed by thought. But gradually you acquire the habit of handling your fingers in a certain way. Gradually you cease to think at all about your finger movements; you "do it instinctively." In other words you have trained your heart, your subconscious mind, to do the thinking for you. Henceforth, instead of thinking consciously about your finger movements you think about them in your heart, that is, sub-consciously.

Psychologists say that not more than five per cent of our mental processes are conscious, the remaining ninety-five per cent being under the consciousness. This means that at least ninety-five per cent of our thoughts are habit thoughts, or "instinctive" thoughts.

It is this instinctive part of us, this ninety-five percent of us, that is referred to in the Bible as "the heart."

Now if this "heart" of us carries at least ninety-five percent of our mentality you can easily see why a man is what he "thinketh in his heart." And you can see why a few affirmations of success, or even a good many of them, will not change the man sufficiently to make any great difference in his surroundings. And you can see why a mere intellectual conception of new thought is not enough to change him and his environment.

Man is a magnet, at least ninety-five per cent of which is habit mind. Therefore by far the greater part of his environment comes to him by its affinity to his ninety-five percent habit or instinct mind, his under-conscious mind, of whose workings he is practically unconscious.

So it is no wonder he so often says, "I don't see why this undesired thing should come to me." He cannot see why it comes, because he is practically unconscious of that great ninety-five per cent of his thinking which draws them. He knows he does not consciously desire these unpleasant things and he can scarcely conceive the fact that he is conscious of only about five per cent of his thoughts and desires.

And, too, he is loath to acknowledge that the greater part of himself has no more sense than to bring such things to him! He feels more complacent when he lays the blame at the door of "environment," or "wicked people," or "malicious animal magnetism," or a "God who chastens whom he loveth," or a devil who got loose from God's leading strings and goes raging about to pester good folks.

Man is a magnet, and every line and dot and detail of his experiences come by his own attraction. "As a man thinketh in his heart so is he." The preponderance of attraction comes through the instinct self, the "heart."

And there is no use in trying to fight off, or run away from, the things which come to us. We only hurt ourselves by fighting. And to run away from the things we have attracted is to run into the arms of similar, or worse, conditions. We have to take ourselves along.

The only way to change conditions effectually is to change "the heart," the habit or instinct mind.

This can be done with more or less ease, according to the degree of setness of character and the degree of will and enthusiasm brought to bear.

The key to all change of character lies with that little five per cent conscious mind, which with all its littleness is a sure lever by which to move the ninety-five percent ponderosity below it. For conscious thought is positive thought, dynamic; while subconscious thought is negative, receptive.

That little five percent mind has stronger compelling power than several times its bulk of sub-conscious mind, and there is not an atom of all that ninety-five per cent subconscious mind which cannot be moved by that little five per cent mind which lies at the top.

The conscious self is the directing power. Just as it directed your fingers to change their fixed habits, so it can direct any change in other lines of mental or bodily habit—by directing persistent, quietly insistent practice on the desired lines.

Insist upon right conscious thinking, and in due time you cannot fail to have right subconscious thinking.

To think good, peace, love, self-command, self-faith, success, long and faithfully enough will fill even the most set "heart" with-habits of good, peace, love, self-command, self-faith, success. And in proportion as the heart becomes filled with such habits the environment and experiences will change to match.

How long will it take thus to transform you by the renewing of your whole mind? All depends upon you. If your practice is fitful and half-hearted it may take another generation or two. If you go at it with a steady will, cutting off all distractions which sap your will and enthusiasm, practicing faithfully and diligently at the new mental habits you may make the desired change in, say, half a lifetime or less.

And if you can bring to your assistance a high spiritual exaltation and faith you can make the change in almost no time at all. For spiritual exaltation and faith and enthusiasm will literally melt the hardest "heart" and permit a quick re-formation.

This is the secret of quick accomplishment in children; their hearts are clean and molten in the emotional fires of enthusiasm and faith, ready to receive deep and lasting impressions.

By [our being schooled in] reason we grown-ups have cooled and even quenched the heart fires of faith and enthusiasm; so it takes time and repetition to re-form us.

This is the secret of miracles. Religious enthusiasm and exaltation are akin to the fires of youth; they melt the heart to receive higher impressions.

The rationalist must receive his new impressions by painstaking hammering in. Repetition and time will do for him what religious or youthful enthusiasm does quickly for babes and fools.

No, affirmations will not do the work of "putting your shoulder to the wheel" when the load is stalled. But they will transform you, heart and consciousness, so that you will attract better horses as well as wheels, better roads, more friends to happen (?) around in the moment of need.

And affirmations of the right sort will wake up your gumption so that you will not overload your horses or your personal energies to the point of needing a shoulder at the wheel.

Success is the natural result of intelligent direction of effort.

Affirmations of success, faith, wisdom, power, good, love, will wake your latent forces to more intelligent uses.

The more enthusiasm you can conjure into the affirmations the more quickly will you realize success.

Your Forces and How to Manage Them

You can overdo anything, even self-treatment. If you keep repeating affirmations to yourself your mental chattering interferes with the real healing.

It is not the conscious mind which heals you; it is the subconscious or soul mind and the super-conscious or Over-Soul mind.

Your soul's expression is guided and directed by your conscious mind. A mental affirmation is simply a word of direction to your soul mind. The soul hears your statements and then builds accordingly.

But what would happen if you called up your housemaids and told them over and over, just what you wanted done and just how to do it? If you spent all your time repeating your directions to them when would they get the work done? And wouldn't they get your directions mixed, too? Of course.

You don't do it that way, of course not; not if you are a wise housekeeper. You call up your maids and tell them quietly and kindly, and in as few words as possible, just what you want done. Then they go cheerfully away out of your presence and do their best to please you. If you later come across something which was not done right you call in a maid and repeat your directions, with perhaps a little further explanation. Then you go away again and trust her to do it aright this time.

What would happen if you tagged around after your maids and tried to watch and criticize and direct every little movement? Why, they would grow nervous and make foolish mistakes and you would all give up in despair.

And what would happen if you directed them to do a certain difficult piece of work and then came back five minutes later expecting to find it all done? Oh, you can't imagine yourself doing such foolish things!

Perhaps you don't with your maids, but evidently you do with your own self. Your objective, everyday consciousness is the mistress or master of your being.

Psychologists say the objective mental activities are not more than one twentieth of all your mental activities. That means that the mistress mind has the equivalent of at least twenty maids under her direction. These "maids" belong to the subjective mind, or soul of you.

Then there is the great Over-Soul, of which your individual soul is but an atom; but an atom whose every demand is heard. That means that your little mistress mind not only has at her bidding the equivalent of at least twenty maids of the subconscious, but she has also at her call the equivalent of ten million billion other helpers of the infinite Over-Soul.

And all the mistress mind has to do is say the word. All these helpers fly to do her bidding.

Perhaps you think all these helpers don't fly to do your bidding. But they do. The only trouble with you is that you don't give your helpers time and chance to work out your desires. You keep repeating your directions over and over, and you keep trying to tag around after all your twenty or more housemaids to see if they are doing the things you want done. You watch them in your stomach and your liver and your lungs, always fretting for fear they are going wrong.

No wonder you get nervous and fidgety and strained all over; no wonder your "feelings" are no better than they were!

Make your statements of health, happiness and success at certain regular intervals, say two or three times a day. Or make them at times when you can't get your mind off your conditions.

Make the statements plainly and positively. Then call your mind entirely away from the subject and give your soul and the Over-Soul a chance to work. Make light of your feelings and go get well interested in some good work.

Take it for granted that all your being, and all creation besides, is working out for you the things you desire. Rest easy and trust yourself.

Don't let your mind tag your feelings and symptoms; give it plenty of useful work and plenty of play and plenty of rest while your soul works things out for you as fast as it can. Just be as interested and happy as you can while the soul is working. Jolly yourself into having a good time.

Say the Word, and then be happy and do not allow yourself to doubt that the soul will do the work. This is the secret of quick healing. The nearer you can come to keeping your mind pleasantly occupied between the times when you give yourself special affirmations and treatments, the more quickly you will realize health of mind, body and environment as well as soul.

Thy faith in thy soul and the Over-Soul will have made thee whole.

The faithless mind is a terrible meddler and creator of discords; and the idle mind, the mind not directed to useful purposes, is always a faithless meddler.

Moral: Get interested in some good work.

Duty and Love

Though you work your fingers to the bone and have not love for your work it profits you next to nothing and your employer less than it ought to.

Duty work robs the doer of the joy of doing, which is the chief compensation for all work.

You imagine you do your work well from a sense of duty. You would do it better still if you loved it. If you loved it you would enjoy every bit of it, and you would glory in every little improvement you hit upon; and you would hit upon a lot because your soul would be playing through your fingers.

The soul of the duty doer is shut away from his work—he works with his fingers and his habit mind only. By the end of the week he is fagged out and his poor soul droops for lack of exercise; then perhaps he takes it to church for relief; and shuts it carefully away again before Monday morning.

And the worst of it is that so many people make a virtue of keeping their souls locked up six days out of seven. They parade duty as their mainspring. And even when they do happen to let a little soul, a little love and joy into their work they won't acknowledge it. They stick to it that it is "duty" which impels them.

When the soul does manage to get out of its shell and express itself in useful work the brain denies it the glory and happiness which belong to it. The worker resolutely shuts off the joy vibrations with that stem word "duty." He robs himself of the pleasure of his honest effort.

There are two ways of robbing one's self of the joy of work. One is by paralyzing joy with "duty"; the other is by scattering the mind and soul all over creation whilst the hands are doing something. In the former case the soul is shut away in idleness; in the latter it is wasted in riotous thinking.

The soul's power is emotion, that which flows from the silence within. The nature of emotion is motion. To let emotion move through the body, out into intelligent effort, is joy and eternally welling life and strength and wisdom.

To let the mind wander while the hands work is to fritter your soul force away at the top of the head—the power which should move from the head down through the body and out into intelligent doing, is simply dissipated into thin air.

The wandering mind robs the body of vitality and joy. It is the prodigal who wastes all your substance.

The duty doer is a niggard. He lets some of his soul into his work, shutting the rest tight within. He puts his thought into his work, but he is stingy with his soul, his love. He works coldly, stolidly, conscientiously, reminding himself constantly that he is to "be good for nothing," as the wise mamma commanded the little boy who wanted a prize for being good.

Now everybody knows that cold contracts things. The cold duty doer shuts off his soul warmth and his body grows gaunt and pinched, his brain cells stiff, his thoughts angular. He shuts off the inspiration of love and joy and works like a machine, grinding out the same old things by the same old pattern.

The duty doer converts a real living, growing, loving being into a mere cold machine. It's a shame. And the whole cause is the old fathers' tradition that duty is greater than love. I wonder where they got that notion?

The same spirit led them that leads us. That same spirit must have led them and us into duty doing.

Why? To gain self-control that we might have the greater joy. That is it! First there is the "natural," the animal way of doing things; just to follow impulse and gratify self at no matter what expense to others. But somehow you are not very happy after you have done it.

Then there is the mental way of doing things, the "duty" way; when we cut off all the old "natural" impulses and teach ourselves to work stolidly, steadily in the "right" line.

It takes about all our thought and effort to control ourselves in this mental way; it requires a firm unrelenting hand upon our impulses. But we were not happy when we didn't control our impulses, and we are at least at peace when we do. So we keep on crushing back the "natural" impulses and sticking sternly to duty.

When we followed the old animal impulses to have things our way right or wrong, without regard to the other fellow, we were always lured on by the hope of joy; and when we got the thing desired, as we sometimes did, it was only to be disappointed. So we were full of unrest. Since we have chosen the ways of duty there are no joys to lure us, but rest accompanies us.

In the old way we were always sure we were going to be happy; in the duty way we have ceased to expect happiness but we really have peace. And a peace in the heart, we have learned from sad experience, is worth two joys in the bush. We have been oft bitten and thus learned caution: so we keep on schooling ourselves to keep the peace and shut eyes and ears to promises of pleasure.

We have learned to follow "conscience" instead of "natural impulse." Conscience is merely spiritual caution. The faculty called caution warns us from outward danger; it was created by many ages of race experience in getting its fingers burned and its shins kicked and its head broken Conscience warns us from inner dangers; and is being created by many ages of human experience at stealing from the other fellow only to find its own heart robbed of peace and happiness.

We tasted impulse and found it sweet at first and bitter, bitter at the last. Then we tasted duty and found its first pungency melt away to a clean sweetness such as we had never tasted before; a sweetness so pure and satisfying that it is no wonder we keep clinging to the duty doing which brought it.

When we lived from unchecked and unguided impulse only we were many times happy on the surface, when we happened to get the things asked for, but we were always restless and dissatisfied within. This unrest is the voice of the universal spirit within, which is ever urging us to take our dominion over self and to direct our energies to higher and yet higher uses; it is the voice of life, which ever demands a high purpose for being and doing.

The spirit of the world which is moving us allows each a few years and many intervals of irresponsible living. We have our childhood when the whole world smiles and flies to gratify every impulse; and when we are good children we have our little vacations and play happily with that sweet taste in our hearts. If we try to take too many play times the spirit in us is frowning and restless again, ever urging us to be up and doing that which will help the world spirit express the beauties it has in mind for us.

When we quit chasing pleasure and begin to live and do after the plan set in our hearts the world spirit whispers "Well done," to us. We find peace. We taste and see that it is good. Henceforth we work for the inner peace, not for the fleeting gratification of the outer senses.

As we follow duty peace deepens and widens. By and by we form the habit of duty and it grows easier and easier. We do what seems best because we have learned that to do otherwise ruffles our peace; and we have learned to love that peace beyond anything else life can hold for us.

Peace keeps on deepening and widening and growing more dynamic. At first it is a solemn calm, and a little deviation from duty ruffles and dissipates it. But by and by as we keep on doing our duty, through this solemn calm, growing ever deeper and broader, there wells the full diapason of a deep joy—very softly at first, with many diminuendos and silences; at unexpected moments it swells again; over little things the tide of life has brought us—things we loved, and thought we had given up forever when we chose duty as our guide.

Fitfully at first the deep joy wells, fitfully and gently, but, oh, so full and sweet and satisfying; such tones as our souls never heard before. We wonder at the deep joy; and, oh, we begin to see that the world spirit was urging us on to duty only that we might find deeper joy than the old irresponsible life could yield us. By taking dominion over self, by using our energies for higher purposes, we have deepened our capacity for joy.

Now the harmony of deep joy begins to swell, and every touch of life but adds to the paeans of praise.

And the good things of life begin to come—houses, lands, fathers, mothers, brothers, a hundredfold more than ever before, bringing joy such as we never knew before. Oh, we thought we had given up the pleasures of life for its duties, and behold we find the pleasures added.

We used to be fascinated and tossed about by life's pleasures; now we find them fascinated and obedient to us—oh, the power and glory and joy of it!

We gained dominion over ourselves and our environment through doing our duty. We gave up the shortsighted impulse "will" to follow the omniscient will which is working through us, and behold the things we once desired vainly are now ours to command and enjoy. No wonder we laud duty!

But duty is a schoolmaster whose work we do not need forever. When we have made its wisdom our own, we outgrow duty. Duty flowers in love.

The more resolution and persistence we put into duty doing the sooner we shall outgrow it.

The more pleasure we can get out of duty doing the faster we shall outgrow it. When the worker puts his soul into his duty, duty is swallowed up in love, and joy grows.

Many a duty worker cheats himself out of the joy which is his, and stunts the growth of his joy and himself, simply by denying that he works from anything but a sense of duty.

As long as our best efforts are called duty they answer to the call as cold, hard duty.

As soon as those same activities are called pleasures, our soul joy and love, are turned into them and they are transfigured.

The worker who calls his work duty shuts his soul back from his body and his work. The soul of you is love, and love has no affinity for duty; so as long as you insist upon working from a sense of duty you shut in, shut away from your work, the sense of love. You thus rob yourself of the joy of doing.

And this means that you rob yourself of the greater share of your power and wisdom for doing.

Love is the essence of all wisdom, imagination and inspiration, as well as power. To hold sternly to duty is to shut out love, and with it the wisdom, inspiration and imagination necessary to improve your work. You are robbed of the joy of doing, and your work is robbed of its highest beauty and usefulness.

Quit calling your duties by that name. Jolly yourself into doing your duty for love of it. Don't you know how you can jolly a child into doing things? Haven't you been jollied yourself until at last you laughed and forgave and did the thing you had sternly resolved not to do? Haven't you seen scores of your friends jollied into doing things? Of course. All nature responds to a smiling good-willed jolly.

And your soul, your love, will respond to the same good-willed jollying. It will come out and smile on your doings, and radiate soul-shine and joy and power and inspiration through you, and down through your fingers into your work, and out into your aura, and on out to all the world.

Smile and come up higher than the duty class—the *joy* class awaits you!

Well Done

"Natural disaster overtakes a man and he loses every cent. Possessing untold aversion to becoming a paid employee, he lives with friends, helping where able, and at the same time reaching out to grasp something by which to start again. Has an overwhelming desire to get money for home and marriage. This could be had in a very short time by successful speculation, if the unlimited Force is there as taught, for use on lines of desire. There is no wrong in the world. Is he then to command the powers for conscious use, go in faith and win; or shall he sit down and build, bit by bit, by uncongenial labor?" —M.T.

The man who possesses such "an untold aversion to becoming a paid employee" that he prefers to sponge a living off his friends rather than to earn it honestly, will never succeed even at speculation.

Such a man could not generate a desire strong enough to attract fortune even at a gambling table.

It takes character to generate a desire of the sort that moves things. It takes steadiness of purpose, positive determination.

And character, purpose, determination, are never found in the sponger.

If he had character he would choose any sort of honest work that would keep him in independence. His "untold aversion to becoming a paid employee" would be as nothing to his disgust for sponging a living, even temporarily.

Character is the outcome of an unconquerable self-respect and self-reliance. A man's character is that which distinguishes him from a jellyfish, which takes the shape of any environment that happens along. It is Something which keeps him upright on his own pins, no matter what happens.

Character is mental backbone and muscle, and is subject to the same laws of development and growth as other bone and muscle.

Bone and muscle and character do not grow by bread alone, but by use. Character grows by the use of self-reliance and self-respect, just as physical character grows by the use of muscles. Character becomes weak and flabby when self-reliance and self-respect are kept on the shelf of another man's pantry.

Character develops by exercise. How is it to exercise except by doing things? How is it to do things when somebody else does them for him?

The first thing a man of character, of self-respect and self-reliance would do under such circumstances as M.T. describes would he to overcome his "untold aversion" to anything which would help him to continue living in self-respect and self-reliance. Indeed the only "untold aversion" held by a man of real character is the "untold aversion" to living off other people.

A person whose aversion to "becoming a paid employee" is greater than his aversion to idleness and sponging is a mere mush of concession to public opinion—he hates paid employment because he thinks his neighbors will "look down" upon him, and because he likes to look aristocratic and give orders rather than to be what he is and take what orders are necessary for the time being.

Such a man cares for appearances above all things. He cares for the outside of things, as a jellyfish does. He seeks first an agreeable resting place, as the Jellyfish does. And he will sacrifice the last vestige of self-respect, self-reliance, character, to that fetish, outside appearance. He thinks it looks better to live off his friends than to soil his hands to take care of himself.

But if he had a real character of his own, if he had mental backbone and muscle worthy the name, he simply could not crouch and cringe as a dependent, a beggar. He would have to get out and express himself in some sort of independent activity, or die.

For character is a deep-down life-urge which will push to expression through any conditions. It simply cannot continue to sit supinely by another man's fireside, or wait by the wayside with cap extended to catch stray pennies from the passers-by.

Character must act, or degenerate.

Character must ex-press, or ex-pire.

Character is to the individual what the channel is to the river. Take away the banks which confine the stream and direct it, and the water gushes out in an endless sloppy marsh.

The inner character of a man confines and directs the life force, the desire force.

The stronger the character the deeper and broader the stream of desire, or life; and the more positively the man will express himself in independent, self-respecting activity.

The stronger the character the greater will be the man's "untold aversion" to depending upon anybody but himself.

And so deep and strong are his desires as they flow through the clear-cut channels of character, that they force new channels through any circumstances. Such a man's desires flow deep and strong enough to carry things his way.

But the man without a strong character is a mere sloppy marsh of sentimentality. He is incapable of anything more than "overwhelming desires"—his desire stream, having no strong banks, simply overwhelms the whole surface of things, with no depth by which to sweep its way through environment. His desire energy spreads out and wastes itself in mere shallow longings, unworthy the name of desire. So the man welters in his own swamp of sensibility, and gets nowhere.

Herein lies the reason that M.T.'s man will not find success at the gaming table, nor anywhere else, except by "building bit by bit" a character strong enough to find its way to the good things he wants.

The first step toward success is to decide that it is yours, and that all creation is ready to help you manifest it.

The next step is to work with the world, taking hold anywhere that the world will let you, in full confidence that the world will promote you as fast as you prove your fitness for promotion.

To prove your fitness for promotion necessitates doing your best with any job the world gives you, and at the same time using your spare time and thought in fitting yourself for a better one.

To do one of these things is not enough. The man who does his work exceptionally well will be kept at that same kind of work until crack o' doom unless he shows aptitude for doing more valuable work. The world is always looking eagerly for men who can fill the more difficult positions. It is always trying to tempt people into higher, better paying positions; and the man who is faithful and efficient in one place, and evinces the slightest capacity for higher work, is always the first man to get a chance of promotion.

The man who thinks he is "kept down" is right; but he is kept down by himself alone. Either he is slack, inefficient, uninterested, gumptionless in his present work; or he is not fitting himself for something better.

Abe Lincoln split rails all day. He split them with vim and intelligence. But at night he studied books by the light of a pine knot. All the way along from rail splitting to the presidency, Abe found some time out of business hours to inform himself on lines beyond his work.

The main difference between Abe Lincoln and Abe Johnson lies in the way they spend their after-business hours. Abe Johnson, too, works with vim and intelligence. And he never had to split rails for a living. He is an A-1 bookkeeper. Been in the same store, with almost the same salary, for twenty-five years. And almost every noon and every evening for twenty-five years he has sat on a sugar keg in the store and discussed politics and economics. And very often he has grumbled to his cronies about his lack of a chance to rise in the world.

Down here in a Massachusetts town, they have been having labor troubles for a long time. The cotton mill owners say the bottom has dropped out of the plain cotton cloth trade and they simply must reduce wages or close down. There is small demand for the sort of plain cotton goods manufactured in these mills. The mill hands say they can't live on any smaller wages and they won't, so there. So one strike follows another, or a lockout. For months at a time the mills lie idle while owners and workers deadlock.

Some one suggested that the mills begin to make the sort of new fancy weaves of cotton cloth for which there is increasing demand. But the weavers refused to learn the new weaves. They said they knew how to do the plain weaving and it "wouldn't pay them" to learn the new kind of weaving on the old wages, which are paid according to the amount of work done. And many of them said anyway they were too old to make such changes now.

So these faithful and efficient weavers go on fighting and striking and reviling "fate" rather than fit themselves for new work which would in the end pay better than the old.

Poor shortsighted weavers.

Poor shortsighted cousins to the weavers.

Poor shortsighted and disappointed Abe Johnson.

What do you suppose life makes us begin at the bottom for, and "build bit by bit"? For the sole purpose of building character; building good, strong channels for desire to run in; channels so deep and full that the desire-stream will be strong enough to accomplish for the individual the thing he wants.

And how are we to know we are building the right kind of character? By the sense of inner satisfaction which witnesses every well-done deed.

That is where self-respect and self-reliance come in. Even a baby feels the "Well done" of its soul when it succeeds in doing something for itself. A child prizes this inner self-satisfaction, self-respect, above all things else. Watch the happy look on a child's face when it has succeeded in doing something for itself.

Only foolish grown-ups value anything on earth above this inner satisfaction. Only grown-ups will let other folks do for them what they can do for themselves. Only grown-ups will quench themselves for the sake of appearances. Some "grown-ups."

To know thyself is to know that the best thing in heaven or earth, the best guide in heaven or earth, is the inner sense of "Well done," the sense of self-respect which comes from doing things instead of letting them be done for you.

As long as the innermost self approves your doings you are building character. And what shall it profit you if you gain the whole world and lose the "Well done" of your soul?

Nothing! Less than nothing!

For in all creation or uncreation there is but one real satisfaction, one real happiness, and that is self-satisfaction, self-respect.

Self-respect springs only from well-doing. It is "Well done," thy soul says to thee, that gives thee joy.

What matter what Tom, Dick, and Harry and Madame Grundy say? Be still and hear thyself.

Eye hath not seen nor ear heard the glory and satisfaction which await him who listens to himself.

"Well done, good and faithful servant; enter thou into the joy of thy Lord"—which is thy innermost self.

What Has He Done?

We were talking about new thought and the increased efficiency it gives to people. Evidently he did not think very highly of the practical side of new thought. It is all very well to help people to bear their troubles, he said, but it does not get rid of the troubles.

And I said I thought if it never did anything more than help people to endure things, it at least helps more than anything else ever did.

But I assured him that new thought rightly applied does change conditions, and I cited my own experience in proof. Then I called his attention to other people, prominent in the new thought, whose conditions and health have been changed for good. One of the names mentioned was that of a successful lawyer well known to us both. "Well," queried he, "what has he done that is so wonderful? Others have done as great or greater things, who never heard of new thought."

Of course. The principles of new thought are the principles of life itself, and in all climes and times there have been people who, consciously or unconsciously, lived according to principle and thereby manifested health (which means wholeness) of mind, body and environment.

Wisdom's ways are always ways of pleasantness and all her paths are peace.

And wisdom is as omnipresent as the ethers, to be used by him who inspires it—by him who desires it above all else.

Every pleasant thing and thought in this world comes by mental breathing of wisdom. And every soul that ever lived has lived by breathing wisdom.

In proportion to his inbreathing of wisdom has been the pleasantness of his ways and the peace of his path.

And his ups and downs have come from the fact that he inspires wisdom in spots only. He keeps on mentally breathing, of course; but he doesn't always breathe wisdom. He is like a man who breathes pure outdoor air awhile, and then goes into a close room, or down in a mine, and breathes poison gases.

As physical health depends upon the quantity of pure air inspired, so physical and mental and environmental health depends upon the amount of pure wisdom inspired.

And nobody will deny that most of us inspire a large proportion of poison gas of the mental kind, instead of pure wisdom. We breathe over other people's thoughts after them, just as we breathe over the air after them. This breathed-over thought destroys our physical, mental and environmental health. We need to get out in God's open air and breathe new thought, or we shall asphyxiate.

Old thought is division, dissension, separateness, competition.

New thought is the great opening of principles, oneness, harmony, God, good, freedom, peace, love.

New thought is from ages to ages everlasting. Those who inspire it, inbreathe it, are the whole and strong ones, whether they breathe it consciously or unconsciously.

By teachings of new thought the world is learning to do consciously, intelligently, what a few have done here and there through all the ages. And need we be reminded of the advantages of knowing how and why we do things?

"What has he done that is so wonderful?" The lawyer we spoke of is not what the world calls "great" in any line. He has not built up a Standard Oil "system," nor torn one down. He is not a Roosevelt or a Togo, or a Napoleon, nor even an Elbert Hubbard. His desires and ambitions have run in other lines. He is not "built that way." He "hasn't it in him" to be a Rockefeller, and he is glad of it.

Why then should he be compared with Napoleon or Rockefeller? Do we measure roses and violets and daffodils and chrysanthemums by the same standards? Is the violet inconsequential because it sheds its sweetness in a shady corner instead of flinging it in midday from the top of a sunflower stalk? No. We measure violets by other violets, not by sunflowers or hollyhocks or peonies.

And men are more diverse than flowers. Every man has his own individuality, his own soul specifications to develop by. Every man comes as the flower of a peculiar ancestry, like no other man's ancestry. To judge one man by another is as foolish as to judge a violet by a sunflower.

This lawyer we spoke of stands in a class by himself. He has not achieved what Rockefeller has, but he has achieved something which satisfies himself better than the doings of a dozen Standard Oil magnates could.

And what is success but self-satisfaction?

To succeed is to accomplish what one sets out to do.

A growing success is a matter of growing ideals and a succession of successes.

Our lawyer is satisfied with new thought and its efficacy in his case. By its use he has accomplished a succession of things he wanted to do. He has literally made himself over, and his environment, too. And he has evolved new ideals and developed new energies which show him a joy-full eternity ahead.

He is satisfied with the new thought as a working principle.

He goes on working by it, growing daily in wisdom and knowledge, daily growing greater graces of character, mind, body and environment.

It is the man who does not live new thought teachings who misjudges them by the outward appearances of other men's lives.

Will and Wills

Nothing before, nothing behind;
The Steps of faith
Fall on the seeming void, and find
The Rock beneath. —*Whittier*

In a copy of an old magazine is an article entitled, "What New Thought Women Say of the Will, by an Old Thought Woman," who fails to sign her name. This article is about as cross-eyed as anything I have read recently. It amuses me. And yet it touches a responsive chord of stored memories, and I sympathize.

That is, I am enabled for the moment to re-enter the same-pathy or condition this woman describes Every step she has passed through I, too, have experienced.

But I have passed through it all and emerged upon the spiral above, where I am enabled to understand the phenomena of wills in relation to each other, and in relation to the whole.

Briefly stated, "The Old Thought Woman's" idea is, "The will is a part of that delusive mortal mind. It is the executor of the world, the flesh and the Devil. 'God's will' is a fiction." "Devil" with a capital D, mind you. Then she goes on to tell how willful she used to be; she dominated her relatives, friends and enemies alike, and even the cats and dogs. "There was scarcely no way in which will can dominate that I did not work to its limits," she says; "I intended to marry without declaring my views, get the property and support, but refuse all sensuality," because she was "adamant against child-bearing."

Decidedly a disagreeable person, I should say. I don't wonder that she was "cordially hated by those whom she hypnotized and outwitted"; I don't wonder "pain, anguish, hatred, suffering, disappointment followed in the wake of every triumph." Do you?

Then she grew sick of it all and "gave up all will." "In a complete loss of will, self-will, God's will, all kinds of will, there is a miraculous condition of affairs," she says. Then she goes on to preach Christ's teaching of non-resistance.

Every positive character, and probably every negative one, too, passes sometime through an experience identical with this woman's. The more pronounced the character the more definite is the change from self-will to self-abnegation.

A negative character will hang on eternally to his self-will, and the giving up of his will causes him all the anguish this woman experienced as a result of using her will.

Now without pointing out to you the mistakes of this writer let me give you my statement of will, its nature and uses; after which I think you will see the Old Thought Woman's understanding needs to grow a bit.

Will is the motive, electric force of the universe; the only force there is.

Will is the energy which forms worlds and swings them in space; which dissolves all forms and creates anew.

Will is attraction and gravitation.

Will is love, and will is hate.

Will is the passion, the active force, of the One.

Will is omnipresent and omnipotent.

Without will there could be only stagnation, death, annihilation.

But there is Will; and there are wills; there is all-pervading, all-evolving Will, and there are countless little tossing, warring wills. There is one great ocean, and there are countless little, tossing wavelets, each taken up with its own aims to rise above its neighbors.

On the unseen side Will is one, the only One. On the seen side there are only wills, beginning and ending within the personal circle.

Will is the executive of omniscience.

Will is the executive of universal, all-evolving Wisdom. "Will of God" is no fiction; it is the one immutable, inexorable *fact* which personal wills ceaselessly and uselessly toss themselves against, to their undoing and the increase of knowledge.

All-Wisdom and All-Will are the one great ocean, from which personal wisdom and will are tossed, and to which all return.

Will and Wisdom are all there is in the universe; they are one and inseparable. Water is correctly formulated as W2W, instead of $H2O$; and every atom in the universe, seen or unseen, is simply Will in definite and varying proportion to Wisdom. The less Wisdom in the mixture the more foolishly will the Will be exercised.

Will is used commonly as a name for volition exercised by the conscious 5 per cent mind. The individual reasons from his own narrow view and sets his will to execute his finite judgments.

For the time, he sets his judgment up as infallible, grits his teeth, clinches his fists and drives through;—until he comes slam up against Universal Will.

It is as if one of your hands set up a judgment of its own and attempted to force the other hand to move after his pattern. Your right hand sees and judges for a right hand, but not for a left hand.

Just so with this Old Thought Woman; she set up her judgment and attempted to bring relatives, friends, enemies, animals, under subjection.

Under subjection to what?—her will? No—under subjection to her judgments. Her will was simply the executive—the sheriff's posse. Having a strong will she had her way in many cases, where a less determined individual would have held just as severe judgments without having the will to execute them.

Was her will "evil," a "delusion"? No. But her wisdom was a minus, a personal, quantity and her will thereby misdirected.

I am a very strong willed woman and I glory in it. But the time was when I made all kinds of a chump of myself by setting up my judgment for other people's guidance, and sending my will to execute my judgments, willy-nilly on the other fellow's part.

My will was first class; likewise my intention; but my judgment was exceedingly narrow and crude. I got into all kinds of hot water, just as this Old Thought Woman did; and finally I couldn't stand it any longer.

I "went to the Lord.'" I prayed and agonized and humbled myself—as I needed to. The trouble with me was that I had not learned yet that my judgments were not the best on earth and my will [was not] the only executive.

All these failures on my part made me look at last for higher judgments and mightier will.

Among men I could not find them. Not a writer or lecturer or friend but showed me plainly that his judgments were as wry and his will as circumscribed as my own. So I turned to the unseen and unbelieved-in, but greatly needed and longed for God. I "gave up my will"—I said, "Not my will but thine be done."

It was hard to do, but being a strong willed woman I did it and did it well. I lived daily with Jesus in that sublime "Sermon on the Mount."

Of course "I found peace." Having laid aside all personal aims and ambitions and given up all efforts to make myself or the world better, I found peace.

An Indian lying full length in his canoe, which is floating softly and surely down the broad Columbia toward the ocean, is an emblem of peace.

The individual who wakes up at last to the fact that what he has been tearing himself in tatters trying to accomplish is already being accomplished by a broad river of Will of which his own will is but a wavelet, finds himself embodying peace.

"He that loseth his life shall find it." He that loseth his will shall find it—for the first time.

I thought I was giving up my will, when it was only my judgments I gave up. And I gained in return the entire will of the universe. I changed my point of view—that was all.

I had been seeing countless myriads of striving, tortured individuals, each warring in chaos to bring order according to his judgments.

Now I saw God as the animating soul and will and wisdom working in and through and by these striving ones.

From a formless wavelet striving to get up, I became the Indian, resting, realizing the mighty Will underneath me that carried me unerringly in the right direction even when I did nothing.

I rested and let the All-Will carry me and everybody else. At times it seemed that I must spring up and make this one or that one go right or do right. But I used my will on myself and kept hands off.

I could not see that the All-Will was bringing this out right; but I had made such a miserable failure when I was running things that in sheer despair I determined to resist nothing, compel nobody, but just trust that the All-Will would bring things out right.

I kept saying to myself, "Hands off—hands off;—loose him and let the All-Will run him," until I really learned to let the All-Will do it.

Of course I thought, just as this Old Thought Woman does, that I was exercising no will at all. But I was, and she is doing it, too.

The only difference between the use of my will before and after this self-abnegation was this: After I "gave up my will" I had the All-Will on my side for the first time, and so easy did it seem to be to let the All-Will do everything, that I did not realize that the All-Will worked through and by my personal will.

It was as if I had been trying desperately to lift something too heavy for me, and suddenly my efforts were reinforced to such an extent that it was easy. Or, as if I had been trying hard to shove open what seemed a door when along came one who showed me where the real door was and how to open it easily.

I had been using all my will to make myself and others "good" and suddenly I found the All-Will reinforcing my little will—as if a mighty power had been switched on to my circuit.

This was not really what happened, you know. It was this: My little will had been striving against other little wills—as if one finger strove to curtail the action of another finger. At last, in desperation and without at the time understanding what I did—I let go my little attempt; and immediately I began to sense the All-Will working through my will for the accomplishment of larger purposes I had not before dreamed of.

It was hard to strive against other wills—hard; and the outcome uncertain, and fraught with suffering and disappointment. But it was easy to let the All-Will back my will—so easy I failed for some time to realize I was using any will.

Like Solomon I asked for wisdom, for understanding. As it came to me I saw that whenever the All-Will backed my will and made action easy I was on the right track; whenever I felt a sensation of pulling against some other will I was on the wrong track and must let go and rest.

Many times the thing I could not at one time do without that pulling against feeling, at another time I could do easily with that sense that the All-Will backed me. Sometimes the All-Will backed me in doing what some other person opposed, and yet I was not backed when I did the opposing.

At first all this seemed like the capricious "leadings" of a "spirit." But at last I began to see a principle in it.

I found the Law of Individuality. I found that when I willed to do anything which I desired, the All-Will backed me, unless I foolishly desired to curtail what some other body desired to do—not what some other body desired me to do, but what he desired to do without interference from me. Do you see the point?

For instance, I desired to teach and heal; another desired me to cook and sew; and the spirit backed me. I serenely taught and healed. That other fumed and fretted, and yet, all serene, I knew the All-Will backed me. But that other smoked; I considered smoking wasteful and detrimental; and every time I expressed my opinions on the subject I felt that the All-Will was not backing me.

This one had a right to smoke, because he was not thereby interfering with the free action of another. But when he tried to put me back in the kitchen he had to use his personal will un-backed by the All-Will; because the All-Will was backing my will to get out of the kitchen. On the other hand, the All-Will backed his will to smoke; therefore, when I tried to interfere I opposed not only his will but the All-Will as well.

Now that is just what gives us all so many hard knocks in the world, dearie. We fail to respect the other fellow's rights, and in so doing we run against not only his personal will but the All-Will into the bargain. No wonder we get some horrible bumps.

When you exercise your will against another's freedom of action you shut yourself off from your source of will supply, the All-Will. This is why you clinch your fists, grit your teeth and contract your lungs and muscles. You are shut off from the source of will supply, and you contract in order to force your will power against another. Then you are exhausted, and have accomplished nothing. For if you succeed in "making him be good" this time he hates you for it. And he will break out with more force at the next opportunity—because the All-Will is backing him even in the actions you judge as "bad."

Remember, the All-Will backs every personal will except when the personal will interferes with the free action (not interference) of another will.

Then, when you attempt interfering with the free action of another you force out your will upon him, just as you force out the breath from your lungs. Then you have to "catch your breath" and your will again.

It takes time to fill yourself again with will, and whilst you are doing it you suffer all those horrible sensations of remorse and weakness and disgust that come over one after one of these tussles with another will. You have all these feelings whether or not you succeed in downing the other fellow.

Oh, it doesn't pay, dearie. It doesn't pay to use your will except when you can feel the All-Will backing you.

What new thought people refer to as "cultivating the Will" is simply cultivating acquaintance with and consciousness of the All-Will. It is simply recognition of will; recognition of the ceaseless, underlying urge of the uni-verse which is working within and through the individual to express more and more of beauty and wisdom and good.

To use the little, personal will apart from the All-Will one must contract and thus force out his will upon other people and things.

To use the All-Will one must first know he is right, then relax and let will flow through him to accomplish according to his word or desire.

In using the little, personal will one recognizes himself a member of a "multi-verse"—a being separate and apart from all other beings.

In order to use the All-Will one must first have learned his relation to it and to all other persons and things; he must have recognized the uni-verse, and himself and others as orderly, useful members of the uni-verse.

Only as he recognizes Oneness is it possible for him to resign the exercise of the small, personal will and let the All-Will accomplish through himself and through every other man.

He that loseth his will shall find it one with All-Will.

And after all it is not his will he has lost, but his beliefs about it and its use. He has come up higher and caught a glimpse of the unity of things. He has hitched his wagon to omnipotence and behold all things are done according to his word.

The All-Will backs the individual in anything good, bad or indifferent, which he wills to do; just so long as the individual does not interfere with other individuals.

So you see, in any effort you may make toward self-development you have All-Will working with and through you. And if you will attend strictly to business nothing on earth or in hell can stem the tide of your will, and so defeat you.

"There is no chance, no destiny, no fate, Can circumvent or hinder or control,
The firm resolve of a determined soul."

Concerning Vibrations

Vibration is Life. Vibration is motion. All motion is vibration. All motion is Life. You expand your chest with an inhalation of air; you contract your muscles and exhale. This is vibration. Your heart "beats." This, too, is vibration.

Every tiny cell in your body is "beating," or vibrating, just as your heart and lungs do.

When your chest expands you take in fresh air, which goes not only into your lungs, but into all parts of your body. The air blows like a fresh breeze around the countless millions of cells which go to make up your body. These little cells in their turn expand and take in the air. Then the cells contract and force out the air, and your lungs, too, contract, and force the air clear out of your body.

Now this air which is thus vibrated through your body serves to clean it. The decaying particles of your body cells are thrown off and carried out in the streams of air which are vibrated through your body. If it were not for this vibration of your body, which keeps the air flowing through, your body would soon become clogged with dead matter.

The nerves and arteries in your body are constantly contracting and expanding, contracting and expanding, to move along the blood, which carries food supply to the cells and bears away their sewage in just the same way that the air is carried to and from the cells.

It is by constantly vibrating—contracting and expanding—that your stomach and bowels digest food.

It is by vibration of the cells of tree and plant that the sap flows through and feeds the tree.

Even a stone is composed of tiny cells which breathe, just as the cells of your body, and just as your body as a whole does.

Every individual, be it cell, plant, animal or man, lives by vibrating; by expanding and contracting to take in the new and force out the old matter. Every mind, too, lives by vibrating—by alternately expanding to receive new ideas and contracting to get rid of the old.

Then there is another sort of vibration by which one individual communicates with another. Imagine to yourself that the ether is made up of infinitely small elastic balls. If you strike any one of those tiny balls it will strike those next to it and rebound, and those hit will strike the next, and so on the blow will travel from one tiny ball to the next, clear to the edge of creation—if you can imagine such a place. The blow you strike sets all the little elastic balls to vibrating, or moving back and forth.

Now if I stand away out in space and I feel the little elastic balls vibrate against me I know it means Something. By experience I learn what each kind of movement means.

If you clap your hands together the vibrations of those tiny elastic balls strike my ear and I say, "I hear some one clapping hands." If I face your way the vibrations strike my eyes and I say, "I see some one clapping hands." In any case your motion caused the ether to vibrate and I felt the vibrations.

If I had no ears or eyes I could not feel the vibrations, but they would be there just the same.

Every movement made sets the ether to vibrating to its particular pitch; and wherever there are eyes or ears the vibrations are recorded. When you talk it sets the ether going just the same whether there are ears to hear or not.

And when you keep perfectly quiet and think you set the ether going, too. Your brain sets vibrations going, just as your tongue does. There are people who can hear thoughts, just as you hear another's speech. In due time we shall all hear thoughts—we are all growing mental ears.

Thoughts are higher vibrations than spoken words; and they "carry" farther. You know a deep, growly bass voice makes a great noise when you are close to it, but a shrill treble call can be heard much farther than the growly bass. The high voice makes short, sharp, far-reaching vibrations.

Now thoughts make infinitely shorter, sharper and farther-reaching vibrations than the voice can; and thought vibrations carry farther and far more quickly. And wherever there is another thinker ready to hear, the thoughts are recorded.

Many times we hear the thoughts of other people and mistake them for our own; for everybody has at least a little mental hearing.

When you speak clearly and distinctly your voice carries much farther than if you speak hurriedly and carelessly; and other people can more readily understand what you say.

If you mumble your thoughts or your words the etheric vibrations carry mumbled meanings.

As people learn to think distinctly their thoughts carry farther and find more listeners. In course of time and with due practice, we shall easily think so that people on the other side of the earth can hear us. Not only that, but we shall think so clearly and high that the inhabitants of Mars and Venus and the sun, too, shall easily hear us.

I shouldn't wonder if what we call sun rays are really the thought vibrations of the sun's inhabitants. What if we receive and respond to their thoughts and think them our own!

The I Was and the I Am

According to the original Christian teaching (as I understand it), all undesirable conditions and circumstances are constituted by illusions that are held by ignorant, immature minds, and that project on to the bodily or material plane what may be compared to shadows. "If thine eye be single"—that is, if thy view be true, if thy understanding of life be sound,—"thy whole body shall be full of light. But if thine eye be evil, thy whole body shall be full of darkness." Undesirable experiences are the darkness wherein a person walks and works and stumbles about, whose notion of the universe, instead of shedding light on the meaning of life, casts on it a shadow. They are the effects produced on the field of our senses, by mistaken thought on the main issues of life, by a misunderstanding of life, by believing, and therefore practicing, a lie. The stuff they are woven of is something like the unsubstantial kind of stuff that makes up nightmares. They are the sort of thing from which Truth, thoroughly known, can set people free. —J. Bruce Wallace.

Some one has said that "an honest man is the noblest work of God." Ten thousand thousand others have repeated his little speech—with a solemn wag of the head and sidewise squinting which conveyed the opinion that God is chary of his noble works.

Then there came another man who paraphrased that. "An honest God is the noblest work of man," he said. And a thousand or so of us wondered why we hadn't thought to say that! Why, of course. And the other thousands of thousands lifted up their hands and cried, "Blasphemy—stone him, stone him—put him out of the church, where the bogies'll get him!" They put him out. But the bogies haven't got him. And many of the thousands are taking up his cry—"An honest God is the noblest work of man."

Why not? An honest God is of greater value than many honest men, is he not? God is the creator of man; unless God is himself honest his honest man is but an accident, instead of an image and likeness of himself.

But, according to the paraphraser, man creates his God. Well, that is a paraphrase only, and true only in a sense.

God is. Man's creation of God is simply his mental concept of God; it is God as he sees him, or it, from his viewpoint.

An honest God is the concept of a man whose soul recognizes honesty and loves it. A God of power is the mental creation of him whose soul recognizes and loves power. A God of love is the mental creation of him who recognizes and loves love. A God of vengeance is the mental concept of him who loves vengeance.

Perhaps you think your mental concept of God is not so very important, since it is all in your mind and the real God is what he is regardless of your idea of him. But it matters vitally to you.

It is not God as he really is, that is creating you; but God as he appears to you. Your concept of God is creating you in its own image and likeness.

If you think of God as a great man on a throne, with a long white heard and an eye-for-an-eye-and-a-tooth-for-a-tooth expression, you may depend upon being made over into a sour-visaged decrepit old man who will want to die and get away from it all.

If you think of God as a God of power, love, wisdom, beneficence, you will aim to be perfect as he is perfect.

If you happen to be one of the fools who has said in his heart there is no God, your life will be a crazy patchwork and your end that of the stoic who defies earth to do its worst by him; which it probably will, being a willing earth and ready to give each according to his demands.

You are being created in the image and likeness of the Lord your God, the God enthroned in your heart.

What kind of a God is in your heart? Is he small and revengeful and capricious, a sort of policeman to tell your troubles to, to receive consolation from, and by whom to send punishment to your enemies?

Or is your God the Principle and Substance behind all creation, the power, wisdom, love, of all creation, a God who loves all, is just to all, generous to all, favors none?

But no matter how lofty a God you carry in your heart he will do you little good unless he is an "I Am" God.

Most men's Gods are "I Was" Gods. They believe God did wonderful things for the children of Israel; that he performed great miracles for the apostles and disciples of Jesus; but to this age they think of him as merely the I Was God, who stands aloof and lets man run things—man and the devil, or "malicious animal magnetism."

Believers in the "I Was" God are also great sticklers for the "I Shall Be" God, who is coming again to judge the wicked and set up his kingdom on earth. And these believers in the I Shall Be God think that their only business in life is to wait around until the great I Shall Be makes his appearance.

People who worship the "I Was" and the "I Shall Be" are never demonstrators. Between admiration of the "I Was" and anticipation of the "I Shall Be" they fall to the ground and—wait for the I Shall Be in themselves and others.

Only the "I Am" God does things. "I Am" love impels you to love now. "I Am" wisdom inspires you to act upon your ideas. "I Am" power performs miracles, not yesterday or tomorrow, but now.

I Am God is the God who works to-day, in you and in me. His ways are not the ways of the I Was God, nor of the I Shall Be God; they are the ways of the "I Am"—new, different, the ways of to-day, not of yesterday or to-morrow.

I know a dear woman who worships the I Was and the I Shall Be. She entertained Schlatter the healer, and was firmly convinced that he was a literal reincarnation of Jesus Christ. She took Schlatter's word for it. She also accepted his excuses for not immediately setting up a literal kingdom here on earth, as described in the book of Revelations. He told her he had other work to do just now, that he was going away, but would soon return and establish a literal kingdom. She swallowed it all—without a single chew. Schlatter went away, and later a body was found in the mountains which was said to be his.

Since Schlatter's disappearance some years ago, this lady has spent her time in writing about him and looking for his return. The I Was and the I Shall Be absorb her entire spiritual attention.

In the meantime she lives in a small mining town where in the life surging about her she sees no God. Not long ago she wrote me to help her speak the Word of freedom for a man on trial for his life. She said he was absolutely innocent and that a "terrible conspiracy" existed against him. The man was condemned to die, still protesting, not innocence but self-defense. It was a case of mix-up with two men and a woman, followed by a drunken brawl and the usual plea of "didn't mean to."

This lady's sympathies were all with the man, and her letters to me were pitiful. Her heart was wrung with agony for him and his bereaved wife, and convulsed with horror and impotent rage at the "wickedness" of the "wretches who falsely swore away his life." The way "evil" triumphed over justice was awful, she said, and she knew when Schlatter returned justice would be done and the wicked wretches annihilated—or words to that effect.

You see, she has no conception of an "I Am" God, who rules now. She sits in judgment on men's acts and prays to Schlatter to come back and set things right.

She remembers that the "I Was" put 10,000 to flight with Gideon's three hundred pitchers and candles—simply sneaked up and scared them into a panic. She knows the "I Was" hardened the heart of Pharaoh to lie repeatedly to the Israelites. She knows the devil had to ask permission of God before he tempted Job. She knows God said "I make peace and I create evil," and that "The Lord hath made all things himself; yea, even the wicked for the day of evil." She knows that "Whatsoever the Lord pleased that did he in heaven, and in earth, in the seas, and all the deep places." She knows all these things of the Great I Was.

But that the I Am works now in the hearts of men; that God now hardens one heart to perjury and another to truth, one to murder and another to lay down his life that his friend may live;—that God now works in these apparently antagonistic ways and thereby works out perfect justice, wisdom, love, has never entered her mind.

She cannot imagine that no man meets any form of death until he himself has ripened for that particular form of death. She has read that eighteenth chapter of Ezekiel, where God explains that every man dies for his own sins, not for the false swearings of another. But the great "I Was" said that, and the "I Shall Be" says it; but the "I Am" is absent—so she thinks.

Somewhere in the Old Testament—in Psalms, I think—the statement is made that those who die are "taken away from the evil to come." I opine that this is literally and unvaryingly true, that death never comes except as the dying one needed relief from worse things than death, things which lay straight ahead in his path.

The man of whom this friend wrote me deserved his death; if not for the specific act for which he was tried, then for other thoughts and acts which preceded that. The man was on the wrong road—a road of many and increasing evils. Death took him off the road at the right time, and gave him a better start in some other state of existence.

I must either believe this or deny the "I Am" God's power, wisdom or omnipresence. I must accept God's wisdom, power, love and presence on faith; or my own judgment on sight.

As I know from experience that appearances are deceitful, and that my personal judgment must perforce be based almost entirely upon appearances, I prefer to hold fast my faith in the presence, power, wisdom and love of the God over all. Therefore I deny that this man suffered an untimely death for the vindictiveness and perjury of others; I believe he died as a result of a mental constitution and tendencies which are hidden from me, but not from the I Am.

I believe it was the spirit of the I Am moving upon the face of his soul-deeps and saying, "Let there be light," which gave him his experiences and his particular form of death. And I believe his soul goes marching on to greater light—freed from the burdens of wrong habits of mind and body which were contracted in the old life of ignorance.

Oh, yes, it is easy to believe thus of one I never saw. It is not quite so easy to apply the same principle in the lives of those near and dear to me, and in my own life. But I aim to do it, even in the smallest details of living; and I am daily growing in the ability to acknowledge the "I Am" God in all my ways. I know this is the only way to live the new thought.

Immortal Thought

The "I Am" of every being is God, the only power, wisdom, will, mind; the only actor in all action; the only creator, disintegrator and re-creator. The I Am of you is One, the Only One.

The "I Am" or ego or spiritual being of you is a thinker. All thinking is done by the one thinker—mortal thinking or immortal thinking.

Your body is an organization within you, the real you, the "I Am," the thinker,—an organization within you of the thoughts you (the I Am or God) are thinking. Your body is the present conclusion of all the thoughts, good, bad or indifferent, true or untrue, mortal or immortal, which you have thought, un-thought or rethought from the beginning of eternity; and hourly it is being changed by the new thoughts coming to you.

The real you does the thinking, recording conclusions in the body—which, mind you, is not you; nor does it even "contain" you; you are omnipresent, omnipotent, omniscient spirit or mind, and your body is within you. In you (God) it lives and moves and has its being, and by you (God) it is held together.

You have all-power to think all kinds of thoughts; and you use that power. You know you do—you know you think good thoughts, bad ones, mortal ones and immortal ones. Why question it?

You think all kinds of thoughts. But that does not make you all kinds of a being. You are the One Being to whom all kinds of thinking are possible, just as you are a being to whom all sorts of acts are possible.

In their essence, thought and action are one. Are you a human being when you play on the piano and an animal when you sweep the floor? Are you a human being when you walk and a fish when you go swimming? Of course not. You are the One Being whatever you choose to do or think—you are God-being.

One time you think mortal thoughts and the next time you think immortal thoughts (results always recording in your body) but always you are the same God-being.

And you feel all sorts of ways; but always you are you—the same One, God-being.

Your mortal thoughts are your thoughts of mortality—of death and all that leads to death—of sin, sickness, unhappiness, all that tends to discourage you from wanting to keep on living and thinking. Your immortal thoughts are your thoughts of life, activity, love, joy—all those thoughts which make you want to live more. One thought differs from another but you go on forever, the same One God-being.

Your mystification all comes from confounding yourself with your thoughts; from thinking of your thought-built body as you—which it is not.

In its deepest analysis your body and all your thoughts are purely mortal thoughts, and only your real you, the thinker, is immortal. To be immortal is to be subject to no change—which is true of Life Principle only. To be mortal is to be subject to change and death—which is true of all thought, even thoughts of life, love, joy.

All thoughts are fleeting and therefore "mortal" applies to them. Evil disappears before good thought, and "Good doth change to better, best."

The body is eternally changing—eternally receiving from the Self or spirit higher thought and eternally sloughing off lower thought. Body is mortal and will never be anything else. It will never cease to change; it will never cease to receive new thought and slough off back-number thought; it will never cease to "die daily." If it could for one hour cease this daily, hourly dying, this casting off thought which is out of date, it would die altogether.

Individual hanging on to dead thought is the cause of all old age and somatic death. The body instead of throwing off its dead and dying thought through its eliminative system, allows it to continue piling up in the body until death of the entire body comes as a relief. And the God-self goes on to new generations.

All bodily energy is the energy of live thought. Death comes to the body when dead thought preponderates. "Except ye become as a little child," whose daily dying is perfect, you shall continue to grow old and die the somatic death.

A child hangs on to nothing. Every new thing charms it completely from the old, and its intense mental and physical activities keep the old moving out and off to make room for more of the new.

Can you give any reason under the sun why human beings should not continue to live the child life and escape death of the body as a whole? There is no reason to be found in science, logic or nature; the one reason lies in our artificial living.

We stuff the mind with unused knowledge; we stuff the body with twice to ten times the food we need (all food is thought, too); we glory in "owning" more things than we can possibly need or use; we spend our time straddling our possessions to keep others from using them; is it any wonder we become literally loaded down until our bodies are too cumbersome for any life more strenuous than that of the grave?

Life to us is too real, too earnest; we want too much; and as long as we persist in living at this dying rate the grave will be our goal.

I said that in its last analysis all thought is mortal thought. This is true of formed thought, or thoughts.

Thought substance is eternal; thought substance is "matter," without beginning or end; and matter in its original state is mind or spirit—the One Thinker and his thought material, one and indivisible.

Thought substance is immortal, unchanging; but all forms of this thought substance are mortal, ever changing. Think of the ocean—the water is ever the same, but the waves, the forms assumed by the water, eternally change; so with thought substance and thought forms. The body being an organization of thought forms, of "mortal thoughts," must "die daily"; but that thought substance from which all its forms are made is immortal mind—is the God-self. Your body is simply a series or growing organization of fleeting eddies in your immortal God-self.

Too wonderful to grasp? Well, never mind—better not grasp it too tightly anyway—it might prove only another weight on your mind! Let the thought come and go in your consciousness, as waves come and go on the ocean; by and by you will "realize" that it is true— that you and the Father, body and soul, are all One and eternal. Just take it for granted, dearie, and love and be radiantly happy. So shall you use mortality to prove immortality.

God in Person

God [Universal Mind] is not a person; he is all persons.

"The Universe is One Stupendous Whole, Whose body Nature is, and God the Soul."

This means that "Nature," which includes man, is the body of God; and God's body is to him what your body is to you—a statement of beliefs which is eternally changing as experience teaches you more.

The only body God has is your body and mine; the only brains he has are your brains and mine; the only experience he has is your experience and mine; the only judgment he has is your judgment and mine.

The only way God has of proving anything is through your experience and mine.

You have heard it said that you cannot teach a man anything he does not already know; that to educate a man is to draw out into consciousness that which is already within him. By his own experience and by the teaching of others he becomes conscious of the wisdom which was all the time within him. All knowledge is latent in God (the Whole) just as it is in you; and God becomes conscious of what he knows by the same processes by which you become conscious. Your real self is God.

Watch yourself and you will see how God does things.

God is Wisdom. But Wisdom and knowledge are not identical. Knowledge is Wisdom proved—by the only proof, experience. All Wisdom is latent in God's soul, which is your soul and mine. God's Wisdom is expressed in his body, or "statement of beliefs," which is your body and mine.

God knows everything; but he knows that he knows only what he has proved through you and me, and all mankind and animal-kind and vegetable-kind.

"Some call it evolution; others call it God."

If God knew more he would not suffer through us. This is equivalent to saying if you and I knew more we would not suffer. There is no you and I; there is only God.

Evolution is simply God coming into consciousness of himself and his wisdom. Your body is a part of God's body; your soul is God, the One Life of all creation.

Do you wish to make his people suffer? Of course not. Do you wish to make yourself suffer? Of course you don't. You are God, and you don't intentionally make anybody suffer unless you think you have to. The rest of the suffering you have not yet learned to avoid. In other words, God has not yet learned how to avoid it.

But evolution still evolutes, and sighing and sorrow are already fleeing before the dawn of Wisdom coming to itself. God is learning how to enjoy himself in the flesh—in your flesh and mine.

What is flesh? It is mind. God is learning to enjoy himself in his own mind, which is your flesh and mine. He keeps on thinking through you and me until his "statements of belief," his flesh body, bring only joy to all creation and un-creation.

Why did he make the Ten Commandments? Why do you lay down laws unto yourself? Because you catch glimpses of higher things than you have yet experienced, and you lay down laws which you mean to live up to.

But you don't always live up to those laws, do you? Why? Because your body is an organization of intelligent cells each of which has a will of its own. You catch a glimpse of the truth that Love is the Greatest Thing in the World; you lay down a commandment: "Thou shalt not be impatient or angry." Before a day has passed you catch yourself breaking your commandment—"you forgot." In other words, the most intelligent cells in your body recognized a beautiful truth and promulgated a new commandment for all the cells to live by. But the less intelligent cells being still unconvinced of that beautiful truth, and being in a great majority, you did their will—you got mad.

Now God recognized through Moses most beautiful truths, and laid down laws to govern those who were as yet not intelligent enough to recognize the truths for themselves. For thousands of years God tried through these laws to make all the people see these truths. Thus his people evoluted—a little.

The God in Jesus caught a glimpse of still higher truth and laid down another law, that ye love one another. And still, after 2,000 years o that law, the people do not all see it, and very few of them obey.

A Moses or a Jesus recognizes truth so much greater than can be sensed by the common run of people, that it takes thousands of years of reiteration of that truth to make even a majority of the common run of people see it. It takes centuries of evolution really to convert the world to an Ideal conceived by a Jesus.

It takes you years of reiteration of your Ideal, and constant effort toward living up to it, before you can really convert your body to that Ideal.

In other words, God glimpses in Moses or Jesus a beautiful Ideal of himself; but it takes Him thousands and thousands of years to work out that Ideal, to evolute all people to the stage of wisdom and loving-kindness.

It is God's effort to work out his Ideals, which causes all suffering. This means that it is your effort to work out your Ideals, which causes all your suffering.

An Ideal impels change; the Established Order, in the Whole or a Part, resents and resists change; hence the pain. The spirit is willing but the flesh is established and refuses to change.

It was this Jesus had in mind when he said, "Resist not evil." The Established Order, the flesh, resists change because it is too shortsighted to see that the change is good. Because we are not yet convinced that All is Good and every change tends to greater good, we fight the change, more or less whole heartedly.

We have within us the same high Ideals, the same backslidings and wars, revolutions and evolutions, the same joys and sorrows, that the children of Israel had, that the universe at large has had and is having. All history is the history of your own thoughts. Man is an infinite little cosmos.

Just as in history ignorance has warred against the Ideal and yet in the fullness of time the Ideal has had its way; so in yourself ignorance wars against the Ideal and may for a time seem to win, but eventually the Ideal has its way. A man in his ignorance may yield to "temptation" but the results will take away the very temptation itself. When a child's fingers are well scorched it loses all desire to play with the fire.

There is no such thing as "ruining our lives forever." Every soul has all eternity in which to learn to live. Every soul is God—omnipresent, omniscient, or omnipotent in potentiality.

And all eternity is its school term, all space its school ground. Death is simply a promotion ceremony, peculiar to the kindergarten classes. A "ruined" life is no more than a "ruined" problem on Tommy's slate—it is wiped off to give Tommy, who has been learning by his mistakes, a chance to do a better sum.

Be still and know that God and you are one, and all things shall be made plain.

How to Reach Heaven

The subjective or emotional self is the best of servants but the worst of masters. All the evil in the world results from transposing authority from objective to subjective, from letting emotion run away with conscience and reason.

All unpleasant reactions are due to the waste of energy which results from this transposition of authority.

The emotional or subjective self is the storehouse of personal power; the objective self is the director of that power. Happy results come from intelligent use of power.

To give unbridled rein to the emotional self is like turning on the power of an automobile and then lying back and laughing—or weeping—whilst the auto runs its pace and kills or maims what comes in its way. The loud, hysterical giggle betrays that emotion is running away with the directing power, and that personal power is ebbing below the point of safety.

And the waste of power—the letting loose of more emotion than the occasion really calls for—is bound to produce its after effects of depression.

Depression of this sort is due to depletion of emotional energy, and disappears as the system recuperates—as more energy is stored.

Nearly all "blues" are caused by such reaction; energy is wasted in mental or physical agitation due to anger or fretting, or "righteous indignation," or excess of sympathy, or "having a good time"; and then we wonder why we are so blue. We go off and have a "good cry," which relaxes us, fall asleep after it, and wake up without the blues—and wonder why. More energy has been generated—that is all.

The secret of real enjoyment, of the kind from which there is no unpleasant reaction, lies in perfect control of the emotional nature; in so conserving your emotional power that it shall never be depleted beyond a certain definite point of poise, the point where there is plenty in well-controlled reserve.

When one first begins to find and maintain this state of poise he feels that he can never "have a good time" again—that he must repress all the fun and be glum and steady. But this is a mistaken idea, which will disappear as he gains control.

There are heights and depths and breadths of fun and joy which can never be touched except by the poised, controlled person. It takes emotional energy to enjoy, and the greater the store of energy the deeper the enjoyment, and the less of it is wasted in boisterous movements and noises.

One does not suppress his enjoyment of an incident; he suppresses unnecessary expressions of his enjoyment; and every such motion inhibited leaves him with that much more energy on hand with which to enjoy. In proportion as he ceases to slop his emotional power in loud laughs and unnecessary movements he deepens his power of enjoyment.

Laughs are on the surface; real enjoyment is in the deeps of being. It is the surface slopping one must suppress, the waste of power, that he may become conscious of the real depths of enjoyment.

Impulsiveness and nervousness are due to depleted emotional energy, and are invariably caused by letting the subjective, emotional self-rule. So much energy is wasted in unnecessary emotionalism that there is not enough left to enjoy with—there are no depths. There comes to be a habitual waste of emotion over the most trivial things, and there is no reserve for the greater things which occasionally come. All due to excessive expression of emotion. People who have not learned to control their expressions of emotion have never even tasted full enjoyment.

The one cure for nervousness, impulsiveness, boisterous emotionalism of all sorts is to be still; cut off all unnecessary waste and let the reservoirs fill.

There are two kinds of "lively dispositions." One is the result of hysterical slopping over of energy without regard to the fact that the reservoirs of personal power are dangerously near the point of utter depletion. This sort of liveliness often ends in tears, nearly always in depression.

The other sort of "lively disposition" is the surface expression of full reservoirs. One is like the slopping of water from a shallow bowl, by shaking the bowl; the other is like the rippling of a clear lake—the depths are clear, still and happy, whilst the surface answers brightly and without waste, to the passing breezes of fun. The bowl of water is exhausted by its expressions of fun; the clear lake enjoys its ripples of laughter without wasting itself.

The larger the lake the larger the waves. The same breeze which causes a pond to ripple will cause Lake Michigan to toss in white-capped glee. The greater the length, breadth and depth, the greater the waves; the greater the personal reservoir of emotional power; the bigger the laugh of which it is capable.

The loud laugh sometimes betrays the vacant mind and reservoirs; sometimes it betrays wide and deep and full ones; and by its ring the hearer can tell which. Who has not rippled in response to the musical, full, contagious loud laugh? And cringed at the sharp, hysterical loud laugh?

The musical laugh loud or soft, invariably indicates well stored reservoirs of emotional power and real enjoyment. The shrill unmusical laugh, the nervous laugh, loud or soft, invariably means nervous or emotional depletion, shallow reservoirs, and shallow enjoyment or none at all.

Musical and unmusical speaking voices are other indications of these states of personal power. Smooth, graceful, intelligent gesticulations are yet other indications of full reservoirs; rough, jerky unnecessary motions indicating depletion.

The curtailing of wasteful laughs and motions is one of the most important things in life. Emotion is soul force, that which accomplishes all the great things of life as well as all the little things.

Every human being has access to unlimited soul force, which is constantly flowing into him from the Universal Reservoir. But if he uses it as fast as it flows in—uses it in overdoing the small and least necessary things of life,—he has no power for the greater things every soul longs to do.

How much power would the world get from the Niagara River if it were not for the great natural dam and reserve power at the falls? If you would do the great things you must see that your energy is not wasted in a steady stream of little things.

Every movement, every thought, uses a definite amount of emotional energy. Every inhibition of a movement or thought stream permits the higher rising of your reservoir; just as every stone added to a dam increases the reservoir and power behind it.

There are enough good things to do and think in this beautiful world without dissipating our power in thoughtless activities, such as tapping our feet or fingers, rocking to and fro, giggling shrilly, and so on. Yes, we learn to do things by doing them; but do we want to do these useless things? Of course not. They are wasteful, unbeautiful.

And we can learn to stop them by stopping them; and have so much deeper power with which to do the useful, beautiful things. A half hour a day used in simply being still, will add almost incredibly to the depth of our reservoirs. And every time we remember to inhibit an unnecessary rock or tap or fidget we add another depth to our power. This is all easily proved by a little practice.

Our energy is soul power, which is also wisdom. As our energy deepens our wisdom deepens also, and our sense of humor deepens. Soul power is love and wisdom, the One and Only Substance of which the individual is an inlet—a small or large inlet according as he lets the energy run out fast, or conserves it for large uses; according as he lets it run, or dams it for personal use.

There is plenty of soul power for everything—yes. But it takes time to build a dam; and the man who lets loose his whole Niagara Falls of emotion upon trivial occasions will have to spend most of his time in patching his dam. And the man who dribbles all his power in thoughtless and useless acts has no power behind his Niagara.

Do you see that self-control is the key of heaven? And the time to use it is now, the place here.

"Earth's crammed with heaven" waiting to be conserved to individual uses. Love, power, wisdom is flowing through you into expression—don't let it flow too fast—don't waste it in thoughtless, foolish expression.

Cut off the wastes; use the power in wise directions, and let the tide rise within you. Thus shall you come to the great things you would do, and behold within you shall be the power to do them with joy; and there shall be no aftermath of depression.

This is heaven—the highest heaven for the deepest soul. And the door is open for everybody.

Vital energy is soul energy—love-power and wisdom mixed—L2W2.

The body is a generator of vital or soul energy.

Heaven and hell are states of bodily being. The body full of vital or soul energy—L2W2—experiences heaven.

The body depleted of its soul energy lives in hell—carried there by riotous living, by wasting its vital or soul energy.

A Look at Heredity

No evolutionist can overlook heredity, nor underestimate it. He believes that every generation comes in on the shoulders of its predecessors, and he fully appreciates the value of good predecessors The world's pride of ancestry is not so foolish as it might appear.

The more intelligence and culture my forbears had the greater my possibilities. There are no breaks in the law of growth or evolution or heredity, though the casual observer often fancies there are.

Every human being comes into the world as an "acme of things accomplished" by his ancestors, and he is an "encloser of things to be" accomplished by himself and his descendants.

But who are my ancestors? Let me tell you that Ralph Waldo Emerson and Jesus of Nazareth are more directly my ancestors than many of those whom the world calls my great-grandfathers. There is a spiritual and mental kinship through which we inherit.

There are spiritual and mental relationships to which we all owe far more of our goodness and greatness than can be traced to those of blood tie. In rare instances only do these spiritual and mental relationships exist within the line of blood relationship.

The world does well to be proud of its ancestry; but it does better when it appreciates its spiritual ancestry. Think you that the poor little waif owes a larger inheritance to the woman who bore it and deserted it, than to the foster parents who nurtured it in love and wisdom?

Our blood relations are not the only relations from whom we inherit; neither when we are born do we cease to inherit. There is One Father of us all, and the oft-repeated statement that we are all brothers and sisters is no fanciful one. The "fatherhood of God and brotherhood of man" is fact; and the man who thinks he is limited by the ignorance of his blood relations is himself an ignoramus. If his blood relations are not to his liking, let him draw a new inheritance from the world's greatest and best. They, too, are his ancestors.

And mark this: Not only does the son inherit from his fathers of blood or spirit tie, but many a father inherits from the son that which the son has gained from other sources than those of blood relationship.

Inheritance by blood tie is not a stream, the outlet of which can rise no higher than its source. Rather, it is a sort of hydraulic ram through which life may be coaxed to almost any height of culture and refinement.

I have heard it said that culture is "the soul of knowledge—the essence of right living" inherited from our ancestors. Where did they get it? I will tell you where; they got it by persistence in the same sort of practices which are decried—by "wresting, by force," the knowledge, wealth and dominion of others; by generations of "monastic seclusion," much of it enforced by others whose turn it was to "wrest by force"; by generations of "rigid self-control"; by hours and days and years of prayer, which is simply a phase of "going into the silence"; and, yes, and even by "breathing like a filthy, crazy Yoga"—though much of the breathing was forced by strenuous endeavors to get away from the raging hordes whose wealth or daughters they were stealing. The Spirit of Evolution which is running this universe is very cunning in devices for inducing self-culture.

Full breathing, going into the silence, affirmations, etc., are not new methods of self-culture. They are as old and their practice as universal as life itself. But heretofore their practice has been in the main compulsory. Humanity had to be persecuted, starved, hunted into breathing, exercising, praying—had to be forced to develop body, soul and wits by using them.

The present generation inherits the wisdom gained through their efforts. Not the least of its inheritance lies in its wits developed to the point of seeing that for self-development, ten minutes of voluntary deep breathing is preferable to an all-day chase to save one's neck; that a half hour of intelligent silence is worth more than the three and four hour "wrestlings with the Lord" such as our great-grandfather John Wesley—and many of his inheritors—practiced regularly.

Herein lies the great difference between our ancestors and us. They were by conditions compelled to self-culture; whilst we, their inheritors, are making intelligent use of it.

Through evolution we are learning to conserve energy. Our ancestors spent all their time—perforce—in half-unconscious physical exercise and breathings; we spend a few minutes a day in intelligent exercise and breathing, and conserve our forces for mental and spiritual uses.

And without them [our ancestors] we should be minus the intelligence to do this. Humanity is a solidarity—on the square; and without the work of his ancestors none shall be made perfect.

But it is by the work of his ancestors that man stands on to-day's pinnacle. What they learned to do by labored effort and mainly under compulsion, we do by instinct.

It is by man's work to-day on this pinnacle, that his great-grandchildren shall be brought forth on yet higher pinnacles, with yet higher instinctive knowledge.

Take the most cultured person you know; trace his ancestry and tell me where his culture began. You cannot do it. Go clear back to William the Conqueror if you will; thus far you may call his ancestors cultured, but even so their culture, all the way back, is a descending scale of boorishness in comparison with what we twentieth century folk call culture. And we must hark back of William for the beginning of his culture.

William the Conqueror was the illegitimate son of Robert the Devil. Did culture begin with Robert? And the mother of William was a miller's daughter. Is she the mother of all culture?

Robert the Devil was the third earl of Normandy; which means that his grandfather was an ordinary everyday scrub who probably murdered somebody particularly obnoxious to the king and was rewarded with an earldom. Did he bequeath "the soul of knowledge, the essence of right living," to William the Conqueror and his exclusive progeny? If so, where did he get it?

His own grandfather and the ancestors of the poor miller's daughter roamed the same woods, fought the same battles, hunted the same beasts and men, and gnawed the same bones. Where did the ancestors of Robert the Devil pick up the "soul of knowledge"? And what were the miller's ancestors doing whilst Robert's grandfathers cornered the "essence of right living"? For I warrant you that William's miller's-daughter-mother was less of a stranger to the "soul of knowledge, the essence of right living" than was that devil of a Robert.

Yes, there are many people who are educated but not cultured. But their progeny will brag of their culture. For what is in one generation mere education, or "monastic seclusion," or "rigid self-control," or "going into the silence," or "breathing like a filthy, crazy Yoga," is by time and unconscious cerebration transmuted into pure "culture."

And if any of us lack culture you may depend upon it our ancestors, by blood and spirit, are numbered among those who failed to "wrest by force" the very things decried as uncultured.

All life is education; and time transmutes education into culture, "the soul of knowledge, the essence of right living."

Not a human effort but is necessary to the development of the soul of knowledge. Not a Yoga breath, not an hour of silence, not a moment of rigid self-control, not a day of hard labor, not a sound or movement or cry of joy or sorrow or rage or despair,—not one but has helped to free the soul of knowledge. Not one could have been dispensed with without leaving culture less cultured than it is.

The difference between education and culture is the difference between the daily drill at the piano and the finished musical expression of a Paderewski.

Education comes first and without it there can be no culture. Education is the work of today; whilst culture is the soul of well used yesterdays. Why exalt the well used yesterdays to the disparagement of today's opportunities?

Inheritance is wealth left us by sanguine and spiritual relations gone before. It is capital left us, to be increased by just such "wresting by force" as some people condemn. Who is the more valuable to the human race:—he who parades his inheritance as he received it or he who adds to it his own efforts at self-culture?

Don't get stuck on tradition and kowtow eternally to heredity. Be an Individual and improve heredity. If your inheritance was poor make it better; if it was good make it better. The world's culture is only just beginning; get busy helping it along. That is the important thing.

Do it now.

Critic and Criticized

"I don't want to be criticized."

"But you want to learn, don't you? You surely are not satisfied that you know it all."

"Oh, of course I want to learn, but I want to learn by myself. I would rather be wrong than be criticized. I hate to be told how to do things. I want to find out for myself."

Solomon the Wise reasons not thus. Solomon prayed for wisdom above all things, and in receiving wisdom he received all else.

The man who thinks he would rather be wrong than be criticized is for the time being a moral coward and no Solomon. He values his "feelings" of the moment above wisdom. He does not want wisdom and knowledge above all things; he wants what wisdom and knowledge he can gain without the sacrifice of his feeling of self-complacency.

He is complacent as long as his friend says to him, "You are a good fellow, a very admirable fellow"; he feels good as long as he thinks his friend considers him wise; he expands and smiles, and works away in his own good way.

In his moments of confidence he will tell his friend that Wisdom and Knowledge are the greatest things in the universe; that we grow only by the acquisition of Wisdom and Knowledge; that growth is Life, and Life is Love or God. He will enthuse a bit and tell you Wisdom is God, the One Desirable One; and that by growing in wisdom man becomes conscious of his divinity.

Just here his friend, who is a prosy, practical sort of fellow, interrupts him. "See here, Smith," he says, "you are not running this branch of your business quite right. You just ought to see how Thomson does that sort of thing."

He gets no farther; Smith freezes instantly, and Jones's confidences catch the vibrations. Smith is "so sensitive, you know"—he would rather not know anything about better methods, than to stand the shock of a criticism. Jones talks about the weather a bit, and departs.

Smith continues to think he desires wisdom above all things. He doesn't. He desires above all things to have his bump of approbativeness smoothed.

He fails to know himself. And he will not learn himself, because he refuses all truth which does not make him "feel" good.

He shuts himself off from a thousand avenues by which wisdom is trying to reach him.

It is said our enemies are our best friends. Emerson bids us listen to them and learn of them.

Burns exclaims:—

"O wand some power the gift give us

To see ourselves as others see us!
O wand from money a blunder free us
And foolish notion."
Our critics are answering Love's attraction to free us from blunders and foolish notions.

Why not? Why resent a criticism? We are all members of "One Stupendous Whole." Why resent and refuse another's suggestion? It is our own suggestion, drawn by our own affirmed love for wisdom and knowledge.

We don't understand ourselves; we don't trust our surroundings. We say we want wisdom above all things; we want to understand. In our heart of hearts we do love wisdom above all things; therefore we attract it through all avenues.

It is our soul's love for wisdom and knowledge which attracts to us the criticisms of friend and foe.

If we really believed that we attract what we receive; that "our own" comes to us; that all things are working together to gratify our soul's desires;—if we really believed all this we would meet criticism in a friendly spirit, with senses alert to find the kernel of wisdom it is bringing us.

To resent a criticism is to re-send, to send away, a bit of knowledge your soul has been praying for. All because your bump of approbativeness has an abnormal appetite for prophecies of "smooth things."

But to re-send a criticism is not to get rid of it. It comes back to you over and over, and perhaps every time in a little ruder form.

If you speak softly to a friend and he fails to hear, you repeat in a louder tone; if he is very deaf you holler, and perhaps touch his shoulder to gain his attention.

All creation is alive, and pursues the same tactics. When you resent (re-send) a criticism, Creation sends it back at you a little more emphatically. If you still resent it Creation puts still more force into repeated sendings. She keeps this up, in answer to your own semi-conscious desire for wisdom and knowledge, until by some hook or crook you take the kernel of knowledge contained in that criticism. Then Creation smiles and lets you alone—on that line.

The way to avoid Creation's kicks is to accept her hints as they come to you in the form of friendly criticism or suggestion.

Not all criticisms are true in their entirety, but every one contains somewhere a suggestion by which you may profit—by which you may grow in wisdom and knowledge.

Don't let that one little bump of approbativeness make you re-send that knowledge—and bring down Creation's kicks to drive it home.

But don't get the idea that that little round nub of approbation is "bad." He is not. He is a good and useful member of your family, and deserves to be well fed and cared for and respected.

But feed him so well on your own good opinions that he will not sulk and kick if he doesn't receive unlimited taffy from others. Get away up high in your own opinion. Know yourself a god, unique, indispensable to Creation. You have powers and wisdom and knowledge not possessed by anybody else in the world. Nobody who ever lived or ever will is any better or any more of a god than you are.

Neither is anybody less good or less of a god than you. We are different—that is all. Every man has his individual goodnesses and his peculiar point of view—no better than yours, but different.

It takes every man in the world to see all sides of anything, or anybody.

Every individual who is at all wise wants to see all sides of things. The only chance he has of doing this is to look at things from other people's points of view, as well as his own; to put himself in other people's places; to see as others see; to vibrate with the other fellow—who sees another side of the same thing.

Listen to your critic. See yourself as he sees you. He is your best friend, drawn in answer to your soul's cry for more wisdom and knowledge. Be friends with him. Hush the clamor of approbativeness with your own high affirmations of your goodness and worth—hush the clamor and listen. The spirit in you will separate the chaff from the wheat of the criticism; a smiling little "Poof!" will blow away the chaff; and your soul will expand and increase in stature by assimilating the wheat.

The Nobility

We always come in contact with the people we live and think up to. If you are not satisfied with the present environment it can be changed by making your very best of it, and in the meantime fitting yourself mentally, physically and in deportment, for the sort of people you want. Get ready for 'em.

And see you waste no energy in impatience over having to wait a long time.

It takes mental and physical culture and gracious deportment to fit you for the sort of friends you want.

There is no place in life which does not offer plenty of advantages for the cultivation of all these things, but especially for the cultivation of a gracious deportment. You may depend that if you can be lovely and gracious to "common people," who may ruffle your feathers the wrong way, you will be at home if a duchess happens along.

Duchesses, you know, belong to the class of people who make a study and lifelong practice of being lovely and gracious. I am talking about real duchesses now—not the kind that get rich quick and marry a title without having the real qualifications of nobility.

Somebody has said that the world is divided into two classes, the civil and the uncivil. The hall-mark of real nobility is the habit of being civil to the uncivil. No better place to acquire this gentle art than living among the uncivil.

The youth who finds himself among the uncivil and who proceeds to cultivate uppishness and contempt for his associates; who "looks down" on those with whom he is compelled to associate; who tries to be "superior" and to impress others with his superiority,—such an one is forever fixing himself in the class of the uncivil—where duchesses don't grow.

You are what you are. Time spent in trying to "impress" people is worse than wasted. Be your gracious self, and honor not only your father and your mother but your next door neighbor and your next door neighbor's kitchen maid if you want to develop the qualities that will fit you for the sort of associates you want—members of the really truly nobility.

Cultivate your brains, dearie; cultivate your body; cultivate your soul; all to the best of your ability. But above all and in all and through all cultivate the mental and physical deportment of the truly noble. Belong always to the civil class and practice civility eternally upon the uncivil as well as upon the civil.

When a brawling enemy followed Pericles home one dark night, with intent to injure him, Pericles sent his own servant with a lantern to light the man home again. Pericles did not descend from his own class to pay his uncivil enemy in his own coin.

Go thou and cultivate Pericles and thine own high self. Then shall all desirable associates seek you, instead of you having to seek them.

Greater credit belongs to him who sees the real nobility through the housemaid's dress and manner, than to him who recognizes it in silk and velvet voice.

We are all members of the nobility, all descended through Adam and Eve, who never saw silk nor made salaams. All are sons and daughters of the Most High.

Don't be fooled into contempt and incivility by our masquerade costumes; and don't value some of our gowns above ourselves—or yourself.

L' Envoi.
When earth's last picture is painted,
And the tubes are twisted and dried,
When the oldest colors have faded,
And the youngest critic has died, We shall rest—and, faith, we shall need it—
Lie down for an aeon or two,
Till the Master of All Good Workmen
Shall set us to work anew.
And those that were good shall be happy—
They shall sit in a golden chair;
They shall splash at a ten-league canvas
With brushes of comet's hair.
They shall find real saints to draw from—
Magdalene, Peter, and Paul; They shall work for an age at a sitting,
And never get tired at all.
And only the Master shall praise us,
And only the Master shall blame;
And no one shall work for money,
And no one shall work for fame;
But each for the joy of the working,
And each in his separate star,
Shall draw the thing as he sees it,
For the God of things as they are.

www.ingramcontent.com/pod-product-compliance
Lightning Source LLC
LaVergne TN
LVHW011155080426
835508LV00007B/426